"Lucid and engaging, *The Blue Tattoo* contextualizes Olive Oatman's life by delving into Mohave culture and history (including interviews with contemporary Mohaves) and by explaining why her story captured the American popular imagination and continued to be retold and revisited so many times, in so many different media."—Kathryn Zabelle Derounian-Stodola, editor of *Women's Indian Captivity Narratives*

"Mifflin's treatment of Olive's sojourns [provides] an excellent teaching opportunity about America's ongoing captivation with ethnic/gender crossings."—*Western American Literature*

"Mifflin engagingly describes Oatman's ordeal and theorizes about its impact on Oatman herself as well as on popular imagination. . . . Her book adds nuance to Oatman's story and also humanizes the Mohave who adopted her. Recommended for general readers as well as students and scholars."—*Library Journal*

"One can read this work of non-fiction as if it were a sensational novel—with progressive feminist implications."—*Irish Times.com*

"The book's already received rave reviews, and for good reason. . . . A fascinating dose of both tattoo and American history."—*Tattoo History*

"Although Oatman's story on its own is full of intrigue, Mifflin adeptly uses her tale as a springboard for larger issues of the time."—*Feminist Review*

"Margot Mifflin is a great storyteller. . . . *The Blue Tattoo* is well written and well researched; it re-opens the story of white women and men going West and Native people trying to survive these travels."—June Namias, *Pacific Historical Review*

"Mifflin catches the poignancy of this story that manages to combine the conquest of the West, life among its victims, and the national myths that justified it."—*Doubleday Book Club*

"Margot Mifflin slices away the decades of mythology and puts the story in its proper historical context. What emerges is a riveting, well-researched portrait of a young woman—a survivor, but someone marked for life by the experience."—*Tucson Weekly*

"Extremely well written, *The Blue Tattoo* is unquestionably a significant contribution to Oatman studies. Mifflin's claims, close readings, and use of primary resources are engaging. We recommend *The Blue Tattoo* to students, specialists, and general readers of the history of the American Southwest."—*Overland Journal*

BISON
BOOKS

WOMEN IN THE WEST

THE BLUE TATTOO

The Life of Olive Oatman

MARGOT MIFFLIN

With a new postscript by the author

UNIVERSITY OF NEBRASKA PRESS

LINCOLN AND LONDON

Manufactured in the United States of America
♾
First Nebraska paperback printing: 2011

Library of Congress Cataloging-in-Publication Data

Mifflin, Margot, 1960–
The blue tattoo: the life of Olive Oatman /
Margot Mifflin; with a new postscript by the author.
p. cm. — (Women in the West)
Originally published: Lincoln: University of Nebraska Press, c2009.
Includes bibliographical references and index.
ISBN 978-0-8032-3517-5 (paper: alk. paper)
1. Oatman, Olive Ann. 2. Oatman, Olive Ann—Captivity. 3. Indian captivities—Southwest, New—History—19th century. 4. Apache Indians—History—19th century. 5. Yavapai Indians—History—19th century. 6. Mohave Indians—History—19th century. I. Title.
E99.A6O185 2011 979.1'04092—dc22
[B] 2010044619

Set in Carter & Cone Galliard by Kim Essman.
Designed by A. Shahan.

To Mark and Thea Dery,
who traveled with me—
at the dinner table
and through the desert.

Contents

Illustrations

Acknowledgments

I would like to thank the many people who helped me with this book: Oatman scholars Jennifer Putzi, who first told me about Olive; Kathryn Zabelle Derounian-Stodola, who consistently advised and encouraged me; and Brian McGinty, who was generous enough to share his knowledge and resources with a friendly competitor; my agent, Laurie Fox, of the Linda Chester Literary Agency, who was a tireless champion of this project; my astute editor, Heather Lundine, and the ever-efficient Bridget Barry, associate acquisitions editor, both at the University of Nebraska Press.

Many Oatman family descendents and their spouses contributed generously to this project: Walter Fields, who got me started and spurred me on; Edward and Dorothy Abbott, who opened their home to me; and Doris Clark, Richard Nolan, Patricia Carreon, Barbara Hawthorne, and Larry Oatman, who all provided important information.

I'm grateful for the wisdom of many Southwest and Native American scholars who fielded questions and offered input, including: Michael Tsosie, Pamela Munro, Timothy Braatz, and Deborah and Jon Lawrence. I was honored and fortunate to consult with Mohave elders Llewellyn and Betty Barrackman at Aha Macav Cultural Preservation, along with Kim Cameron.

I could not have written the book without the guidance of the following librarians and archivists: Tom Berman and the reference staff at the Nyack Library; Stephen Yale of the California-Nevada Conference Archives of the United Methodist Church; Lehman College librarian Susan Voge; and Ardis Kay Smith of the LDS Church History Library and Archives.

Lehman College of the City University of New York made my

work possible through a series of grants, including three Shuster Fellowships, a 2004–5 Faculty Research Award, and a 2006–7 PSC CUNY grant.

The collections at the following institutions were crucial to this project: the Arizona Historical Society in Tucson; the University of Arizona in Tucson; the Arizona State Library, Archives and Public Records; the Sharlot Hall Museum in Prescott, Arizona; the San Diego Public Library; the Huntington Library in San Marino, California; the El Monte Historical Society Museum in El Monte, California; the Siskiyou County Historical Society in Yreka, California; the Bancroft Library at the University of California–Berkeley; the New York Historical Society; the New York Public Library; the Newberry Library in Chicago; the Oregon Historical Society Research Library in Portland; the Research Library of the Southern Oregon Historical Society in Medford; the Knight Library at the University of Oregon in Eugene; the Eagle Point Historical Society in Eagle Point, Oregon; the Jackson County Public Library in Medford, Oregon; the Rogue Valley Genealogical Society in Phoenix, Oregon; the American Antiquarian Society in Worcester, Massachusetts; the Berkshire Athenaeum in Pittsfield, Massachusetts; the St. Lawrence County Historical Association in Canton, New York; the Bloomfield Academy Museum in Bloomfield, New York; the New York State Library in Albany; the Potsdam Public Museum in Potsdam, New York; the Troy Annual Conference of the United Methodist Church in Saratoga, New York; the Beineke Rare Book and Manuscript Library at Yale University; St. Catharines Museum in Ontario, Canada; the Brock University Library in Ontario, Canada; the Berrien County Historical Association in Berrien Springs, Michigan; the National Museum of the American Indian Cultural Resources Center Archives in Suitland, Maryland; the National Anthropological Archives of the Smithsonian Institution in Suitland, Maryland; the Jerome Library at Bowling Green State University.

Thanks to my friends: Michele McCarthy, who gave me sage advice; Kerrie Chappelka, who entertained me after long days at the

Bancroft Library; and Bill Mullen, who mentioned the right book at the right moment. My mother, Lynne Schloesser, provided hot and cold babysitting and warm support. I thank my husband, Mark Dery, for critiquing multiple versions of my manuscript, and for listening.

THE BLUE TATTOO

PROLOGUE

Emigrant Song

> Within our newly acquired possessions on the borders of Mexico and the Pacific coast, and the recently organized territories in the interior of the continent, are numerous powerful and warlike tribes, of whom little is known, and whose history has no connection with that of the people of the United States, except the fact that they were original occupants of the soil, and that some of them, especially the California Indians, yet dispute our right to sovereignty. | BENSON J. LOSSING, "The Extreme Western Tribes," *A Pictorial History of the United States: For Schools and Families*

In the early 1850s, Olive Oatman was a typical pioneer girl heading west on a wagon train full of Mormons in search of gold and God. By the end of the decade she was a white Indian with a chin tattoo, torn between two cultures. Orphaned at fourteen after her family was massacred by Yavapai Indians in northern Mexico (now southern Arizona), Oatman spent a year as a slave to her attackers before she was traded to the Mohaves, who tattooed her and raised her as their own. Four years later, under threat of war, the Mohaves delivered her back to the whites in exchange for horses, blankets, and beads.[1]

This much is true. But the fine points of Oatman's transformation from forty-niner to white savage have been replayed in countless books and articles—modern and Victorian—that read like Rashomans of revisionist history and romantic conjecture. In her day, Oatman was freakish enough to invite speculation and guarded enough to ensure that the speculation never ended. Because her story was saturated with violence, military intrigue, and sexual innuendo, it quickly became legend. She was the subject of a lurid, best-selling biography published in 1857 called *Life Among the Indians*, by a Methodist reverend named Royal B. Stratton, who stripped her Mormonism from her narrative and portrayed the caring Mohave Indians who raised her as "degraded bipeds."[2]

Stratton also launched Oatman's nearly decade-long public-speaking career. Her experience inspired plays, artworks, and, in the 1880s, theft, when the first tattooed circus ladies used it as a script for their own Wild West fabrications about being taken captive and tattooed by "redskins." Today, in the Arizona town that bears her name, her cheerless, tattooed face adorns the Olive Oatman Restaurant, across the street from the Oatman Hotel where, in its better days, Clark Gable and Carole Lombard spent their honeymoon.

In 1943 the *Galveston Daily News* claimed that a group of Southwest scholars had voted the Oatman saga Americans' "favorite Indian story" of the West. "It is still told constantly around campfires, in college lectures, even on radio programs," the paper asserted, perhaps a bit too promotionally, because this was the reason for telling it again—incorrectly.[3]

Because the Mohaves have no written language, their impressions of Oatman's captivity were not recorded during her lifetime. But in the mid-twentieth century, anthropologist A. L. Kroeber published an interview he had conducted in 1903 with a Mohave who had known her that contradicted what Stratton had written about her allegedly shabby treatment by the tribe, as did Kroeber's publication of Oatman's first postransom interview, with the military commander, Martin Burke, who retrieved her. What Oatman told Burke (as well as the first journalists to interview her after her ransom) differed markedly from the Stratton account and raised questions about whether she ever wanted to leave the Mohaves in the first place. Today, any Mohave who knows her story will say the tribe saved her life. "They felt sorry for her," said Llewellyn Barrackman, a tribal elder and spokesperson who died in 2006. "We have a feeling for people."[4]

What is merely a historical footnote for the Mohaves has become a lovingly burnished, ever-evolving myth for white Americans. A hundred and fifty years after Oatman's return, writers—amateur and professional, religious and scholarly—continue to rework it, invariably reflecting their own cultural fantasies as vividly as Oatman's particular experience. It was the subject of a 1965 episode of *Death Valley Days* (starring Ronald Reagan), an Elmore Leonard story, two novels, and four children's books, including a Christian title sold with a collectible Oatman figurine (worth $695)—facial tattoo and all. Since the 1990s, feminist scholars have revisited Oatman, exploring her status as a white captive and her importance as the author of one of the last captivity tales in a literary genre as old as the colonies. In early 2006, on the sesquicentennial of Oatman's rescue, more than a hundred people met at Yuma, Arizona, and drove eighty miles into the desert to the site of the Oatman massacre, where the family is buried, to hear Olive's ordeal reprised once again, this time by one of her Mormon descendants.

For all its recycling, the only constant about the Oatman story is that no two authors agree on what happened. It's as if the minute she stepped back into the white world and rinsed the mesquite dye from her hair, the truth was washed away and fiction would forever infest her biography. When her family was attacked, for example, Oatman's mother was in labor *or* she was carrying a newborn baby who was skewered by the Yavapais. Before her ransom, Oatman was fully absorbed into the Mohave family she had come to love, possibly with a husband and children *or* she was desperate to return to her own people. The day of her delivery from the Mohaves, she tried to bury herself in the sand on the bank of the Colorado River because she didn't want to go home *or* because she was embarrassed to appear topless before her white liberators. She was ecstatic to see her countrymen again *or* she cried hopelessly for two days. She married a wealthy banker and lived happily ever after *or* she died, "physically wrecked and mentally numbed," in an insane asylum.[5]

Some Oatman enthusiasts boldly wrote themselves into her life. In 1913, a decade after her death, an eighty-five-year-old bailiff in Omaha boasted, in a half-page profile in the *Sunday World Herald*, that he'd single-handedly saved her from the Mohaves by carrying her out of a teepee and delivering her to Fort Whipple, in central Arizona.[6] Apparently, no one told him that the Mohaves didn't use teepees, or that Fort Whipple hadn't been built at the time of her ransom. Five years later in the *Oakland Tribune*, a California farmer made the same claim, but his tall tale ran away with him. He said he had been a scout with Kit Carson and Buffalo Bill, battled Sitting Bull, saw Custer take his last breath, and, like Oatman, had been taken captive as a child by Indians who tattooed his chin, conveniently hidden by a full beard at press time. He claimed not only to have rescued the prisoner but also to have canoed three hundred miles through the rapids of the Grand Canyon—"a route that no white man ever traversed before"—to get her to back to civilization.[7]

Why has Oatman commanded so much attention? Unlike more prominent women of the 1850s and 1860s, such as Susan B. Anthony, Sojourner Truth, and Harriet Beecher Stowe, she wasn't a social activist, though her public-speaking career pushed the limits of feminine convention. She was no feminist—at least not after her ransom. She had lived with a tribe in which women enjoyed a greater degree of physical, sexual, and domestic freedom than white women in America, as well as higher social status in regard to men, even by Native American standards, but in her lectures, she encouraged women to enjoy their homes and be glad they didn't live as she had. She was not a defector, like some famous captives who chose to stay with their tribes, such as Mary Jemison, taken by Shawnee Indians a century earlier and traded to the Seneca at about the same age as Oatman, or Cynthia Ann Parker, who lived with the Comanche from the age of nine until she was forcibly—and tragically—returned at age thirty-four, in 1860.

Oatman's mysterious persona accounts for a small piece of her star power. She had a gothic beauty; the dozen or so surviving photos of her betray a brooding intensity that reads as a reflection of either her lonely trial or her cleaved self. In all the documentation of her life—articles, interviews, reminiscences by friends, and even her biography—she laughs just once, in an interview conducted on the day of her repatriation, and even then, the source of her amusement is unclear. The Mohaves were terrific mimics who loved a good tease and a bawdy joke; almost every description of them before their reservation days mentions their laughter, and they were considered "notoriously outspoken and uninhibited."[8] The unanswerable question of whether Oatman ever relaxed into their utterly un-Mormon social style only compounds her mystery.

The greater part of her fascination, however, lies in her unresolved duality. No American immigrants or captives have worn their hybrid identities so publicly. Like the nation's most famous fictional branded woman, Hester Prynne (who also seized the public imagination in the 1850s), Oatman wore a permanent symbol of soul-searing transgression. She was, in the parlance of her day, "redeemed" as a captive, but there's little redemption in her story. She was a half-finished woman who neither fully renounced the Mohaves nor settled back comfortably into white culture, which may explain why she contradicted herself: her affection for her Mohave family, for example, bleeds through the pages of her biography (which includes long stretches of first-person narrative) even as she disparages them, following Stratton's virulently racist agenda.

The Blue Tattoo attempts not only to sift out the truth of the Oatman story but also to offer a historical understanding of it, particularly concerning the Mohaves, a once charismatic and idiosyncratic tribe—the largest in California—now vastly diminished and all but purged from national memory. In the mid-nineteenth century they, too, were hybrids of a sort, blending Southwest and Californian Indian traditions, such as face painting and tattoo, respectively, and straddling California and Arizona geographically, on either side of the Colorado River. An accidental ethnographer, Oatman recorded her memories of them in their last decade of sovereignty. Soon after she left them, they were forced off their land and pressed into a life of poverty; today, only about a thousand survive.[9]

Oatman stood at the crossroads of history when the West was stolen. At the end of the Mexican–American War, with the 1848 Treaty of Guadalupe Hidalgo, half of Mexico was swallowed up by the United States, expanding the nation's girth by 66 percent and pushing its western boundary from Texas to California. "Manifest Destiny," a phrase minted in 1845 by the *New York Morning News* and circulated by an aggressively expansionist president, James K. Polk from Tennessee, encouraged citizens to stampede toward the Pacific and claim what they believed — and were told — was theirs. For Northerners, this was an opportunity to open the West for democracy; for Southerners, to secure it for slavery. For California Indians, who were in the way, it meant genocide: between 1848 and 1865 an estimated fifteen thousand out of seventy-two thousand Indians were killed in the Golden State. The bloodshed was no accident. "A war of extermination will continue to be waged between the races," California's first governor told the legislature in 1851, "till the Indian race becomes extinct."[10]

The land grab that made this extermination possible happened under Oatman's feet, in the space of a decade. She was living with the Mohaves during the signing of the 1853 Gadsden Purchase, by which lower Arizona, formerly part of the Mexican state of Sonora, was ceded to the United States (with a corner of New Mexico) as the last puzzle piece in the map of the Southwest. Americans were now traversing a million square miles of newly acquired land, blind to the borders—cultural, geographical, and psychological—that had previously set them apart from Mexicans and Southwest Indians.

Oatman's story reflects the crossed boundaries and trampled frontiers that marked this transaction. She survived the botched pursuit of the American Dream, arrived at a geographical and utopian terminus—California—where, as Joan Didion famously put it, "we run out of continent."[11] Then, reborn as a white Mohave, she turned around and went east again. Her blue tattoo became a poignant, permanent, ethnic marker, invoking both the cultural imprint of her Mohave past and the lingering scars of westward expansion.

||||
||||

The challenge of separating fact from fiction in retelling the Oatman saga has not been easy. Debunking the rumors that swirled around her in life and death is a fairly simple matter of fact checking; distinguishing between what she truly experienced in captivity and how Stratton presented it in *Captivity of the Oatman Girls*, the biography he ghostwrote for her, is more challenging. But by analyzing Stratton's motivations in telling her story, his knowledge of and attitude toward Indians and his theological and colonial vision of the West, and by examining the passages in *Captivity of the Oatman Girls* that are provably false, a clear pattern of manipulation emerges, and it is possible to disentangle—to a degree—his story from hers.

Chapter 1 reconstructs Oatman's journey west, drawing from Stratton (who had little reason to distort this portion of the narrative beyond excising its references to Mormonism), historical documents, newspapers, and the letters and diaries of people who traveled with the family. Chapters 2 through 10, chronicling Oatman's time among the Yavapais and the Mohaves, rely on only the parts of *Captivity of the Oatman Girls* that accord with ethnographic, military, and historical records, newspaper interviews she gave immediately after her ransom (before she met Stratton), and the memories of Musk Melon, a Mohave who knew her. Details that cannot be cross-referenced, such as Oatman's relationship with her Mohave family and her brother Lorenzo's postmassacre travels alone in the desert (chapter 5), are included only if they contain no historical or ethnographic inconsistencies and if they fall outside Stratton's schema of distortion. Some of Lorenzo's story can be checked against accounts he gave decades later. Chapters 11 and 12 identify Stratton's modifications to the story, his motivations for changing it, and the ethnographic errors that flag his meddling. Chapters 13 and 14, chronicling Oatman's adult life in New York, and later, in Texas, are based on correspondence by, with, and about her, and on newspaper stories about her.

Finally, Stratton's book appeared in three editions published by three different publishers from 1857 to 1858, each longer than the last; in a 1909 edition of the *Oregon Teacher's Monthly*, which was reprinted by Dover Publications in 1994; and in a 1983 edition published by the University of Nebraska Press. For concision, my citations refer to the latter comprehensive edition by the University of Nebraska Press, except where I have specifically identified an earlier edition.

I

Quicksand

"It was starvation to stay, and almost inevitable disaster to go forward."
| J. ROSS BROWNE, "A Tour through Arizona"

The Oatman family spent their last night together marooned on a tiny island surrounded by quicksand in the Gila River in Mexico. California bound, they had left their farm in Illinois in May of 1850, joined twenty other families in Missouri in July, and by February of 1851, they were alone—seven children and their parents, Royce and Mary Ann—in what would become southwestern Arizona, trying to cross the swollen Gila in three-foot water and failing miserably as their cattle foundered on the river floor. An island little bigger than a sand bar would have to do for the night. Royce unhitched the oxen, led them to the land, then waded across the river to gather firewood. With the help of her older children, Mary Ann unloaded supplies and prepared a dinner of bean soup and stale bread, which the family ate by moonlight.

Their situation was desperate. Their horse had died, and their scant remaining cattle were so weak that some of the children, aged two to seventeen, had been forced to walk long stretches of their route from Maricopa Wells, eighty miles back. They were on a barely blazed trail eroded by recent storms. The food they'd packed under the floor of their prairie schooners before starting west was nearly spent—enough jerked meat and dried fruit, flour, meal, bacon, and beans to last eighteen months, or so they'd thought. They had abandoned

FIG. 1. Olive Oatman, 1857, by Charles and Arthur Nahl. The engraving appeared at the end of the first edition of *Life Among the Indians: Being an Interesting Narrative of the Captivity of the Oatman Girls* and was moved to the front for subsequent editions.

one of their wagons in New Mexico after their oxen had dwindled to the point where they had no way to pull it. They had no money, nothing to trade, and over one hundred miles to go across the scorched desert before they would reach Fort Yuma, an army post just over the brand new California border.[1] Soon they would have another mouth to feed: Mary Ann was nearly nine months pregnant.

Still, the Oatmans feared one thing more than famine: Indians. Before leaving Maricopa Wells, they had been warned that the Apaches were attacking emigrants up and down the Gila, and their fellow pioneers had urged them to stay. But a famine there made prospects for survival slim, so when a traveling entomologist named John LeConte arrived from Fort Yuma, loaded with fossils and beetle specimens, saying he had seen no trace of Indians on the trail, Royce decided to move on, leaving the remaining two families in his party behind, shaking their heads.

Seven days after the Oatmans left Maricopa Wells, LeConte overtook them on his return to Fort Yuma. By now Royce recognized that his supplies and cattle couldn't possibly carry the family through to Yuma. He wrote a letter to the commander of the fort, asking for help, and LeConte promised to deliver it. "I am under the necessity of calling upon you for assistance," he pleaded, requesting horses and harnesses. "There is my wife & seven children and without help sir I am confident we must perrish [*sic*]."[2]

The next day, thirty miles down the trail, LeConte and his Mexican guide met a band of Indians, four of whom distracted the two men at their camp by feigning friendship and making small talk while others stole their horses from a nearby valley. Concerned that the Oatman rescue would be delayed for days while he walked the remaining one hundred miles to Fort Yuma, LeConte posted a card on a tree warning the family about the Indians.

Though he didn't mention LeConte's card to the children, Royce had probably seen it by the time they reached the Gila, where he began to fray. At the start of the trip he believed that, treated well, Indians were inherently friendly, and he even blamed their violence on cruel treatment by whites. When he'd worked as a traveling merchant in Iowa, Royce had mastered an attitude of unflappable cool to placate them, and his approach had always worked. But this journey had tested his theory. Some Indians had shared his tobacco and traded with him; others had stolen his cattle or pressured him into bartering irreplaceable pots and pans along with beans and bread. One night, as he and his fellow emigrants camped on the Arkansas River, Apaches on the other side had massacred a group traveling in a government expedition and stolen a hundred mules. Now the information he'd chosen to ignore back in Maricopa Wells was roiling in his mind: though LeConte hadn't been assaulted by Indians himself, he *had* said Apaches were moving in the hills, and Royce knew they were much more likely to menace a family traveling alone than members of a wagon train.

That night, a high wind swept river water onto the two-hundred-square-foot island, threatening to snuff out the fire and forcing the family to move its camp repeatedly. No one, including the spooked cattle, got much sleep. Fifteen-year-old Lorenzo spent much of the night tending to the frightened animals while the older children shivered around the fire and their parents conferred inside the wagon. Mary Ann, who had her own worries, not the least of which was kicking inside her, comforted Royce as he broke down and wept for a solid hour, lamenting the dangerous situation he had brought his family into. She assured him he was simply exhausted and his mind was working overtime. Only seventeen-year-old Lucy, the eldest, heard her father cry.

The gravity of the situation hadn't fully impressed Olive and her younger siblings, Royce Jr., eleven, Mary Ann, seven, and Charity Ann, five, who blithely fantasized about what they would do if Apaches attacked them. One would run; another would "fight and die fighting"; another would hold them off with a gun or a club.

"Well there is one thing," said fourteen-year-old Olive, a dark-haired beauty with deep-set eyes and a serious brow. "I shall not be taken by these miserable brutes. I will fight as long as I can, and if I see that I am about to be taken, I will kill myself."[3] Shortly after dawn, the family reloaded their wagon, hitched the cattle again, forded the river, and stopped to let their team graze. At noon they continued, but the trail led to a lime rock mesa where the beleaguered oxen balked at the steep ascent. The Oatmans unpacked the wagon and began hand-carrying their belongings up the two-hundred-foot-tall bluff. That day, Lucy confided in Lorenzo, describing Royce's tears the night before, and together they noted a change in their forty-one-year-old father. Five feet tall, solidly built, and bearded, Royce was a man who exuded confidence and readily expressed his feelings. Restless and drawn to novelty, he jumped into new situations with conviction and—some said—arrogance. Until now, despite everything, he had seemed optimistic. But as he mounted the hill, he looked like a defeated man. Royce sat on a rock, turned to his wife and said, "Mother, in the name of God, I know something terrible is about to happen."[4]

After hauling the first load of supplies, the Oatmans stopped for lunch, sitting atop black lava rocks and looking out at the mountains looming north and east of the Gila River. It was a lunar landscape, a parched expanse stippled with patches of dried grass and studded with Saguaro cacti, some as many as two hundred years old, standing alone and in clusters, like alien sentries lifting their spiky arms to the sun. Red plumes of flowering ocotillo shot up from gangly stalks, and golden brittlebush bloomed in low clusters across the desert floor. The region was populated by a network of Indians, including friendly Pimas, Maricopas, and Tohono O'odhams (then called Papagos). The Yavapais, hunter-gatherers with links to the Apaches, roamed to the north, carrying bows, arrows, and clubs. Two years later, this stretch of northern Mexico would be absorbed into the territory of New Mexico with the signing of the 1853 Gadsden Purchase, mainly because it contained the only navigable southern route to California, running just south of the Gila. Called Cooke's Wagon Road, it was the road the Oatmans now traveled.[5]

Once the second load had been carried up, Royce started back down the slope, and the family helped the bony cattle pull the empty wagon to the top to be repacked. It was late afternoon. They had advanced just a few miles since dawn and planned to continue in cooler weather at dusk to ease the trip for the animals. By now the Oatmans had spent hours getting their provisions up the hill and reloaded. The sun was hot and there was no sound, save for the lowing of the disgruntled livestock. "Thank God, we are on our road safe," Mary Ann said to her husband. "There is no appearance of danger."[6] Lorenzo studied his father, who glumly repacked the wagon. When the boy turned and glanced back down the hill, he saw movement: a procession of Indians, their wolf-skin skirts gently flapping against their thighs, meandering up the incline from the west. They were Yavapais—possibly the same group that had bamboozled LeConte and his guide a day or two before. When Lorenzo turned to his father and pointed, he found Royce's reaction as alarming as he did the arrival of the Indians themselves: his face reddened then went pale, and Lorenzo saw from his father's twitching mouth that he could barely control his panic. The other family members turned to look. Olive counted nineteen Indians.

Royce finally found his voice. "Do not be alarmed," he said. "The Indians won't harm you."[7] It was the last thing he would say to his family. As they poured into the camp, Royce addressed the Yavapais in broken Spanish, the lingua franca of the Southwest, inviting them to sit down. They asked for tobacco; he lit a pipe and shared it with them. The Yavapais glared nervously around the mesa as they smoked, exchanging knowing glances even as they claimed they had come in peace. When they requested food, Royce resisted, explaining that if he fed them, his family would starve. Still, they insisted. He gave them bread and they demanded more, standing up and rummaging around inside the wagon themselves. When Royce again refused, they stepped aside and formed a circle, conferring in their own language.

Lorenzo stood near the Indians as they spoke while his father reorganized the wagon, keeping an eye on the intruders and struggling to conceal his terror. Royce had always believed that if you didn't show fear around Indians, they wouldn't attack, but he was now far beyond feigning self-possession. Mary Ann climbed inside the wagon, taking three-year-old Roland with her. Lucy and Olive stood to one side near the three younger children. Little Mary Ann sat on a nearby rock holding the rope to the cattle teams between her knees, waiting. They were ready to go.

It took mere minutes for the Yavapais to bludgeon most of the family to death. Pulling knives and war clubs from their skirts, they jumped, shrieking, and assaulted Royce first then clubbed Lorenzo on the back of the head until he fell face down in the dirt, bleeding from his ears. They pushed Olive aside to get to her mother, the baby, and Charity Ann. Eleven-year-old Royce Jr. stood mute with shock until a single blow took him writhing to the ground. Untouched, Mary Ann crumpled, crying into her hands, the rope at her feet, on the other side of the wagon. Olive took in the spectacle and fainted.

"When I recovered my thoughts," she later wrote, "I could hardly realize where I was . . . and thought I was probably dying. I knew that all, or probably all the family had been murdered; thus bewildered, confused, half conscious and half insensible I remained a short time, I know not how long. . . . Occasionally a low, piteous moan would come from some one of the family as in a dying state. I distinguished the groans of my poor mother, and sprang wildly toward her, but was held back by the merciless savage holding me in his cruel grasp, and lifting a club over my head, threatening me in the most taunting, barbarous manner."[8] It was an empty gesture: she and Mary Ann would be spared.

For the next hour, Olive and Mary Ann watched as their attackers ransacked the wagon and looted the bodies of the dead and dying. Lorenzo stirred as they yanked off his hat and shoes, so the Yavapais dragged him by the feet to the edge of the mesa and threw him off. Olive turned away to avoid seeing his head dashed against the rocks. They ripped the cover off the wagon, removed parts of the wheels, unhitched the teams, broke open boxes, and packed up what food they could carry, including two sacks of smoked beef Royce hadn't offered them. Marveling at the odd domestic conveniences they found in the white man's wagon, they pulled out a duvet and tore it open, releasing the down to the wind. Olive watched the feathers float to the ground and blow along the dusty mesa, sticking to the carnage of the family she would leave behind.

With a shove, Olive and Mary Ann were driven down the hill, barefoot, to begin a journey of about sixty miles over four days.[9] As she stumbled forward, searing her feet in the sand and sweating clear through the bodice of her dress, Olive wished the Yavapais would kill her too, but there was Mary Ann, crying, drooling, and tripping along behind her.

Olive's life as a frontier woman had begun.

2

Indian Country

"The [Gila River area is] so utterly desolate, desert, and Godforsaken, that Kit Carson says a wolf could not make his living upon it."
| U.S. Representative THOMAS HART BENTON addressing the house of representatives, June 26, 1854

Forced to discard their shoes to avoid leaving a recognizable trail, the Oatman girls found themselves being marched barefoot at warrior speed back across the river and through a dark ravine to an Indian camp in the hills. They traveled in two groups: one leading the captives, the other the animals. At the camp, the Indians slaughtered a cow and cooked the meat over a fire made with flint and wild cotton, then they baked dough made from the Oatmans' flour and soaked it in bean soup. They scornfully offered the food to the girls, perhaps mocking Royce's claim that he had had no food. But they couldn't eat. They watched in silence, their stomachs rumbling, as their captors ate under the full moon, to the sound of coyotes crying in the hills. Olive's worst fear was that she and her sister would be burned alive. Mary Ann was more concerned about leaving her dead family behind.

After the meal, Olive and Mary Ann huddled together by the campfire, terrified, as the Yavapais jeered at them—especially Mary Ann. "When her feelings became uncontrollable," Olive recalled, "she would hide her head in my arms, and most piteously sob aloud, but she was immediately hushed by the brandishing of a war club over her head."[1]

The Yavapais periodically pointed at the mesa in the distance, where Olive could still see the exposed bows of the Oatman wagon, stripped of its covering. "Mangled as I knew they were," she said, "I longed to go back and take one look, one long, last farewell look in the faces of my parents." She remembered the impossibly trusting expressions of the little ones, Charity Ann and Roland, when Royce Sr. had told them not to fear the Indians, and she recalled how Royce Jr. had convulsed as he died.

Wary of being discovered by whites near the site of the massacre, the Yavapais pushed on an hour later. Tears stung Olive's eyes when she looked back to see that the ravaged wagon—the last vestige of her former life—had disappeared into the mountains behind her. They traveled for several hours—too fast for the girls, whose feet were now bleeding. If the Oatmans slowed down, the Yavapais threatened them with their clubs. When Mary Ann gave up, collapsing in a heap, she was beaten and told she would be left behind. She asked Olive to let them kill her.

"I resolved," said Olive, "in the event of her being left, to cling to her, and thus compel them to dispose of us as they had the remainder of the family."[2] She begged them not to leave her sister, and as she pleaded her case, one Indian removed his pack, handed it to another, threw Mary Ann on his back and continued on. Scrambling to keep pace, Olive watched Mary Ann surrender to exhaustion. "I managed to look into her face, and found her eyes opening and shutting alternately, as if in an effort to wake, but still unable to sleep; I spoke to her but received no answer. We could not converse without exciting the fiendish rage of our enemies."

The Yavapais were worried about making time, and seemed fearful. Heading northeast, they raced over a series of small bluffs and into a winding valley, making a single brief stop in the middle of the night then walking until noon the next day. Along the way, Mary Ann quietly slipped into shock. Olive looked into her eyes to see if she was conscious and saw that her sister had become "utterly indifferent to all about her; and, wrapped in a dreamy reverie, relieved of all care of life or death, presenting the appearance of one who had simply the consciousness that some strange, unaccountable event had happened, and in its bewildering effects she was content to remain."[3] They rested for two hours at a camp in an open space surrounded by mountains. The Yavapais killed the rest of the Oatmans' animals and sliced them up, broiled another meal of meat, bread, and bean soup, and packed the rest to be carried on their backs. Overcome by hunger, the girls now ate the stringy beef. Again, Mary Ann was told to walk, refused, and was beaten, then carried. The Yavapais tied leather to Olive's bleeding feet to protect them, and that night they stopped to camp in a clearing in the woods. The girls slept in the sand, guarded by Indians.

Breakfast was, as Olive put it, "beef, burned dough, and beans, instead of beans, burned dough, and beef, as usual." They resumed their journey on hillier roads that Olive later deemed the roughest she ever traveled as a captive: "*That day* is among the few days of my dreary stay among the savages marked by the most pain and suffering ever endured."[4] By now her death wish was overriding her impulse to protect Mary Ann. Twice she gave up, begging to be killed and left behind, but instead was pushed and dragged along.

Around noon, the party met nearly a dozen Comanches, a tribe notorious not only for its ferocity but also for its sadistic torture methods.[5] One of the Comanches took one look at Olive, strung his bow, and shot at her, piercing only the ragged skirt of her dress. "He was in the act . . . of hurling the second," she later recalled, "when two of our number sprang toward them with their clubs, while two others snatched us [to] one side, placing themselves between us and the drawn bows." Olive later learned the man had lost his brother to whites on the Santa Fe Trail and had vowed to kill the next white person he saw. The two tribes nearly came to blows. One group of Yavapais stayed behind to wrangle with the Comanches while another hurried the girls along. Mary Ann confided to Olive, "I wish they had killed us."[6]

On the fourth day, they arrived at the home of the Yavapais, near modern-day Congress, Arizona. With all they had endured, said Olive, "to get even into an Indian camp was home." Surrounded by hills, the camp consisted of low, thatched huts sunk into the ground. All three hundred inhabitants were called out to inspect the white prisoners. One man made a speech then unpacked the spoils of the Oatman raid and proudly exhibited them. The warriors who'd captured Olive and Mary Ann were hailed as heroes, and a ritual of ridicule began.

The sisters were forced to stand on a pile of twigs and branches while the Yavapais, male and female, young and old, wearing blankets, bark, skins, or nothing, gathered around them. "Music then commenced," wrote Olive, "which consisted of pounding upon stones with clubs and horn, and the drawing of a small string like a fiddle bow across distended bark."

Circling the girls, the tribe yelled, spat, and threw dirt at them. Some Yavapais reached out and slapped them as they revolved around them. "It seemed . . . that their main ambition was to exhibit their superiority over us, and the low, earnest, intense hate they bore toward our race," said Olive.[7] The Yavapai children especially elicited great guffaws from their elders by taunting the girls, who clasped each other in fear, terrified that the worst was yet to come. If the tribe had kidnapped them to torture them to death, they wouldn't have been the first to meet this fate. But this wasn't the Yavapais' intention. The abuse the Oatmans now endured set the tone for their relationship with their captors over the next year. They were slaves.

"Now when you remember our ages," wrote Olive, "our journey

of . . . four days and four nights, the scene of slaughter witnessed; our fears & the attack of the Comanches; our bleeding, aching limbs; & this introduction of two young girls to Indian life; & then you get something of an idea of our situation, & the Providence that sustained us."[8]

3

"How Little We Thought What Was Before Us"

Oh the Good time has come at last,
We need no more complain, Sir,
The rich can live in luxury
And the poor can do the same, Sir,

For the Good time has come at last,
And as we all are told, Sir,
We shall be rich at once now,
With California Gold, Sir.

Campfire song, 1840s

If a belief in Providence sustained Olive and Mary Ann in captivity, it was also what had propelled them into the hands of Yavapais in the first place. The Oatmans were Mormons who had joined a wagon train headed to the mouth of the Colorado River to settle in the "land of Bashan," which they believed would be a Mormon paradise. They were Brewsterites, a splinter sect started in 1837 after eleven-year-old James Colin Brewster claimed to have had divine revelations that Mormon founder Joseph Smith deemed phony. With the help of his father, Brewster published his translation of the writings of Esdras, a figure he alleged was an ancient Hebrew prophet who had predicted the world's end in 1878 as well as the reorganization of the church under the boy "revelator" himself.

Smith was unimpressed by the vision and irked by the boy's chal-

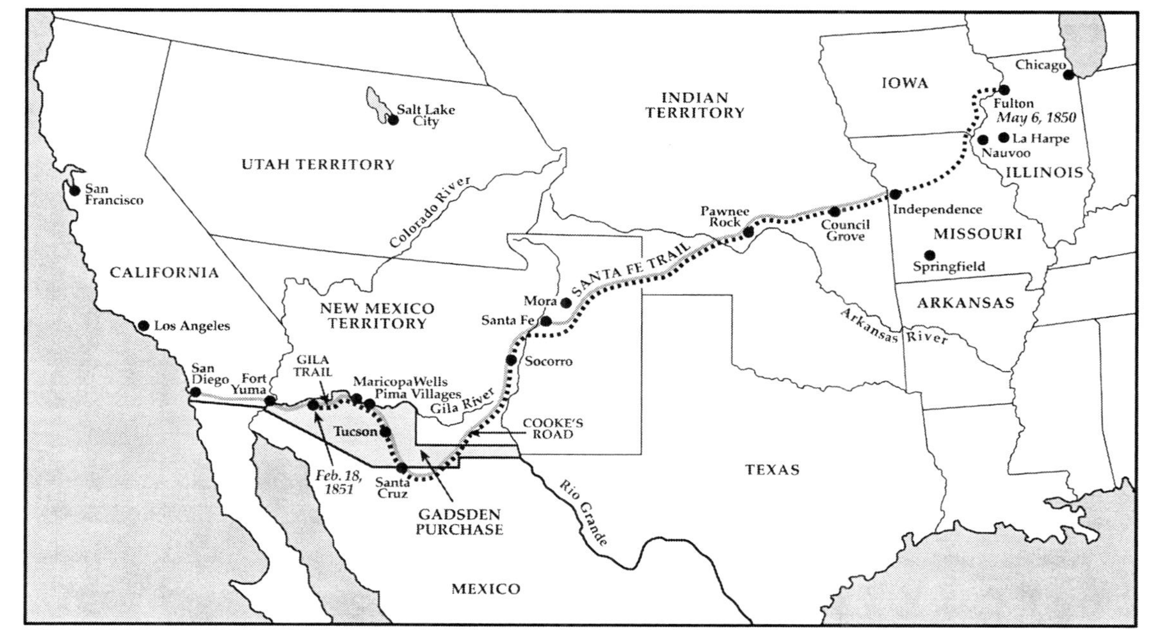

MAP 1. The Oatman route west, 1850–51. California gained its statehood in the fall of 1850 while the Oatmans, on the Santa Fe Trail, were arguing with Brewster about whether to continue to California or settle in Socorro, New Mexico.

lenge to his authority. Mormon doctrine stipulated that only Smith could channel God, and Brewster's strong objection to polygamy didn't endear him to Smith, who had dozens of wives.[1] The church condemned Brewster in its newspaper, *Times and Seasons*, declaring in 1842, "We have lately seen a pamphlet, written and published by James C. Brewster; purporting it to be one of the lost books of Esdras; and to be written by the gift and power of God. We consider it to be perfect humbug."[2]

Brewster subsequently claimed to have found a passage in Esdras designating the mouth of the Colorado River—fertile, wooded, and temperate, as he mistakenly believed it was—a promised land for Brewsterites. Unlike Brigham Young, who succeeded Smith in 1844 and led the Mormons to the Great Basin in 1847 specifically because its extreme climate would repel his enemies, Brewster sought genuine paradise.[3] In the January 1849 issue of his monthly newspaper, the *Olive Branch, or, Herald of Peace and Truth to All Saints*, he announced plans for his road trip to Shangri-la. But Brewster was clearly as misinformed about Southwest Indians as he was about the desert geography of Bashan. He quoted, for his followers, a passage from an 1846 travelogue called *Scenes in the Colorado Mountains, and in Oregon, California, New Mexico, Texas and the Grand Prairies*, written by Rufus B. Sage, a man who had never ventured south of Taos, New Mexico: "The bottoms of the Colorado and the Gila, with their tributaries, are broad, rich and well timbered. Every thing in the shape of vegetation attains a lusty size, amply evincing the exuberant fecundity of the soil producing it. There are many sweet spots in the vicinity of both these streams, well deserving the name of earthly Eden. Man here might fare sumptuously, with one continual feast spread before him. . . . The natives, for the most part, may be considered friendly, or at least not dangerous."[4]

The 1830 *Book of Mormon* painted a more menacing picture of Indians. It posited two warring tribes that emigrated to North America from Israel around 600 BC: the humble Nephites, "white and exceedingly fair and delightsome," and the Lamanites, "dark and loathsome, and a filthy people, full of idleness and all manner of abominations." Godless and "bloodthirsty," the Lamanites lived in tents, shaved their heads, wore leather loincloths, and captured women and children. Once white, they'd been cursed with dark skin for their faithlessness. Mormon scripture held that when they were converted, the Lamanites' skin would turn white and they would be "numbered among the Nephites"—a revealing parable about the nineteenth-century white man's assimilationist vision of Indians.[5]

In the *Olive Branch*, Brewster promised that the "saints" (the Mormon term for followers) who followed him would "receive their inheritances" in the valleys of the Gila and the Colorado rivers. He envisioned a refuge where "none shall be poor, neither shall there be any that are rich." If he had pulled it off, his would have been one of California's first utopian experiments, built on a foundation of collectivism. One convert wrote, "We are all brethren, and one is not above the other. . . . Some of the brethren may get more teams than they need, others a greater amount of breadstuffs or dry goods, in exchange for their property; in such cases, let all aspire to deeds of charity among their more unfortunate brethren, by giving or lending them of their substance."[6]

Throughout 1849 the *Olive Branch* called for saints to send in their names and occupations, asked them to state how much money they had and how soon they could leave, and laid plans for the new nation. "The form of government is to be Republican, in the strictest sense of the word," wrote Brewster. People would elect their own governors, capital punishment would be forbidden, and liquor would be banned, as would, interestingly, "construction of military works and all warlike preparations." There would be taxes. And though Brewster had conceived Bashan as a new nation, he specified that "we are not required to violate any of the laws of our country." That included strict adherence to monogamy, a principle that set him apart from Brigham Young.

Bashan would be laid out on a grid and divided into blocks a mile square. A hundred blocks would form a township, and a town would occupy a square mile in every township. Ten blocks would be set aside for churches and schools. Beating Congress by mere months to the idea of luring pioneers west with free property (the September 1850 Donation Land Claim Act allotted homesteaders in the Pacific Northwest free acreage), Brewster promised the remaining blocks would be divided into farms, and though the land was not his to give, he planned to parcel it out.[7]

If his sense of community planning was arbitrary, Brewster's instructions about how to pack for the westward journey were quite specific: the wagons, he emphasized, should be two-horse wagons suitable also for oxen; provisions should last at least six months and ideally a year. Travelers should bring enough summer and winter clothing for a year, farming utensils for two years. Flour, rice, and beans (a pound per day, per person) were recommended; meat was not. A good rifle and five hundred rounds would ensure that game would be on the menu. Boxes and chests, he said, should all be the same height to allow beds to be laid on them, and each family needed a twelve-foot tent that could sleep eight. Brethren were urged to bring "good books," which meant nonfiction, ideally pertaining to science or history.[8]

Though it served both as an outlet for Brewster's overheated sermons and as a platform for his utopian visions, the *Olive Branch* was tinged with anxiety. In it the boy prophet, now barely a man, compared Bashan favorably—if defensively—to Salt Lake City ("more than 500 miles from any navigable water communicating with the ocean") but wrestled publicly with the troubling knowledge that the Salt Lake Mormons, misguided though he felt they were, were thriving.[9] The *Olive Branch* published letters from Brewsterites who had recruited new converts or dissuaded other Mormons from following Brigham Young to Utah and answered potential converts who wanted to know precisely how Brewster knew the Truth.

In February of 1850 Royce Oatman announced, through the *Olive Branch*, his interest in securing a ticket to paradise. He spent the month traveling around Iowa and Illinois preaching and, he claimed, healing people. In Davenport, Iowa, he reported, "the Lord confirmed the word spoken by healing the sick," and in Muscatine County, "the sick were healed, and I left some who were ready to commence in the great work of the Lord."[10] He would sell his farm, close his business, and go west.

Born in Vermont in 1809 and raised in western New York by parents of Dutch ancestry, Royce had moved to La Harpe, Illinois, at age nineteen, where his parents ran a hotel, and where he met Mary Ann, nee Sperry. Like him, she came from a moderately wealthy and well-educated family—one into which three Oatmans married (two of her brothers married Royce's sisters). The couple spent two years farming in La Harpe, then Royce launched a dry-goods business that prospered until the notorious 1842 run on the banks caused a crash that ruined him. After spending a year in Chicago, the family moved to a farm in Fulton, Illinois. Mary Ann's sister and her husband, Sarah and Asa Abbott, followed in 1847, buying an adjoining property, and Asa's parents followed them.

The Oatmans lived less than a mile south of what in 1912 would become the first coast-to-coast highway in the country: U.S. Route 30, or the Lincoln Highway, about 120 miles north of Nauvoo, where Joseph Smith had moved his church in 1839, attracting thousands of followers and organizing a militia that was almost a fourth the size of the U.S. Army.[11] On land—flat and featureless—said to have been farmed originally by Fox and Sauk Indians, they first occupied a cellar then built a wooden house over the cellar; this was the home in which their youngest children, Charity Ann and Roland, were born.

A singular irony of the Oatman saga occurred in 1846, just before Olive's grandparents (Mary Ann's Mormon parents) left La Harpe on their own westward exodus. Royce and Mary Ann spent a week visiting with them in La Harpe before the Sperrys' departure, during which Royce argued with his father-in-law, Joy Sperry, about who should lead the Mormon Church until a worthy successor to Joseph Smith was found. At the time, Royce supported the theologian Sidney Rigdon, Smith's running mate in his 1844 campaign for president, an antipolygamist who was organizing his own church in Pittsburgh. Sperry had chosen to follow Rigdon's rival, Brigham Young, and join sixteen thousand other believers in what would become Salt Lake City, Utah, where they would soon build their capital.[12]

On the last day of the visit, the men bickered at the breakfast table. As Mary Ann's brother Charles remembered it in his diary, "Finally Oatman said, 'I see Father Sperry it is no use to talk to you. I prophesy in the name of the Lord, that if you go west with your family, your children will go hungry and some will starve to death. Your throats will be cut from ear to ear by the Indians.' My father replied, 'Be careful how you prophesy in the name of the Lord.' Strange to say, that particular prophesy was fulfilled . . . not on my father's family, but upon [Oatman] and his family. It took place on the Gila River in Arizona."[13]

For their part, the Sperrys and their son Aaron died of illness and exposure before they even left Iowa; their two other sons made it to Salt Lake City. Later that year Royce and his family visited Rigdon on his Pennsylvania farm and, possibly turned off by Rigdon's penchant for fainting spells and panic attacks, decided to follow Brewster.[14]

In late 1849, after months of preparation and correspondence with the other members of the expedition, Royce sold the farm and his belongings for fifteen hundred dollars—just enough to buy cattle and wagons for the westward journey. Now, three years after losing her parents, Sarah Sperry Abbott bade her sister what would be a last good-bye, bearing a gift: a lilac bush she planted in Mary Ann's yard. The bush still blooms on the old Oatman property.

The Oatmans left Whiteside County on May 6, 1850, took a ferry across the Mississippi, and collected church elder George Mateer and his family in West Buffalo, Iowa, then the Ira Thompson family in Moscow. In late June they arrived in Independence, Missouri, on a stretch of the Missouri River known for its "jumping-off places"—settlements where emigrants met traveling companions or killed time until their parties arrived, before heading west. Especially after 1848, when news spread that gold had been found in California, Independence had become a springboard for westward emigrants (dubbed forty-niners a year later) from Missouri, Illinois, Iowa, Indiana, and sometimes New York and New Hampshire. Over the next few weeks the Oatmans and Thompsons bought supplies and coordinated with the other families in the outfit. Their food, most of which had been prepared during the previous spring, was stored with clothes and bedding beneath the wagon floor. Guns, ammunition, water kegs, churning barrels, lanterns, fabric, and farm tools were packed above it. The wagons would be drawn by oxen and horses, and trailed by milk cows and supplemental teams.

In mid-July the Brewsters arrived late from Springfield, having left first a cat then a wagon behind, returning each time to get them and forcing the others to wait for two weeks. "We are all tanned very bad indeed," wrote one frustrated pioneer eager to get moving, "and if we continue growing black as fast as we have done, we shall be as black as the Indians."[15] It was now perilously late in the season to be embarking on a cross-country journey—most parties left in May or June to ensure the grass was deep enough for cattle grazing en route and to avoid bad weather in the fall. But when the Brewsterites were finally assembled, they discovered they didn't have enough communal supplies to make it to Bashan and were forced to stock up in Independence, where, like modern-day airport vendors, suppliers took advantage of their captive consumers.[16] On July 15 the group elected Jackson Goodale, a recent convert to Brewsterism, captain of the train, which consisted of more than a dozen families and a handful of bachelors—in total, between eighty-five and ninety-three people, including Brewster, his parents, and his five siblings.[17] A week later they moved their camp to a point twenty miles west of Independence, where one family complained about sharing provisions with others and one pioneer, suspected of being a Salt Lake Mormon sent to cause trouble among the Brewsterites, turned back. Though the journey had hardly begun, Brewster wrote in the *Olive Branch*, "during the past two weeks, all that the power of Satan and the iniquity of the ungodly could accomplish has been done to produce discord and division among us."[18] Not just discordant and divided but now a month behind schedule, the party pulled out on Friday, August 5.

In leaving Independence, the Oatmans joined a migration unparalleled in modern history. Between 1849 and 1853 a quarter of a million Americans went west to settle on free land in Oregon and California, to mine gold and silver, or, in the case of the Mormons, to find Zion.[19] Royce's initial religious commitment seemed clear from the letters he wrote to the *Olive Branch*; whether it survived his trip west is questionable. Certainly, not everyone joined Brewster's party for strictly religious reasons. Seventeen-year-old Susan Thompson, who became fast friends with Lucy Oatman, later recalled, "Father was the first in our part of the country [Muscatina, Iowa] to decide upon the westward journey after the news of the finding of gold in California had reached us."[20]

The trip began on the Santa Fe Trail, the biggest trade and government supply route linking Independence to Santa Fe until the railroad reached Santa Fe in 1880. It had also been the main artery between the United States and Mexico during the Mexican-American War of 1846–48. Thompson remembered "the excitement as we formed into long columns, traveling in parallel lines according to the way the government parties had found to be most safe. There were about thirty of the great canvas-topped wagons, each drawn by three yoke of oxen and saddle horses. We were divided into companies and each band was governed by a captain. Royce Oatman was the man from whom we received directions and counsel." For the children, worries were few and fears—of Indians, disease, or exposure—were minimal. "We were a happy, carefree lot of young people and the dangers and hardships found no resting place on our shoulders," said Thompson. "It was a continuous picnic and excitement was plentiful." In a masterstroke of understatement, Olive later wrote, "How little we thought what was before us."[21]

There was no way these families could know what was in store for them. Guidebooks of the day said the trip would take just three or four months. Typically, though, it took closer to six or eight months, by which time the cattle were often gaunt and depleted and the weather was turning. One book merrily assured readers, "As nothing is required upon this route but such teams and provisions as the farmer must necessarily have at home, it may truly be said that it costs him nothing but his time."[22] Often, because no one in the outfit had previously traveled west, it was impossible to predict whether the roads would be passable or when supplies would give out.

Settlers rolled along in covered wagons that heated up to 110 degrees, slept in crowded tents, and herded cattle across rivers and streams. Mosquitoes could be relentless, and a good storm could drench the tents and bedding, leaving them soggy for days and sending women and children to sleep on muddy makeshift beds under wagons. The same water was used for washing, waste, and drinking, creating Petri dishes for disease. Measles could strike at any time; in 1850 alone, cholera killed an estimated five thousand people who had left on wagon trains from Independence. Gravesites littered the roadsides, sometimes a dozen or two at a pass, with multiple bodies piled into a single grave. Discarded beds and clothes along the road also marked a death—by illness, snakebite, or childbirth—a risky prospect in those years even for women who weren't bouncing along in wagon trains. Women's voluminous skirts often got caught in wheel spokes and pulled them to their deaths.[23]

Finally, Apache Indians, inflamed by white incursions into their land, were terrorizing people up and down the Rio Grande. Known for their horsemanship and guerilla tactics, they had lately begun to unleash their fury on the U.S. Army and the emigrants it protected, and they were formidable foes. For two hundred years they had thwarted Spanish and Mexican efforts to develop the Southwest, acting as well-organized robber barons who demanded food or livestock in return for safe passage through their lands, which spanned parts of New Mexico, northern Mexico, and Arizona. The newly arrived whites were no exception, but the stakes were raised when the northern Mexican states of Sonora and Chihuahua placed bounties on Apache scalps and white mountain men began trading these "hairy banknotes," commanding two hundred dollars for the scalp of a warrior and one hundred dollars for that of a woman or child, sometimes killing whole villages to get them.[24] If the westward migration hadn't fully enraged the Apaches in the region, bounty hunting did.

The Oatmans' first few weeks were uneventful and, by Susan Thompson's account, delightful. Every few days the group stopped to allow the women to bake and the men to hunt for antelope, buffalo, rabbit, or pheasant. When they camped near water, the men fished and the women washed clothes and bedding. "Often," wrote Thompson, "during the daytime halts, we ran races or made swings."[25] The drivers rested in the shade of the wagons, their hats pulled over their faces, and the mules, freed from the weight of the wagons, grazed and rolled around in the grass.

At night, the wagons were drawn into a circle and ropes were tied between them to corral the animals. Cooking was back-straining work done over an open fire—one for each family; it required stooping over a pot strung up on a pole balanced on two stakes pounded into the ground. But there was one time-saving advantage to the bumpy wagon ride of the day: each morning, cream was poured into a pot hung from crossbeams of the wagon, and by evening the butter was effortlessly churned. After dinner, the women unpacked the

FIG. 2. The first night of the journey, from *Captivity of the Oatman Girls*.

tents, made the beds, prepared the next day's food, and—to prevent mildew—cleaned out the wagons so that they could air overnight. The children played games and told stories around the campfire or made music and danced in the glow of lard-burning lanterns. If they had time, the adults also socialized, circulating from wagon to wagon.

At first, there was no travel on Sunday, and the families worshiped every night. "I fancied we were God's Israel journeying to the promised land," Olive wrote.[26] While the drivers slept beneath the wagons, women and children slept in tents, with two men guarding the camp through the night while coyotes howled in the distance. In the morning, Olive, Lucy, little Mary Ann, and their mother pulled their gingham dresses over their heads, buttoning each other from behind, and emerged to bank the fire and prepare breakfast—pancakes or fried bread, reheated beans, fried meat, and tea or coffee—with the younger children at their feet, while Royce, Lorenzo, and Royce Jr. tended to the stock. After breakfast, the mules were hitched, the children were counted, and the crack of a bullwhip sent the creaking wagons rolling back down the trail.

The countryside was magnificent. A pioneer named Marian Russell described what it was like to travel the Santa Fe Trail in the early 1850s: "I remember so clearly the beauty of the earth, and how, as we bore westward, the deer and the antelope bounded away from us. There were miles and miles of buffalo grass, blue lagoons, and blood-red sunsets and, once in a while, a little sod house on the lonely prairie—home of some hunter or trapper."[27] Children delighted in coaxing long-legged tarantulas from holes in the ground and stomping on them, or chasing lizards and road runners.

Where wood was scarce, women collected pieces of dried dung, called "buffalo chips," for fuel. "I would stand back and kick them," wrote Russell, "then reach down and gather them carefully, for under them lived big spiders and centipedes. Sometimes scorpions ran from beneath them. I would fill my long dress skirt with the evening's fuel and take it back to mother." Buffalo trails cut across the open country, running north and south in corridors that led to water that flowed east out of the Rocky Mountains. Sometimes the animals themselves could be seen walking single file along the rutted trails.

The emigrant families, most of whom had never met before the westward journey, got to know each other well. Thompson recalled how one night she and Lucy Oatman forgot to fill the water buckets for the next day and stole down to the river in the dark, in hopes of avoiding a scolding:

We were just starting back with our dripping pails when we heard someone coming. We clutched each other in terror, remembering all too late the warnings we had heard of the fearful Apaches.

In a moment we were reassured by the sight of a boy who was the worst tease in the company. He, too, had forgotten his pail of water. A time for revenge for many practical jokes had come and with a great crashing of underbrush we rushed at him through the darkness. There was a banging of water buckets, a flying of heels, and a volley of blood curdling yells, "The Apaches are coming! The Apaches are coming!"[28]

Though Indians were the pioneers' greatest concern, the party's biggest problem, even at that point, was itself. A hundred miles into the journey, the squabbling began, and Olive noted that even "the most enthusiastic of the party were subdued . . . & the brightest countenance was soon changed to sadness and reflection."[29] Some wearied of the monotony of travel or worried obsessively about Indians. Others argued about religious correctness, including whether one member had been rightfully ordained to serve in the church. Brewster himself proved to be a contentious and unlikable zealot.[30] On a bluff at Pawnee Rock in what became Kansas, he found a stone he claimed was inscribed with hieroglyphics (more likely they were Indian pictographs), and translated them, à la Joseph Smith, into Mormon revelation about the "armies of Kish" and "people of Gerad" who had sojourned in the region centuries earlier.[31] To complicate matters, along the way he had a new revelation that the promised land described in the Book of Esdras was not near the Colorado River but rather on the banks of the Rio Grande, near Socorro, New Mexico—conveniently closer by more than six hundred miles. When he proposed settling there, some of the others—Royce among them—objected.

A traveler named Max Greene would be the only outsider to describe the Brewster party, having jumped aboard mid-journey "on the lookout for novelty." He identified Royce as a key troublemaker, characterizing him as "a fine fellow enough in most respects, but sinfully reckless, and . . . a most dangerous companion on the Grand Prairie." According to Greene, Royce simply wouldn't compromise his private wishes for the benefit of the group. "Could we, therefore, have exchanged him for the small-pox," he said, "the measure would have had a majority vote."

The group discussed splitting up, and during a halt one rainy day a young Pennsylvania printer made a speech in which he described the dire things that would happen if they divided. "It was a hopeless, singular spectacle," Greene later recalled, "that slender youth earnestly talking to a hundred bearded, uncouth wranglers, encamped in the wilderness, four hundred miles from civilized habitation." The printer persuaded the women—but not the men—to stay together, and was subsequently fired at, while reclining in the grass, by someone who mistook him for an antelope. Later, another "accidental" shot whistled through his empty wagon bunk before he'd retired for the evening.[32]

Though they couldn't agree on where they were going, the outfit stayed together for protection from Indians, who were particularly predatory on the western half of the Santa Fe Trail, where Texas settlers had driven many Kiowas and Comanches out of the state. Disaster helped to sustain the group's fragile sense of unity. Early in the journey Roland fell off the wagon—a common accident for emigrant children—and nearly died after a wheel ran over his neck. Still invested in his identity as a preacher, Royce claimed to have saved his son: "I took him up, and saw that he was about to depart this life," he wrote in the *Olive Branch*. "But not feeling willing to part with him, I administered to the child according to the law and order of the gospel, and the Lord Blessed him, and he soon recovered, and is now hearty and well."[33]

On September 16, nineteen-year-old Mary Lane died of tuberculosis, and for lack of timber on the prairie, each family donated a board from their wagons to form a casket. Susan Thompson described how "a kind of terror of the plains came over me as in the dusk of the evening we left the grave on a little hillside and heard the howling of the wolves drawing nearer and nearer."[34] The group's fear of Indians was fueled by increasing reports of raids. A year earlier, nearly one hundred Apaches had killed six travelers in northern New Mexico and captured a woman, her servant, and her daughter. Months later, the mother was located, but as the search party pursuing her approached, the Indians dispensed with her by shooting an arrow into her heart. Her servant and daughter were never found.[35] Brewster recorded the mileage the group logged, and his table of distances included notes about Indian encounters. "Party of thirty or forty Indians remained in camp about two hours and then went away peaceably," he wrote about a stop along the Arkansas River. A little farther west he wrote, "Ten well-armed men guarding Santa Fe mail were chased into camp by Hostiles." And more than one hundred miles farther: "During three days encampment Indians were sighted looking down upon emigrant camp from surrounding cliffs."[36]

Imagined Indian threats could be as heart-stopping as real ones. One day during a halt, two men in the party set out to hunt antelope in the hills, lost their sense of direction, and routed their prey directly toward the wagon train. Several children ran up from behind a nearby hill to try to scare the animals back toward the hunters. The hunters mistook the children for Indians and panicked. Thinking an attack was imminent, the older man, Ira Thompson, turned to his hunting partner and said, "Charles, let us pray."

"I'll be damned if I'll pray; let us run," Charles answered and took off.

When Thompson outran him, Charles begged him not to abandon him to the Indians. Together they sprinted back to the camp, where they discovered, to the hilarity of the party, that they had been running from their own children.[37]

As the wagon train trundled along the north bank of the Arkansas River, the weather was perfect and the party's troubles subsided until early October, when the settlers crossed the river and entered the New Mexico Territory. But in the village of Mora, about one hundred miles north of Santa Fe, order began to break down. For unknown reasons, Ira Thompson and Royce wanted Goodale removed as captain and simply stopped heeding his instructions. Then Brewster charged Goodale with being "guilty of a transgression of the Law of God" and demoted him.[38] Royce was chosen to replace him, but before long he and Brewster were tussling about directions and their dispute fractured the party once and for all.

Brewster was determined to take a side trip to Santa Fe to retrieve his mail, even though the road was said to be sandy and difficult. Royce preferred the quicker, newly blazed southern route. The men bickered then took their grievances to the mayor of the local town and agreed to part ways, but not before Oatman offered to share his food and made a last, unsuccessful effort to convince the others to go with him. Nonetheless, Max Greene called Royce "the nucleus of our troubles." He was not malicious, said Greene, "but simply a facetious quarreler." Of Royce's decision to go it alone, he reflected without sentiment, "He paid the penalty of his temerity."[39]

On October 9 nearly half the party, about thirty-two people, followed Brewster toward Santa Fe en route to Socorro, near which they purchased land and began building a new settlement called Colonia, named for a prophet in the writings of Esdras. The others, about fifty people, including the Thompson and Mateer families, elected Royce captain and continued west. Olive had just turned fourteen. "These," she wrote, "were the beginnings of our sorrow. . . . Inclemen[t] weather, swollen streams, hostile tribes, scarcity of provisions & failing teams; were among the difficulties we began to meet with." The party, she said, now smaller by half, "seemed somewhat discouraged."[40]

In mid-October, just before they reached the Rio Grande, two of the Oatman horses were stolen (because of "poor guarding," one member claimed) and later seen among Mexicans, who said they'd bought them from Indians who raided emigrant trains and sold the spoils in Mexican settlements.[41] Possibly in response to the theft, Norman C. Brimhall replaced Oatman as captain, and Ira Thompson became company secretary.

For nine days in early November the Oatman party stopped in Socorro, where their reencounter with the lost half of the Brewster party was chilly. Brewster took a final swipe at the mutineers in the *Olive Branch*, reporting that "by their bad conduct," Oatman's company "gained the reputation of being the most dishonest men that had ever been in the country," without specifying why.[42] Oatman and his allies used the opportunity to make some fast cash by cutting and gathering hay at a nearby army post, then they left the Brewsterites behind. Over a year later the *Republican Compiler* of Gettysburg, Pennsylvania, reported on the Brewster party, saying, "Sickness, starvation, and the savages have about used up the balance of these misguided people. The few left would return to the states if they had the means to get back."[43]

With money in their pockets and meat, produce, and grain in their wagons, Oatman's group followed Col. Philip St. George Cooke's 1846 route, which would become the main overland route through the Southwest to southern California during the second half of the nineteenth century. It ran from Santa Fe to San Diego, heading south through New Mexico's Rio Grande Valley and cutting west into the future Arizona, where it hugged the Gila River (which then marked the U.S.-Mexico boundary), and turning northwest across the Colorado at Yuma Crossing to the Pacific, where it merged with the Gila Trail.[44] November was not a good month to be braving this landscape, especially where the road passed through the mountains of northern Mexico, more than five thousand feet above sea level. The rugged terrain reduced them to a quarter of their normal speed and forced them to tie fallen trees to the back of the wagon to serve as brakes during downhill travel.

In late November, Asa Lane, like his daughter Mary, died, probably of tuberculosis. He was, said Olive, "a man of stern integrity, appreciated and loved by us all, and his death was an irreparable loss." By now they couldn't afford to collaborate on a coffin, so the body was covered with a blanket and buried in a grave strewn with wildflowers and marked by a crude wooden stake bearing his name. "I remember," said Susan Thompson, "how even the faces of the roughest men showed pity when . . . we made [a] grave for Mr. Lane and attempted to console the daughter, Isabel, who was now the only member of the little family that had hoped to find health and fortune on the great western road."[45]

Days later, the party awoke to three inches of snow. They had had no water for twenty-four hours and trudged for a full day through the mounting snowdrifts in search of a stream they spotted about four miles away; there they found not only water but also timber and game. If not for the firewood they discovered there, they would have had to use pieces of their wagons for kindling. The mountain was filled with turkey, deer, antelope, and wild sheep. The group spent a week hunting, fishing, and feasting on wild meat cooked over coals in pans inside the wagons.

"It was rather cold weather to live in a wagon and cook out of doors," recalled Mrs. Wilder, who wrapped herself and her baby in blankets and kept a pan of coals burning inside the wagon. "I baked bread to last some time while we tarried. [Husband] Willard would make the coffee. So we lived without any actual suffering. We fared better than those with more children."[46] Royce, his seven children, and Mary Ann, now seven months pregnant, were all crowded into two wagons. They surely dreamed of Bashan's "temperate" valleys, aware, possibly, that in September, California had become the thirty-first state.

Indians approached the camp almost daily, and the women appeased them by cooking pots of beans for them and sending them away. When they failed to appear one day, the pioneers sensed trouble. The next morning three Apaches entered the camp and made friendly overtures but acted suspiciously. The party managed to deflect them, but that night the dogs barked incessantly, running back and forth between their masters and the woods. Royce and the other men put out their fires, took up their guns, and kept watch. The next day Indian tracks ringed the campsite, and a dozen animals were missing. The men tracked the cows, oxen, and a horse into the mountains for awhile then gave up on what was clearly a pointless and dangerous pursuit. When the group finally departed, the Oatmans, with no cattle to tow it, were forced to leave a wagon—and its contents—behind.

By the time they pulled out, the snow was melting. Flowers grew on one side of the trail and snow cascaded down the other. "These same little flowers served to break up many a cold for us," said Thompson, "for we had learned from the Indians to use them in place of quinine."[47] They passed Mexican shrines and pioneer graves, walked along the San Pedro River, and tried not to dwell on the roadside detritus marking other emigrants' defeats: bleached cow bones, abandoned baggage, mining equipment, beds, and wagons. By now, Royce was frantic to get to the Colorado. "He drove so long," Mrs. Wilder later said, "the oxen did not have time to eat and we were afraid our cattle would not be able to take us through, so we let them go ahead."[48]

Though it was a walled city protected by fifty Mexican troops, Santa Cruz was constantly assailed by Indians, and the Oatman party arrived just after both a winter drought and an Apache raid that had left the town with nothing but pumpkins to trade. The Mexicans urged them to stay for a year, hoping an infusion of whites would fortify them against Indians, who surveyed them from the nearby hills. But though the pioneers liked both the town and its residents, they declined, moving on to what they hoped would be safer havens. From there, Royce allotted each person just one and a half dry biscuits a day. The women tried to innovate by cooking hawks and other unusual fare, but not always successfully: when Susan Thompson's mother made soup from coyote meat, she got sick.

In early January, 120 miles later, the group arrived in Tucson, where they soaked up the winter sun and witnessed the Mexicans celebrating the Feast of Epiphany, marked by dancing, feasting, and firecrackers. "Luck favored us," said Thompson. "Almost the first day of our stay I had an opportunity to make a soap, sugar, and white of egg poultice to draw a mesquite thorn from an old Mexican's foot. The poultice is reverenced among the superstitious people. To them, it was also a sign of my super-natural ability that I could go outside the town and call our cattle to me, as they had never heard of controlling their animals by kindness."[49]

Thompson claimed that they were the first white women to enter the village, and though they were tainted as Yankees in light of the Mexican-American War, her poultice won her the gratitude of the Mexican she healed: he offered to rent her family a house. The party spent nearly a month in Tucson then split again: five families, including the Thompsons, stayed behind to farm and await other emigrant trains who could help them. But Royce insisted on pressing on. Mary Ann said good-bye to her friend Mrs. Thompson, one of three women, including Mary Ann, who had been pregnant on the journey. Mrs. Thompson had her baby girl about a month later at the mouth of the Gila River, just before her family reached Fort Yuma.

Determined to keep moving, the Oatmans, Kellys, and Wilders traveled another forty-five miles to Maricopa Wells, a common stop on the southwest route between Texas and California, arriving February 5 to find atrocious conditions after a winter drought and about a thousand nearly starving Indians. The local Pima and Maricopa Indians spoke different languages and occupied separate villages scattered along the Gila and connected by canals that sustained the Pimas' sophisticated farming practices. They were friendly with each other and welcoming to whites, but they lived in fear of Apache attacks. Two days after they arrived, Mrs. Wilder had a baby boy. Mary Ann was now the last of the pregnant women on the train, just weeks away from having her eighth child.

The group planned to stay for a week and urged the Oatmans to do the same. The area Royce planned to enter, especially near the Colorado River, was considered a war zone at best, a natural disaster at worst—a land so barren that the legendary scout Kit Carson had said a wolf couldn't survive on it. It had deteriorated since 1850, when an outlaw and former scalp hunter named John Glanton and a gang of men had seized the ferry service run by Quechan (then called Yuma) Indians at the intersection of the Gila and Colorado rivers and launched a booming business, robbing and sometimes killing their passengers, who arrived every few days. The Quechans had retaliated by killing fifteen men and taking Glanton's scalp. No one who knew better traveled the Gila Trail without a convoy.[50]

Still, having come fifteen hundred miles with less than two hundred miles to go, Royce refused to wait. He had consulted with LeConte, the entomologist who had traveled from Fort Yuma to Maricopa Wells, reporting no trouble on the route. Ignoring the remaining party's advice as well as warnings from the Pimas, who knew the region better than LeConte, the Oatmans set out for Yuma alone. By now Royce had given up his vision of utopia on the Colorado River and was set on mining gold in California.

"The decision was a severe trial to my father," wrote Olive. "If he went on he must now go alone with his helpless family & expose them to the dangers of the way; & if he remained starvation & perhaps death, from the treachurous [*sic*] savages, would be their fate."[51] The family left with four milk cows and two oxen pulling their wagon into a 190-mile desert wasteland.

4

A Year with the Yavapais

> At the period of its [1853] purchase, Arizona was practically a *terra incognita*. Hunters and trappers had explored it to some extent; but their accounts of its resources and peculiarities were of a vague and marvelous character. . . . Few people in the United States knew anything about it, save the curious book-worms who had penetrated into the old Spanish records. | J. ROSS BROWNE, *Adventures in the Apache Country*

The Oatmans' darkest fantasy, lovingly cultivated if averted along the way west, featured an attack by brutal Apaches. Now, Olive and Mary Ann were in the hands of a tribe with no significant reputation for raiding—for that matter, with no reputation among Anglos at all, because until the late 1840s they'd rarely if ever seen—or been seen by—anyone but Indians. Though Olive later identified her captors as Apaches—commonly assumed, in her era, to encompass a variety of dangerous Southwest tribes—they were likely much less notorious.[1] Their proximity to the murder site, regular contact with the Mohave Indians, hunter-gatherer lifestyle, and small-scale farming practices suggest they were one of four fluid groups of Yavapais. Most likely they were Tolkepayas, a name that distinguishes them more geographically than culturally from other free-ranging yet interconnected Yavapais: they lived in western Arizona, north of the Gila and east of the Colorado rivers.[2]

Unlike the Apaches, the Yavapais had not adopted the horse and did not regularly conduct raids, except against their traditional rivals, the Pimas and the Maricopas. The Oatman incident was somewhat atypical for them. The Yavapais had had minimal contact with emigrants along the Gila Trail, which marked the southern border of their territory. With between thirty thousand and forty thousand miners and pioneers traveling between Arizona and California from 1850 to 1851 alone, the tribe had found little need for plunder there, possibly because so many emigrants shed their belongings on the trail that it had become a free-for-all for scavengers.[3] But hair-curling tales of cholera deaths and defeated gold seekers had temporarily staunched the flow of emigrants through Arizona in 1851, leaving fewer pickings.

The Oatman massacre was evidently inspired by the Yavapais' typical late-winter hardship, exacerbated by the previous year's bone-cracking drought. The tribe had, after all, asked Royce for food before attacking, and had cooked and eaten the Oatmans' cows immediately afterward. The Yavapais' primary interest in livestock was as food, which also explains why they had stolen LeConte's horses days earlier. The smaller number of emigrants on the trail that year made the Oatmans, as well as LeConte, easy targets.

Why the Yavapais took the girls, which meant more children to feed, is another question. Native American tribes from east to west had many motives for seizing captives: revenge (which could involve torture and killing), ransom, slave labor, adoption (to increase their numbers or replace dead relatives), and, for some Southwest tribes, the flourishing slave market in Mexico. The Yavapais had, on occasion, practiced ceremonial cannibalism. Just a few years earlier, after an attack on Halchidhoma Indians who had entered their region, they had killed twenty people and captured a mother and daughter; they then roasted the girl alive and had eaten pieces of her. By one account, the woman was forced to eat her daughter's flesh. Fortunately for the Oatmans, cannibalism was rare among the Yavapais, and its sole purpose was to avenge a death or terrorize tribal enemies. Their interest in the girls was more mundane. After a few days in captivity, the sisters' value was clear: they were slaves to the women, and sometimes to the children, who also gave them orders. They carried water in pots and wood in bundles on their heads, collected from miles around. They were taught to dig roots, which they did for a mind-numbing year during which the women, wrote Olive, "took unwarranted delight in whipping us on beyond our strength."[4]

The Yavapais were mountain (and sometimes cave) dwellers who lived on deer, sheep, quail, rabbit, prickly pear, yucca, roots, and the roasted meat of the agave plant. They boiled their meat in clay pots but, according to Olive, did not believe females should eat meat unless they were at death's door. Olive said that "their own children frequently died, and those alive, old and young, were sick and dwarfish generally." There is no record, however, of such a practice among the Yavapais; Olive probably did not know that the tribe was struggling to survive a particularly bad winter and that older women and girls were at the bottom of the food chain, thus the last to eat meat. Females were also forbidden meat while menstruating or after giving birth.

Olive's belief that the women were slaves to the men was similarly mistaken. In fact, the Yavapais had a clear division of labor: women gathered and prepared food and, with their children, harvested the meager crops; men hunted, guarded the camp, dressed skins, built huts, and sometimes farmed. Having been consigned to the female realm, Olive may have seen the women working while the men rested, without understanding that the men had their own responsibilities. Women also walked behind men on marches, which likely reinforced her perception that they were subservient.

The Oatmans' culture shock began with the Yavapais' appearance: Olive called their clothing "needlessly shocking."[5] Children went naked to the age of nine or ten. Men sported buckskin breechclouts secured with a belt, and sometimes a buckskin shirt tied with a string in front, with fringes swinging from the shoulder and seams.

Women, including, ultimately, Olive, wore two-piece belted buckskin dresses that hung from a strap around the neck and extended to mid-calf, with a three- or four-inch fringe. Unmarried women sometimes rolled pieces of tin into the hem of their fringed skirts. If a woman had just one deerskin, the dress was slit on the sides and showed her legs to the hip.

If their clothing was "savage" by Victorian standards, the Yavapai women's beauty practices were positively twenty-first century: during menstruation, girls and women were discouraged from smiling for fear of developing wrinkles and forbidden from stooping to gather wood from the ground because it would make their breasts sag. Instead they were instructed to break the branches off of trees, which allowed their busts to grow round and full.

Face painting was popular for adults and children mainly for decoration, though the pigments were sometimes mixed with deer fat to provide warmth or applied in black stripes beneath the eyes to improve vision. Most boys had decorative facial tattoos by their midteens: a cross or circle on each cheek, wavy lines or zigzags on the forehead, or rows of dots on the nose. But tattoos were much more consequential for women, who received them on the chin between puberty and marriage so they could reach the land of the dead to greet their relatives. As captives who were not members of the tribe, Olive and Mary Ann were spared the procedure. The Yavapais didn't care whether they mounted the stairway to heaven; their souls could wander indefinitely.

To Olive's repulsion, when food was scarce, the Yavapais ate caterpillars and grasshoppers, boiled and salted. The tribe also practiced an erratic form of floodplain agriculture, planting corn, beans, and squash in the banks of streams and rivers in anticipation of seasonal floods. They migrated seasonally depending on whether they were hunting or farming. From spring to fall they lived in clusters of domed open huts—enough to accommodate a single extended family during planting and harvesting season. To facilitate group hunting, the winter villages were larger, consisting of as many as fifty people who lived in closed huts, caves, or sunken huts with flat roofs. Olive was impressed by how little they needed to survive and was soon forced to do the same. Often, she said, when a party returned from hunting deer or rabbit, she and Mary Ann were thrown scraps and told, "You have been fed too well; we will teach you to live on little."

The girls soon learned the Yavapai language to the extent that they understood their orders. Mary Ann, who was prone to illness even back in Illinois, became sick but was still expected to work, carrying water to the men or gathering roots for the tribe with her sister. "We were compelled to heed every whimper and cry of their little urchins with promptness," Olive wrote, "under no less penalty than a severe beating." They plotted an escape, but couldn't muster the courage to attempt it, especially when they had no idea where to go and no food to take with them. Clinging to the hope that some mention of them would make it to the whites and they would be rescued, they waited, hungry and anxious, their chances, as Olive put it, "like that of the dogs, with whom they might share the crumbs."[6]

In the summer of 1851, the U.S. boundary commissioner, John Russell Bartlett, traveled through California and Arizona to mark the newly established border between the United States and Mexico. Through the Treaty of Guadalupe Hidalgo, which had ended the Mexican-American War, Mexico had ceded California and the province of New Mexico (which included Utah and Nevada, southern Colorado, and parts of Arizona and Wyoming) to the United States, along with ninety thousand Hispanics, and even more Indians.[7] When he spent a few weeks at the Pima and Maricopa villages, Bartlett asked the Maricopa Indians if they knew about the Oatman murders. Of course, they did—some had surely seen members of the Oatman party before they had departed nearby Maricopa Wells the previous winter—but they had no idea where the girls had been taken. Bartlett promised them a reward if they could find the children and return them to Fort Yuma or to the Mexican commanding officer at Tucson. But they never did.

Within a few months, as the girls became more fluent in Yavapai and were able to communicate with more nuance, the Yavapais softened. They became curious, drawing the Oatmans into their conversations, and were amazed at how far they had traveled from home. "They became more lenient and merciful, especially to my sister," Olive reflected. "She always met their abuse with a mild, patient spirit and deportment, and with an intrepidity and fortitude beyond what might have been expected from her age. This spirit . . . was plainly working its effect upon some of them." The women gathered around them and asked questions: How many white folks are there? How far does the ocean extend? Do the whites own the worlds east of the Atlantic? How many *Americanos* (a term they'd borrowed from the Mexicans) are there? How are the women treated? Do the men have multiple wives?[8] They themselves were monogamous, and violently so: if a man caught his wife and her lover together, he might kill her. The wife of an adulterer would fight the mistress or simply take her children and leave.

The tribe's cosmology centered on a destruction myth: they believed the world had been destroyed and reborn three times, most recently in the Red Rock area of Sedona—and that a fourth apocalypse was imminent. When the girls discussed their religion, the tribe was incredulous, especially when Olive described the whites' belief that "the stars above us [are] peopled by human beings and . . . the distance to these far off worlds [has] been measured by the whites." The women wanted to know if the Oatmans had been there, and called them liars, charging that "if the stars were inhabited, the people would drop out." Olive said they believed an evil spirit ruled the whites and that he was "leading them to destruction."[9] At the very least, such exchanges humanized the Oatman sisters in the eyes of the Yavapais, who, having discovered their entertainment value, treated them better.

Endurance was highly valued among the Yavapais, who perceived complaining under torture as a sign of weakness that only invited more pain; consequently the girls became quick studies in stoicism. They settled into a routine: obeying the women and children by day, slipping off to pray together, Olive said, when they could, and listening to the men recount the adventures of their youth by the campfire at night.

In the autumn of 1851, the Mohaves came on their annual trading run with the Yavapais, bringing vegetables to exchange for furs. Olive called them "superior Indians," with "a much more intelligent appearance" than the Yavapais, and heard that having seen the unhappy white girls, they had bargained for them. When no agreement was reached, the Mohaves left without them. But the Yavapais subsequently spent hours discussing the pros and cons of releasing the girls, their greatest concern being that if they got back to the whites, the U.S. government might retaliate for the Oatman family killings. Selling them to a remote tribe like the Mohave, however, which had had little truck with Anglos, could forestall such a scenario. Throughout the winter, when they were alone, Olive and Mary Ann put aside their root baskets and sat down to ponder their fates.

"I believe they will sell us," said Mary Ann, who had overheard a Yavapai leader talking about the Mohaves' return. "From what I saw of them I think they know more, and live better than these [Yavapais]."

"But maybe they put on the best side when here," said Olive. "They might treat us worse."

"That would be impossible without they kill us, and if we cannot escape, the sooner we die the better."[10]

Again Mary Ann was sick with a cold that was getting worse every night, and she feared that even if they were traded, she would never survive another journey like the one that had brought them to the Yavapai camp. It was late 1851, just a year after the drought; the tribe had minimal supplies and the girls were living on little more

FIG. 3. Stratton's map of the New Mexico Territory (which included the future Arizona), showing the massacre site, the Oatman girls' two areas of captivity, and Fort Yuma.

than roots. Olive noticed that her sister's cheeks were pale and her eyes were sinking.

In the spring of 1852, five Mohave men and a young woman came to the village with a contract approved by a "chief" named Espaniole.[11] He had sent his seventeen-year-old daughter, Topeka, to cut a deal with the Yavapais and bring home the Oatman girls. "The daughter of the chief was a beautiful, mild and sympathizing woman," wrote Olive. "Her conduct and behavior toward [the Yavapais] . . . bespoke a tutoring, and intelligence, and sweetness of disposition that won their interest at once." She also spoke their language, and using it, told the girls directly she had come to take them. But the trade wasn't easy; the Yavapais argued about it all night while the girls waited in their hut. The Indians who had killed the Oatman family objected to the trade, thinking it would ultimately invite revenge from the whites. Others asked Olive and Mary Ann whether they wanted to go. A Yavapai woman named To-aquin, who had ingratiated herself with the girls by learning a bit of English, approached them that night and assured them the Mohaves would either sell them or kill them. "I hoped to see you free in a short time," said To-aquin, "but I know you will never get back to the whites now."

The Mohaves said the exchange was inspired by kindness, asserting that they wanted to save the girls from the cruelty of the Yavapais. But Olive was skeptical: "Their real design it was useless to seek to read until its execution came." By sunrise, an agreement was reached. The Yavapais would get two horses, three blankets, vegetables, and beads in exchange for the white girls. By way of a goodbye, the tribe insulted or laughed at them, though a few children whom they'd cared for cried. "We found that there were those . . . who were ready to tear us into pieces when we left, and they only wanted a few more to unite with them, to put an end to our lives at once," Olive recalled.[12] The Oatmans were each handed a pound of beef which, along with whatever roots they could find on the way, would be their only food for ten days as they marched through the moonscape of western Arizona.

5

Lorenzo's Tale

> A boy of fourteen years with the mangled remains of my own parents lying near by, my scalp torn open, my person covered with blood, alone, friendless, in a wild, mountain, dismal, wilderness region, exposed to the ravenous beasts, and more, to the ferocity of more than brutal savages and human shaped demons! I had no strength to walk, my spirits crushed, my ambition paralyzed, my body, mangled. | LORENZO OATMAN, *Captivity of the Oatman Girls*

With their immediate family slaughtered and their relatives in Illinois too far away to help them, Olive and Mary Ann had every reason to believe they were alone in the world, buried in the mountains beyond the reach of white culture. But they weren't alone. On the night of the attack, while the girls stood by as the Yavapais devoured the remains of the Oatman larder at the first camp, Olive had regarded the full moon, an inappropriately lovely moon, while back at the Gila River, Lorenzo lay bathed in its brilliance—blinded and paralyzed in the ravine where he'd been rolled toward—but not to—his death. He had witnessed the culmination of the assault: his mother shrieking, "In the name of God, cannot anyone help us?" followed by the groans of his siblings and the lengthening silences through which his family, one by one, fell away from him.[1] He heard the agitated murmurings of Indians and recognized Olive's voice but couldn't tell who was with her.

Lorenzo fully believed he was dying—his body, he felt, was already dead and his mind was stalling out. As the footsteps on the hill subsided and the voices receded, he hallucinated lavishly. He sensed a light above his head, dwindling to a pinpoint, and then he was moving for what seemed like hours through a gallery of paintings levitating in open space. He heard grating and scraping sounds, then rapturous music. He had no idea who he was, but he was happily engaged, drunk on the distractions his mind threw up as a buffer for his pain.

And then it was morning. The sun was shining. He wiped the caked blood from his eyes and took in the spectacle of the new day, then he clasped his head as a thundering pain slammed through it. His scalp was torn and blood still oozed from his ears and nose. He was certain his brain was loose in his skull; he knew he was not physically right. But he could move now. He pulled himself up on his hands and knees and fell, tried again, and fell again. He saw a ribbon of blood that led up the mesa—a clue, surely, to how he'd ended up in the ravine into which he now inexplicably found himself. Where was everyone? His eyes followed the trail to the top of the bluff where the bowed struts of the abandoned wagon floated like the mast of a ghost ship, and the gothic memory of the previous day rolled back and flattened him.

His family was dead; his sisters were gone. The coda to the attack, he remembered, was the sound of Mary Ann crying as the two girls' voices faded into the desert. And now, somehow, his friends from Illinois were standing around him; boys he had pitied because they would never make the journey west and start a new life; boys who'd grieved when he'd left and warned him not to go because of the danger, and because they would miss him. He begged them to help him, gesturing toward the ridge and sputtering about the carnage on the hill, but they were home in Illinois—he could see their houses behind them—and they were happy.

Partly standing now, he tried to get up the incline and managed to crawl fifty feet, then he peeked over the rim to see his family's bat-

FIG. 4. Lorenzo Oatman, 1858, by Charles and Arthur Nahl, from *Captivity of the Oatman Girls*.

tered bodies and scattered belongings. He edged over, picked up a few crusts of hard bread, and ate them. Fearful that Indians might see him, he turned back and continued his crab dance along the path from which the Oatmans had come, toward Maricopa Wells. When he stopped to rest under a dry shrub, the massacre replayed itself relentlessly and his mind whirled with the torture he imagined his sisters suffering at that moment.

Supporting himself on a stick, Lorenzo crawled and then walked fifteen miles by the next morning. His brain had taken on a life of its own and seemed to be trying to jump out of his head, forcing him to cup his skull and press to keep it in place. By mid-afternoon, starving and dehydrated in the heat, he passed out on a plateau in the simmering sun. A few hours later he opened his eyes to an audience of gray wolves that came sniffing within arm's reach. He jumped to his feet, swatting one on the nose, and yelled at them—surprising himself at the sound of his own voice. They backed off as he hurled a stone at another, then they scattered and returned to howl mournfully at him. "A fit requiem for the dead," he thought as he journeyed on, reanimated by the jolt of adrenaline this new threat had induced yet afraid he would ultimately faint again, providing a tasty meal for his predators.[2] They trailed him until nearly midnight, pulling back every time Lorenzo whacked one with a rock, until some limit was reached and they stopped to huddle, then went wailing into the hills to the north.

Lorenzo continued in the cool of the night, slept, and dreamed of the ordeal. In the morning, with the wolves no longer driving him, he was weak with hunger; his foraged bread crusts of two days earlier had been his last meal. He knew he couldn't make it to Maricopa Wells without food. With dry scrub and saguaros surrounding him, he examined the flesh of his arm and considered cutting it off and eating it—then hobbled on.

At noon, he was slurping at a canyon slick with water when the sound of horses' hooves alarmed him: two Pima Indians in red shirts appeared, froze at the sight of Lorenzo, and drew their arrows. In Spanish, he begged them not to shoot. They dropped their bows and rode up to him, squinting, and dismounted. One, it turned out, was a friend from the Pima villages who barely recognized Lorenzo through the blood and swelling, but now remembered him as the eldest boy in the family that had left the camp a few days earlier. "He embraced me with every expression of pity and condolence," Lorenzo later said.[3] The men laid him on a blanket under a tree and gave him ash-baked bread and water from a gourd, then rode back to the disaster site to investigate. When they returned, carrying some of the family's belongings, they escorted Lorenzo back toward Maricopa Wells to find the remainder of the party.

The trio traveled slowly through the night, and the next morning—the third day after the attack—Lorenzo saw something moving in the distance: two white covered wagons. Miraculously, they belonged to the Wilder family and the Kelly brothers, who had traveled fifty miles west since leaving Maricopa Wells, days after staying good-bye to the Oatmans. Robert Kelly climbed down and scrutinized Lorenzo's battered, sunburned face. "My God, Lorenzo, what in the name of heaven has happened?"[4]

The boy could only cry. When he finally told them his story, the women wept and asked him not to reveal the gruesome details of their friends' slaughter. The group concluded it was too dangerous to go on and agreed to retrace their steps back to Maricopa Wells. "Those miles wearily traveled we were as badly off as ever, not wanting to go back and afraid to go on," said Willard Wilder.[5]

Once Lorenzo was safely returned, Wilder and the Kellys rode out to the murder site to bury the dead. Susan Thompson later said that when the men saw the bodies, they remembered a dream that had "cast a cloud of morbidness" over Royce for days before he left Maricopa Wells. "He had dreamed of floating in the air above the top of a hill and seeing beneath the bodies of himself and his wife. The fact that his wife's feet rested against his left shoulder seemed to impress him vividly. The finding of the bodies in this exact position seemed too strange to be true."[6]

Coyotes had eaten the flesh off the corpses. Because the men had no shovels and the ground had been hardened by the sun, they simply covered the ravaged bones with mounds of rocks. This was the first of many burials for the Oatman family, whose gravesite would be regularly disrupted—by wild animals, natural forces, and mischievous humans—for the next 150 years.

Lorenzo was dangerously ill with a high fever during his first week at Maricopa Wells, but the next week, with his wounds washed and his body rested and refueled, he recovered somewhat. The party wanted to get back on the road to California, but they needed protection. Help came in the form of seven army deserters who rolled into town seized with gold fever, heading west with stolen mules. Lorenzo was laid on a bed in a wagon and the motley group headed down the sandy road to the Gila, no questions asked. "We hailed them with as much joy as if they had been strictly on government duty," said Wilder. "We were in just the hard up position to help each other without any special prying into previous conditions."[7]

The low point of the ten-day trip came when Lorenzo was forced to pass the scene of the massacre on his second try for California. "It was haunted ground," he later wrote, "and to tarry there alive was more dreadful than the thought of sharing their repose. I hastened away."[8]

When the Kelly-Wilder party arrived on March 31, Fort Yuma was a barely established, undersupplied post in a state of slow-motion collapse. Founded the previous winter, after the deadly Quechan attack on the Glanton gang, it was established to aid emigrants and miners en route to California and to quell the local Indians. Perched on a bluff eighty feet above the river on the west side, it offered panoramic views of the Southwest desert and the river crossing, and was elevated well beyond the reach of local Indians. But getting food there, two hundred miles from San Diego, was slow and difficult. One supply load took twenty days to cross the desert, during which time the drivers were forced to kill an ox and drink its blood to avoid dehydration. The camp's one-armed lieutenant, a Mexican-American War veteran named Thomas Sweeny, called it "an occurrence but too common in this desert."[9]

Just four months old, the camp already had an attitude problem. Its prickly commander, Samuel P. Heintzelman, a short, bearded West Point graduate who had served in the Mexican-American War and later became a major general in the Civil War, didn't want to be there and was preoccupied with making extra cash through the thriving ferry service. His ranks of about one hundred men were weakened by scurvy (which he tried to remedy by planting his own garden), dysentery, drunkenness, and desertion. He clashed with the camp surgeon, Dr. Henry Hewit, one of the first doctors in the Southwest, who proposed, among other things, excusing the guards from wearing full uniforms in the sweltering heat, putting roofs over the soldiers' quarters, and building a proper hospital. The commander also bickered with LeConte, Hewit's old friend from New York, and elicited contempt from Sweeny, who gloated in his diary, "It is true that I am under the Major's command, but only in a general way. . . . Nobody thinks of disputing my orders, while there is not one *he* issues that that is not objected to by somebody under his command."[10] Heintzelman confided in his diary, "Dr. Hewit & Sweeny are quite thick together. . . . They agree on one thing—that is hating me most cordially." By all accounts, Heintzelman gave them good reason to loathe him.[11]

The Oatman incident made bad relations worse. In late February, after receiving Royce's letter asking for help, Heintzelman had done nothing. He said he couldn't send a rescue party because all his horses were being used to transport rations to the fort from a ship on the Colorado. This may have been true, or he simply may not have believed the letter's carrier, "Dr. Bugs," as he called LeConte, whom he detested, partly because he suspected him of masking an interest in prospecting with scientific study, but more likely because Heintzelman disliked almost everyone he met at the camp. Only pressure from a captain named Davidson compelled him—belatedly—to send two soldiers with pack mules after the Oatmans. After finding the wagon and removing the stones Wilder and Kelly had laid over the nearby bodies, they found what they'd feared. The wagon was empty except for a few planes, chisels, and scattered tin dishes. The men collected some letters and a lock of hair and saw footprints, both of shod and barefoot travelers, heading toward the Pima and Maricopa villages.

In the privacy of his diary, Heintzelman blamed LeConte for the disaster: "[If] Dr. LeConte had so much charity," he snarled, "he should have staid [*sic*] and accompanied the family, particularly as the woman expected daily to need his services. If he and his [companion] had staid [*sic*] and come on with them, they probably would not have lost their lives. Some people like charity at other people's expense."[12]

Oddly, he sent a report to headquarters in San Diego three days later, saying, "I cannot believe they have been murdered & if so it is too late to pursue with any force I have the means to send . . . we are much in want of a male mounted force, or some 25 horses to mount a portion of the infantry to go on these expeditions."[13] How he thought the family ended up brutalized in the desert, their wagon ransacked and looted, without having been murdered, is a mystery.

Even with the knowledge that some of the Oatmans were missing, Heintzelman refused to send out a search party for survivors, which prompted Hewit to file charges against him for "cruel and inhuman conduct" and "neglect of duty" in light of direct orders to protect emigrants in the region.[14] Sweeny sided with Hewit, laying the blame for the Oatman fiasco wholesale at the commander's feet. Heintzelman claimed that the Oatman slaughter, which occurred in Mexican territory, wasn't his problem (without considering that the victims might have been taken across the border into the United States) and insisted that entering Mexico would be a violation of the 1848 Treaty of Guadalupe Hidalgo, which decreed, at the close of the Mexican-American War, that no one from either country would cross into the other bearing arms.

Heintzelman also clearly believed that Royce Oatman got what was coming to him. "Oatman was of an obstinate & contrary disposition & would take advice from no one," he rationalized in a report to headquarters. "He was warned of the imprudence of going it alone."[15] Finally, the commander, who had likely given the children up for dead, was probably loath to invest his limited resources in a seemingly hopeless cause. What a surprise, then, when Lorenzo rode into camp with his chilling story of murder and kidnapping.

Although in one report Heintzelman referred to Lorenzo as "the boy in the celebrated Oatman family," he wasn't particularly interested in the survivor, whose appearance was merely another pretext for a squabble with Sweeny, this time over the use of the army boat to ferry the emigrants across the river to the camp. "That boy that escaped the murder of his family came here today," his March 31 journal entry reads. "His story does not vary materially from what I heard before. Sweeny asked me for the boat for himself and then took Bugs over and brought back the boy. I let him know he should have told me he wanted the boat for Bugs."

After a journey marred by droughts and snowstorms, illness and death, the remains of the Brewster party pursuing the land of plenty on the Colorado River stepped off the ferry and took it in. One look at the landscape told them that the boy prophet James Colin Brewster's visionary powers were as bankrupt as his revelations were changeable. Here was Brewster's land "of hills, of vallies [*sic*], of plains and pleasant places, which brings forth in abundance, that they who go there shall prosper."[16] It was a wasteland. True, two tongues of fertile terrain licked the river, but the mountains were bare and the only thing growing in abundance was chaparral and weeds. In the past ten months, the ferryman told Mrs. Wilder, it hadn't rained enough to soak his shirt.

The emigrants would stay long enough to raise crops where the river flooded, then they would move west. Heintzelman gave them permission to camp on the hill below the fort, where they dropped posts in the ground and wove willow branches into them for protection. Willard Wilder took a job working for the quartermaster, helping with the food and equipment of the troops, earning sixty dollars a month, and getting soldiers' rations. At some point, Heintzelman got wind of Brewster's glowing description of "Bashan" and snorted in his journal, "I wish he could see our starved mules."[17]

Lorenzo was installed in the hospital, where he spent months before he could even perambulate the grounds, which consisted of eight or ten small adobe buildings and a dozen officers' quarters—roofless brush sheds constructed of young willow, spanning about an acre. Here he would see his fellow travelers, the local guard, and Quechans—there were thousands of them in the region, whom Sweeny had subdued with threats, invoking "the Great White father" in Washington.[18] In his journal, Sweeny described their magpie fashion sense: one man wore a calico loincloth and a cast-off officer's cap, "strutting among his tribe with the air of an emperor," and a woman wore a traditional bark skirt with a pair of soldier's shoes. The Quechans could also be seen floating in the river with mud packs on their heads to kill lice and cool themselves in the heat. As one visitor to the fort put it, "It is enough to make a man stare with amazement to see a group of mud-balls floating on the current of a hot day, laughing and talking to each other as if it were the finest fun in all the world."[19]

LeConte left a few days after Lorenzo's arrival, which Heintzelman noted in his journal with seething sarcasm: "Bugs is on his way to New York and we shall not have the pleasure of seeing him here again—much to the sorrow of all."[20]

Word trickled back from the Pima villages that Maricopa Indians were selling the Oatmans' looted clothing, and the debate about whether to send men out in search of the Oatman children continued. Heintzelman dug in his heels, claiming he had no authority to do so. In April, LeConte and Hewit published complaints about Heintzelman's conduct in the *San Francisco Herald* and the *Daily Alta California*, which didn't faze the commander. He published a response in July, reiterating his position on sending forces into Mexico and taking a gratuitous jab at his critics, implying their letter was a misplaced act of vengeance: "Both were disappointed because I would not furnish them with the means of the Government placed at my disposal for the wants of the troops, to use for their gold speculation."[21] In his diary, Heintzelman called the charges "a sheet of fools-cap." The army, in evident agreement, ignored them.[22]

When the Wilder-Kelly party left for Los Angeles, Lorenzo stayed behind under Hewit's care, hoping to find a way to save his sisters. "He became a parent to me," said Lorenzo, ". . . at a time when but for his counsel and his affectionate oversight I might have turned out to wreck upon the cold world." The boy also befriended the camp carpenter, Henry Grinnell, who advised him to go to school in San Diego. But by mid-June, fed up with the camp politics and poor medical equipment, Hewit resigned his post and left to pursue a private practice in San Francisco, taking the boy with him. Lorenzo said his good-byes, saving a special farewell for Grinnell, who promised to do everything he could to "liberate" Lorenzo's sisters.[23]

Five years later, Lorenzo would have every reason to thank him.

6

Becoming Mohave

> Mohave nationalism, since it is not imposed on the individual by a tyrannical government or inflexible codes covering all aspects of life, must be held to have sprung from the general satisfaction of the Mohave with his socio-cultural milieu. This world gives him his emotional anchorage, and he, in turn labors for its perpetuation.
> | GEORGE DEVEREUX, "Mohave Culture and Personality"

As terrific runners whose barefoot marathons took them over rock, sand, and gravel, sometimes as far as the Pacific coast, the Mohaves drove Olive and Mary Ann too fast, until their feet were nicked and raw. On the second day after leaving the Yavapais, their guides made them makeshift shoes from skins and agreed to travel shorter distances each day on the journey home. Topeka carried a roll of blankets and shared them with the Oatmans each night when they camped in the sand. Olive found her to be good-natured, even jovial, and sympathetic to the malnourished sisters she had come to liberate.

In the late afternoon on the eleventh day, they entered the Mohave Valley, a lush green expanse stretching for thirty miles, flanked by mountains and bisected by the Colorado River, which marked the boundary between California and the future Arizona. The Mohave lived in villages scattered up and down the river on both sides. Thus the tribe's name: Aha Macav, meaning "along the river."

It was early spring and the river, running high, was lined with cottonwood trees putting out new leaves. "Isn't it a beautiful valley?" asked Mary Ann. "It seems to me I should like to live here."

"Maybe," said Olive, "you will not want to go back to the whites anymore."[1]

The girls saw the Mohave settlement nestled in the hills above the river: a cluster of large, low wicker and straw huts framed by wood posts. They were taken directly to the home of a local leader, Espaniole, whose house stood in a one-hundred-foot square of cottonwood trees above the water, with a sweeping view of the valley and the village below.[2] It was a ten-foot-by-ten-foot log structure with a roof of sticks and mud, a grassy front yard, and a fire burning inside by the front door which, said Olive, was always open. This would be the Oatmans' new home.

When Espaniole and his wife, Aespaneo, greeted Topeka, Olive observed what anthropologists noted about the Mohaves over the next century: they showed their feelings openly and loved their children lavishly.[3] The family smiled at Olive, unable to communicate with her verbally, and treated Topeka as if she'd been gone for months. After the reunion, Topeka promptly grabbed a cake she saw roasting in the ashes, tore it in three pieces and invited the girls to eat, giving Olive the biggest piece.

Espaniole was most likely a *kohota*, or festival chief, who was responsible for receiving captives, planning dances, and overseeing celebrations. At his prompting, the Oatmans were taken out on the grass, where the Mohaves celebrated their arrival with singing and dancing. Olive described the leader as a happy man with a mild disposition, a sense of ease in his authority, and a serious demeanor that was not typical of the Mohaves. He told the tribe, "Let everyone help raise them. If they are sick, tend to them. Treat them well."[4] Still, the girls went to bed that night wondering what value they had for the Mohaves and what was in store for them, as Olive put it, "plunged now in to the depths of a wild country where the traces of a white foot would be sought in vain for hundreds of miles."[5] She didn't realize that having traveled from an area northwest of Phoenix to the California border, she was now closer to civilization than she had been with the Yavapais—about 250 miles from Los Angeles and an even shorter distance to Fort Yuma.

Olive and Mary Ann had walked into a culture entering the twilight of its independence. The tribe, which had probably inhabited the Mohave Valley for at least a thousand years, had largely eluded Spanish, Mexican, and American influence and was living as it had for centuries.[6] In 1776, Father Francisco Garces of Spain, who hailed from Tucson, then the northernmost outpost of New Spain, visited the Colorado, where the Mohaves guided him across the desert to the Pacific coast. By way of visual aids, he carried religious paintings on a banner, one side bearing a portrait of the Virgin Mary, which the Mohaves liked, the other showing a sinner burning in hell, which they found hideous and refused to contemplate. When he promoted the mission system of justice administered by a local *alcalde*, or mayor, they retorted, "We do not steal, and we very seldom disagree; what use have we for an alcalde among us?"[7]

Garces, who called them "Jamajabs," said the Mohaves were of "gentle and sincere character" and claimed he had never met Indians who talked more, though their exchanges did not lead to many conversions. He found a more receptive audience farther south in the Quechans, and he subsequently built two missions in their area. But his goodwill didn't hold: five years later he was clubbed to death during Mass, in an uprising of furious Quechans over the Spanish soldiers who had followed him and seized their land.

After Garces's visit, the Mohaves lived undisturbed until fur trappers, including Jedediah Smith and later Kit Carson, arrived in the 1820s, precipitating more than a decade of Anglo-Mohave violence. The Mohaves revered beaver and were appalled to see their skinned bodies thrown on the banks of the river by trappers from both north and south of their valley, who nearly trapped out the region before a vogue for silk hats ended the fur craze. The tribe's retaliation against these intruders gave them a reputation as fierce warriors. Still, history shows they always met strangers with hospitality. Garces, who had traveled from Mexico to San Francisco, said no one had treated him better than the spirited and obliging Mohaves.[8] Even Jed Smith, whose relationship with the Mohaves ended badly, reported his first encounter with them in his journal by saying, "I was treated with great kindness."[9]

Though the tribe, then about four thousand strong, had endured and often enjoyed their white visitors, their perception of them was changing. They had seen the Quechans, their cultural and linguistic brothers to the south, bullied by missionaries, and starting in 1850, attacked by troops at Fort Yuma. Lieutenant Sweeny's journal routinely mentions burning Indian fields, driving Quechans from their planting grounds, destroying their villages, and handling warriors who surrendered themselves at Yuma.[10] By now, the Mohaves surely sensed that the Great White Father might have designs on them as well, which may explain their interest in the Oatmans.

The Mohaves took captives—usually women and children—to employ as laborers or savor as symbols of victory. But the term they used to describe them, *ahwe*, meant "stranger" or "enemy," not "slave" or "captive." Women captives were sometimes given as partners to older men (who were not as spooked by the prospect of enemy sickness as younger men, because they did not have long to live); children were often adopted into families. They were seldom mistreated. Some were used as pawns or peacemakers in negotiations with the tribes from which they'd been taken, then they were returned when peace was made. But Olive and Mary Ann weren't spoils of war, and as white girls they carried no diplomatic currency among neighboring tribes. The Mohaves wanted to keep them, possibly as curiosities, but also, perhaps, because they anticipated the need for a new kind of diplomacy: one requiring leverage with whites, who would begin muscling them off of their homeland within a decade. Espaniole later said he had hoped the Mohaves' good treatment of Olive would encourage the whites, in turn, to treat the Mohaves well.[11]

The blueprint for their ruin had already been drafted. Just as they had had no idea that their land had been handed from Spain to Mexico in 1821, the Mohaves were probably unaware that the United States had acquired the region at the end of the Mexican-American War in 1848. Soon after, with no perceived conflict of interest, the Department of the Interior had combined the government agency that was designed to protect Indians (the Bureau of Indian Affairs) with the departments responsible for assessing, dividing, and redistributing their land (the General Land Office and the Geological Survey and Territorial Office). "Indian Removal" was the precursor to a transcontinental railroad, and in its first two years of statehood, California spent over a million dollars executing it.[12]

Though the Mohaves were highly nationalistic, their sense of patriotism had always been more a mental than a territorial construct—one that would soon be tested. The U.S. War Department had sent its first surveyor, Lorenzo Sitgreaves, to map potential routes across the desert to the Pacific in late 1851, just months before Olive and Mary Ann's arrival from Yavapai country. Nearly two hundred Mohaves—men, women, and children—met and traveled with Sitgreaves's party one November day, and when their curiosity overwhelmed them and they crowded Sitgreaves's camp that night, they were thrown out, as Sitgreaves put it, "hardly without the use of violence," and responded by hurling insults and shooting arrows into the camp. Sitgreaves's was the first of four government-sponsored parties to explore the Mohave Valley as a thoroughfare in the 1850s (Whipple, Beale, and Ives would follow) and the first to see the tribe as an obstacle on the road to Manifest Destiny.

If Sitgreaves cleared the way for the Mohaves' displacement, he also provided, in his government report, the first detailed visual portrait of them. He called them "striking," averaging at least six feet in height, and said their athletic figures offered proof of the benefits of a mostly vegetarian diet. Their hair was cropped at the forehead and hung in a cascade of loose braids down the back—the longer the better. They carried bows and feathered arrows, spears and clubs, and in cold weather, firebrands. The women wore willow bark skirts that fell to the knees and tied at the waist—and nothing else. Both sexes went barefoot.[13]

By all subsequent accounts, from the explorers who soon followed Sitgreaves to the anthropologists who studied the dwindling tribe in the early twentieth century, the Mohaves, especially the men, were beautiful. They were described variously as majestic, Herculean, and as one of the Smithsonian Institution's first ethnographers put it, "as fine a race of men physically, perhaps, as there is in existence."[14] They painted their faces coal black, with a red streak from the hairline to the chin, and were known for their tattooing and face painting, on both men and women, which communicated everything from military might to grief over the loss of a child. Like most of the Colorado River tribes, their primary diversion was swimming. As one observer reported, "During the greater part of the year more than half of their time is spent in the river; men, women, and children swimming, as only they can swim, hours together without fatigue or rest."[15]

For Olive and Mary Ann, the handsome Mohaves and their verdant homeland presented a mighty contrast to mountain life and famine among the Yavapais. One explorer who met the Mohaves in the mid-1850s compared them to the "hideous" Yavapais leading "the lives of wolves in the mountains": "It was a real pleasure to see these finely-developed forms, as they came bounding towards us in immense leaps over stones and bushes, with the agility of black-tailed deer, and their pleasant, almost open looks, which even their frightful styles of decoration could not disguise, and to watch the perpetual good-humor that seemed to prevail among them, their playing and romping with each other, and the shouts of laughter that followed their reciprocal jokes, the whole day long."[16]

The Oatmans joined other girls and women carrying wood and

FIG. 5. Mohave Indians, photographed by Timothy O'Sullivan, 1871. Edward Palmer, an early ethnographer for the Smithsonian Institution, called them "as fine a race of men physically, perhaps, as there is in existence." U.S. National Archives, Washington DC, and American Indian Select List no. 136.

water, as they had done for the Yavapais, along with farming in the swollen banks of the Colorado River during the summer of 1852. Nicknamed the American Nile because it flooded its channel from May to midsummer as the snow melted in the Rockies and thundered down to the Gulf of Mexico, the river ran wild and deep (that is, until the creation of Hoover Dam). In a good year, when the high tide subsided, the residual silt fertilized the seeds the Mohaves planted in the riverbed with their bare hands, and the blistering sun caused the crops to sprout and ripen supernaturally fast. The tribe planted wheat in the fall and corn of various colors in the spring, along with beans, pumpkins, watermelon, cantaloupe, and wild herbs. In a bad year, they relied on roots and hard-to-collect mesquite beans. They hunted infrequently—sheep, deer, and rabbit—and used nets and sometimes arrows or hooks made of cactus needles to catch fish stranded in the overflow of the river in late summer or early fall.

Olive disapproved of the Mohaves' ineffective—or rather intermittent—farming methods. "What was to them a rich harvest would be considered in Yankee land, or in the Western states, a poor compensation for so much time and plodding labor," she wrote. She couldn't understand why they planted only enough to last four months, which forced them to rely on mesquite beans when supplies ran out. Still, seeing the crops growing brought the girls closer to home, said Olive, and "placed us in a nearness to the customs of a civilized mode of life that we had not realized before."[17]

A good harvest called for a feast, and the first Olive attended, where she saw Mohave social life in full swing, was shocking, not just by nineteenth-century standards but also by comparison to the social rituals of the more solemn and conservative Yavapais. For these galas, the Mohaves came together wearing bark masks and face paint or mud-slathered hair, marched upriver to the feasting area, built a fire, and danced until midnight. The next day they ate. The women arrived carrying soup, cakes, or boiled vegetables in dishes and baskets on their heads. Their cakes were made of ground wheat and boiled pumpkin rolled into a dough that was placed in the sand, covered with a leaf, and baked. At one such banquet, said Olive, "I witnessed some of the most shameful indecencies, on the part of both male and female, that came to my eye for the five years of my stay among Indians."[18]

She didn't say precisely what she saw, but the sexual practices of the uninhibited Mohaves surely gave a young Mormon from the Midwest ample reason for embarrassment. The Mohaves considered sex natural, fun, and emotionally inconsequential. Children witnessed it at a young age because they lived in one-room houses with their parents and other adults. Many lost their virginity by the time they reached puberty, and most girls had sex soon after they began menstruating. Adult Mohaves encouraged the young to indulge themselves sexually while they could, so that by their mid-teens, they were jaded, at which point, wrote the psychoanalyst George Devereux, "frills" were added to keep things lively: "The Mohave will actually devote some time to thinking up sexual 'stunts,' to make the act more exciting." If their hosts' sexual frankness didn't kick the girls' culture shock to new heights, their flexible definition of gender did: children's gender was not considered fixed until after puberty and transvestism was not only accepted but merited its own confirmation ceremony, after which some homosexual Mohaves crossed over to become same-sex wives or (less often) husbands.[19]

There's no way of knowing whether, once settled into Mohave life, Olive joined in the sexual activities of other Mohave teens. If so, she would never have revealed it to the whites to whom she was returned—it would have sealed her doom as a perpetual outsider and, sexually, as hopelessly damaged goods. As a teenager not long out of the Midwest, she surely balked at the prospect, at least initially, and it's difficult to imagine the laissez-faire Mohaves pushing anything on her. Her ethnicity probably disqualified her from Mohave sexual escapades at first; as ultranationalists, the tribe prided themselves on their racial hygiene and feared sex with other races would cause illness or even kill them. But ultimately, says Michael Tsosie, a Mohave who is the director of the Colorado River Indian Tribes Museum, because she was adopted and given a clan name and therefore was considered a Mohave, she was most likely initiated sexually into the tribe.

She had a nickname that bolsters this theory. Olive was primarily known as "Ali" or "Aliútman," a rendering of Olive Oatman for which the Mohaves, whose language includes a "v" sound, deliberately—and seemingly affectionately—elided the two names.[20] She was also called "Olivino," and "Oach," the clan name for her Mohave family.[21] But the Mohaves, like their allies the Quechans, loved bawdy sobriquets referring to—or flatly advertising—genitalia. Quechan names for men at the time, for example, included "Big Cock," "Cock-with-a-Blue-Head," and "Good Fucker." One Mohave woman was nicknamed "Charcoal Testicle," indicating she liked sex so much that she burned men's testicles.[22]

At some point, Olive acquired the nickname "Spantsa," which meant "rotten vagina" or "sore" vagina.[23] She may have been menstruating when she arrived, wrapped in rags, or she may have been perceived as unhygienic by comparison to the Mohaves, who bathed every day in the Colorado River, unlike whites, for whom a splash of toilet water was considered a substitute for washing.[24] Tsosie believes the name indicates that she was very sexually active, implying that she was having so much sex that she was "sore" and had a vulgar smell ("rotten") or that she was with someone so virile he was wearing her out.

Alternatively, the name, which the commander at Fort Yuma printed on the travel pass that was ultimately used to ransom her, may have been invented by Quechans who interacted regularly with the troops at Fort Yuma, one of whom was recruited to attempt her rescue. If she had spurned one of their advances or somehow offended him, Tsosie theorizes, he may have passed the name on to soldiers at Fort Yuma to get back at her. But it's unlikely that "Spantsa," as used by the Mohaves, was intended to be hurtful, because Mohave insults more often revolved around dead relatives, the mention of which was considered a slur. Tsosie alleges that the very fact that Oatman was nicknamed confirms her acceptance within the culture; if she had been marginalized within the tribe, she would never have warranted one. Along with "Aliútman," the name stuck, and Mary Ann, perhaps too young for teasing, went by her given name.

It was Olive's clan name, Oach, however, that carried more solid evidence of her tribal status. Mohave women used clan names passed down from their fathers, which they retained even after marriage. The names were shared by all the women, and individualized by descriptions. The clan name Whalia, for example, meant "moon," and all the daughters in the family carried it, but were given variations on it, like Whalia Quarai ("clear moon"), or even Whalia Davov ("the moon at certain seasons, balanced with the sun—when you see the moon just coming up, the sun just going down").[25] Tsosie says Olive would only have been given a clan name if she were considered a full Mohave. But her clan name also masks her marriage status. If, after some period of adaptation, she was married—and Mohave girls of the period did so in their early to mid-teens—her name wouldn't show it.

The Mohaves were serial monogamists with no wedding ceremony. Marriage meant living together; moving out signaled divorce. Boys and girls met at feasts; if they liked each other, the boy went to the girl's house, where they talked for a few nights then had sex. In the morning they were considered married—unless the girl's parents disapproved, in which case they made the boy uncomfortable enough that the lovers broke up. If a couple divorced, the children stayed with the mother. Although polygamy was uncommon and generally frowned upon, adultery was not, but it did sometimes provoke a fight between women, inspire a cuckolded partner to get a lover of his own to get even, or lead to divorce. It was no problem if a pregnant woman left her husband for another man; the Mohaves believed that a fetus's biological identity was shaped by the man the mother lived with; it became his child by exposure to him. Likewise, stepfathers raised other men's children as their own.

The Mohaves' temporary marriages were a keystone of their social structure: children's socialization was vitally important to them. From an early age, children lived in multiple homes and were raised by a large circle of ever-present if permissive adults who provided a fluid family that became more significant than the nuclear family. Children were heaped with affection, never struck (the tribe considered hitting them an abomination), and the principal value they were taught was generosity. By the time they reached adulthood, this had become a reflexive attitude rather than a point of etiquette. It also fed the tribe's communal sense of ownership: hoarding or coveting was not just uncivilized, it was barely human.

When they weren't farming alongside the other Mohaves, the girls spent their first summer with the tribe gathering mesquite, collecting wild vegetables with the women, or swimming naked in the Colorado. They probably played dice (which the Mohave made of cottonwood), cat's cradle, or ring toss (using pumpkin rinds and a willow pin). Girls also ran races, played tag, and climbed trees. They watched the men play a popular game called shinny, resembling field hockey, in which teams chased a wooden ball with a curved stick in a chaotic spectacle at which onlookers sometimes risked getting run over—there were no positions and the goal lines could be five hundred yards apart.

And the Oatmans continued to sing their Sunday school hymns. Once, when some Mohaves overheard them outside Espaniole's house, they were asked to sing more and were subsequently paid strings of beads or pieces of red flannel to perform for a few hours. Singers were well regarded among the Mohaves, who believed they received their power in dreams. The girls tied the beads together

FIG. 6. Mohave dwelling, with men playing the hoop game described by Whipple. Illustration by D. Lancelot, after H. B. Mollhausen.

and wore them, said Olive, "squaw fashion" and threaded the flannel pieces together to make clothing.

The Mohave language was linguistically akin to Yavapai, though the two were not mutually intelligible. The girls mastered it fairly quickly, and Olive was soon having lively and sometimes contentious exchanges using it. When a young man named Ccearekae asked Olive how she liked living with the Mohaves, for example, she replied that she didn't have enough to eat.

"We have enough to satisfy us," he countered. "You *Americanos* work hard, and it does you no good; we enjoy ourselves." Olive then critiqued their farming practices, angering him by calling him lazy for raising so little. When she explained how breaking up the soil would promote the growth of seeds and drew a plow in the sand to illustrate, her Mohave audience was interested but unconvinced. "You whites," said one Mohave, "have forsaken nature and want to

FIG. 7. Mohave Indians by H. B. Mollhausen, ca. 1854.

possess the earth, but you will not be able."[26] Olive's freedom to speak her mind so pointedly to the Mohaves—something that would surely have backfired with the Yavapais—confirms her greater sense of freedom within her new tribe.

They also discussed religion, which for the Mohaves focused on origins and guidance, not worship. They had no gods or religious ceremonies, but their central spirit was Matavilya, a being who had performed a great service (killing a sea monster named Sky Rattlesnake) and flown away. Dreams and legends were the source of wisdom and information, providing models for behavior and decision making, and they were all traced back to Matavilya. When Olive told them she worshipped a god who lived in the sky and said she planned to join him in his palace above the clouds, one of the women quipped, "When you go to your heaven you had better take a strong piece of bark and tie yourself up, or you will be coming down among us again."[27]

The girls noticed that the Mohave women, like the Yavapais, wore chin tattoos as a passport to the afterlife; the Mohave believed anyone without facial tattoos would end up in a desert rat hole instead of in the land of the dead.[28] One day after digging for roots, they were sitting in Espaniole's house when two doctors and Espaniole himself approached. Aespaneo instructed the girls to go out in the yard to be tattooed. They belonged to the tribe, they were told, and thus needed the tattoo.

The girls lay down in the grass, their heads in the laps of the tattooers, who drew charcoal designs on their chins. Using a cactus thorn, they "pricked the skin in small regular rows on our chins with a very sharp stick," Olive wrote, "until they bled freely. They then dipped these same sticks in the juice of a certain weed that grew on the banks of the river, and then in the powder of a blue stone that was to be found in low water." The stone was burned, then pulverized, then applied to the pinprick patterns that had been etched into their faces.[29]

The procedure took a few hours, but it was most painful during the healing process of the next three days, when they could eat only soft foods like roasted pumpkin so the wounds would not open. Because the Mohaves prized broad faces, tattoo patterns were designed to create or enhance this impression.[30] Broad-faced tattooees, such as Olive, got wide lines that stretched across the chin to highlight their facial structure. Unlike the Maoris of New Zealand, whose strikingly similar (still extant) facial tattoos carried tribal designations, the Mohaves' designs were purely decorative, with no symbolic or referential significance. They were also not specifically linked to puberty rituals.[31]

Whether she wanted the tattoo or not, the clean lines of Olive's pattern indicate that she cooperated thoroughly with both the process and the aftercare it required. Tribal elder Llewellyn Barrackman believed that Olive, like most Mohave females, *chose* to be tattooed, because, he said, the tribe never forced the tattoos on anyone. Indeed, some Mohaves resisted chin tattoos until they got older and were either persuaded or chose to get them for fear that they would

FIG. 8. Mohave chin tattoo designs, from *Mohave Tattooing and Face-Painting* by Edith S. Taylor and William J. Wallace. Courtesy of the Autry National Center, Southwest Museum, Los Angeles. Southwest Museum Leaflets, 1947, no. 20, p. 2, fig. 1.

be held back in the afterlife without them. Once healed, Olive wore five thick vertical bars that stretched from her jaw line to her lower lip, with a pair of horizontal cones extending from the outside line on each side. She also wore a vertical band on her upper arms, a typical tattoo for women. Mary Ann's pattern was never described or recorded.

Olive's tattoo marked the first stage of her transformation into a Mohave. She was now visually integrated into the tribe and physically traceable as a Mohave because of it. She also stood on an adopted ancestral continuum: one purpose of tattooing, says Tsosie, was to allow people's descendants to recognize them in the afterlife, especially if they were generationally too far separated to have met. But Olive knew this emblem of Mohave civilization would have a reverse value in the white world, where it would brand her as a savage, diminishing her chances of ever living normally again. If, with her immediate family gone (as far as she knew), she had trouble imagining who she and Mary Ann would return to if they were rescued, she now had the added complication of being stigmatized forever in the eyes of Anglos, not just as an outsider, but as a freak.

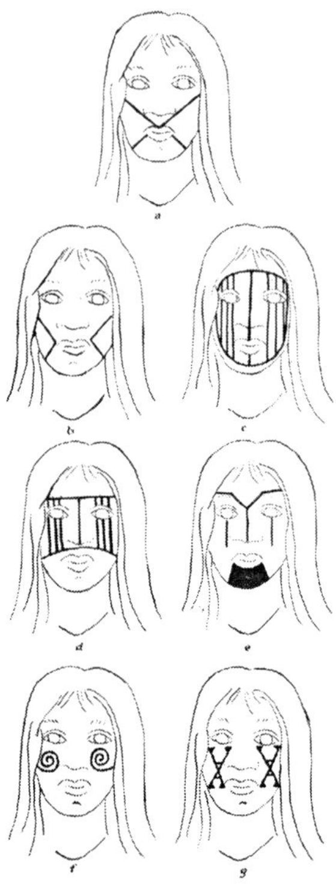

FIG. 9. Mohave women's face painting, from *Mohave Tattooing and Face-Painting* by Edith S. Taylor and William J. Wallace. In the nineteenth century, chin tattoos were common for tribal women throughout California. In the Southwest, face and body painting was widespread, and tattooing was specific to the tribes of the lower Colorado River. The Mohave men and women practiced both. Courtesy of the Autry National Center, Southwest Museum, Los Angeles. Southwest Museum Leaflets, 1947, no. 20, p. 7, fig. 5.

FIG. 10. Mohave men's face painting. Courtesy of the Autry National Center, Southwest Museum, Los Angeles. Southwest Museum Leaflets, 1947, no. 20, p. 9, fig. 6.

Standing now astride two cultures, Olive had unwittingly made history: she was the first known tattooed white female in the United States. The tattoo, both in its timing and meaning, made her a fascinating cultural counterpart to other tattooed Anglos of her era. Tattoos, which had just begun to settle in the American consciousness, were tokens of crossed borders and encounters with exotic people. In the late 1700s, Captain James Cook had returned to England from Polynesia with sailors bearing Tahitian "tatau" marks, and by 1848 the first professional U.S. tattooist, Martin Hildebrandt, had opened a shop in New York and began working on seamen there. The year Olive was captured, 1851, saw the publication of *Moby-Dick*, the first American novel in which tattoos defined an important character, Queequeg. But unlike Queequeg's tattoos, which were reminders of his native identity wherever he traveled, Olive's showed how far she had strayed both physically *and* culturally from her roots. Like Melville's hero, Ishmael, Olive had survived an epic journey, led by a man, her father, every bit as monomaniacal as Ahab in his determination to push as far into the unknown as he wanted. Her voyage had taken her deep into the wilderness of her own nation.

7

Deeper

> It would seem as if these simple people were really pleased with the first dawning of light of civilization. They feel the want of comfortable clothing, and perceive some of the advantages of trade. There is no doubt that, before many years pass away, a great change will take place in their country. The advancing tide of emigration will soon take possession of it, and unless the strong arm of the government protects them, the native population will be driven to the mountains or be exterminated. | LT. AMIEL WEEKS WHIPPLE, *Pathfinder in the Southwest*

Mary Ann had always been a frail child. During the summer of 1853, the girls' second with the Mohaves, she was chronically sick, sometimes too weak to wander the desert plucking the seed buds off the mesquite tree and hang them to dry for the winter. A basket a day was all the girls needed to fill, and even that much was hard to find. "I often felt as though it would be a sad relief to see her sink into the grave," wrote Olive. "But there were times when she would enliven after her rest."[1]

The excellent harvest of 1853 both sustained Mary Ann and fortified the tribe with supplies for what would be a major trading opportunity that winter—and a test of the girls' allegiance to the Mohaves.

With almost all of Mexico's northern provinces folded into the United States at the close of the Mexican-American War, the War

Department was busy charting the nation's new borders and exploring its expansive lands. A railroad would link the far-flung states and territories together, so in early 1854 Lt. Amiel Weeks Whipple was sent to map a route from the Mississippi River to the Pacific Ocean. Whipple was a thirty-seven-year-old West Point graduate from Massachusetts, known for his competence and conscientiousness, who later fought and died in the Civil War. He had surveyed along the Gila River in 1849, spending months observing and engaging with the Quechans in the region, and later submitted a Quechan dictionary to the five-year-old Smithsonian Institution. His 1851 report on the journey was respectful, expressing concern for the tribe, poised for attack by the U.S. Army (ultimately at Commander Samuel Heintzelman's hand) for their retaliations against trespassers in their territory.

A member of an elite corps of scientists closely associated with the Smithsonian Institution, Whipple was also an amateur ethnologist who proposed "lifting the veil" of the "singular people" who were disappearing "before the westward march of the Anglo-Saxon race." He had prepared for the expedition by reading an early history of Indian tribes by a famous Indian agent and pioneering ethnographer, Henry Schoolcraft, and took with him comparative vocabularies to ease communication with the Indians whose lands he would survey. He also asked the Bureau of Indian Affairs for extra money to buy gifts for them. Traveling with more than a hundred men, from engineers, cartographers, and geologists to astronomers, meteorologists, and botanists, as well as soldiers and guides, Whipple trudged through present-day Oklahoma, Texas, and New Mexico, into what would become Arizona, on a path that vaguely foreshadowed today's Route 66. The group was guided along the way by Indians—Creeks, Shawnees, and Zunis. But it was the Mohaves who would lead Whipple on the final leg of the journey.[2]

On the afternoon of February 23, 1854, the Whipple party was camped in the Chemeheuvis Valley, just south of the Mohaves' homeland, unpacking the two wagons they intended to leave behind in order to get across the river and piling their supplies on mules. A group of Mohaves appeared, led by a man named Manuel who wore a turquoise pendant suspended from his nose. He was trailed by three tall, chiseled warriors wearing rats, squirrels, and frogs swinging from their bronzed bodies, ready for roasting. Their faces were painted, in typical fashion, black with a red stripe from forehead to chin. Strands of small beads hung from their pierced ears. Their black hair was twisted into thick strands styled with colored clay. They strode barefoot into camp, recalled Whipple, "with the dignity of princes."[3] And they looked spectacular.

Manuel approached, wrote Whipple, "to welcome us to their country." Eyes to the ground, he "submitted to the ceremony of an introduction." He, like the four other leaders Whipple would meet, used his Spanish name, probably because the Mohaves were reluctant to reveal their Mohave names to strangers. With apparent indifference, he took the few presents Whipple offered. What might have registered as arrogance was in fact humility—Mohave headmen simply didn't accept gifts, except as communal property to be distributed to the tribe.[4]

When Whipple accepted a basket of maize in exchange for three strings of white porcelain beads, all hell broke loose: a crowd of Mohaves descended on the party, trading maize, beans, wheat, squash, and peas for beads and calico, and an impromptu bazaar bustled until dusk. Women arrived with clay pots on their heads, carrying bags and baskets of goods, then knelt on the ground and spread their wares out at their knees while the men wandered around the camp soliciting trade and overseeing the deals. Whipple called the Mohaves "cool and determined" traders.[5] Pleased with the activity, the Mohaves hoped to spend the night, but Whipple gently drove away the exasperated Indians, except for Manuel and a few of his friends. The next day they returned in good humor—armed with bows and arrows. Two of them led the way north into the Mohave Valley, past the Needles, a trio of mountain peaks on the east side of the Colorado. This was where the main body of the tribe resided—including Olive and Mary Ann.

Here Whipple met a second leader or captain who called himself Francisco, this one less impressive than the first. Wearing a bandless black hat pulled down to his eyes and a "half stupid, half ferocious" expression, the old man looked like a scrawny beggar to Whipple.[6] His interpreter, a Quechan named José, formally presented Francisco as a dignitary of the tribe, even offering a letter of recommendation from Heintzelman, whom Francisco had visited at Fort Yuma. Francisco knew that the letter—written in English he could not read—explained that he and a group of warriors had visited Major Heintzelman at Yuma after a battle with the Cocopas; what he did not know was that in it Heintzelman, no friend to Indians, advised Americans not to trust him. Unfazed, Whipple shared a pipe with him and explained his mission: to find a suitable crossing where the Old Spanish Trail met the Mohave River (near present-day Barstow) for the purpose of building a railroad.

Francisco approved the plan, assured Whipple his people would help, and declined the gifts he was offered. The minute the meeting ended, the trading began anew. White cotton, calico blankets, and white or blue porcelain beads commanded high prices from the tribe; glass and coral beads were nearly worthless to them. Some women traded their bark skirts to men who had ethnographic collections; likewise Mohave men bartered weapons and ornaments for blankets, fabric, and clothes. Later, Whipple said, the Mohaves "ranged about camp in picturesque and merry groups, making the air ring with peals of laughter."

Some young Mohaves cleared a forty-foot area for a game in which pairs of players rolled and chased a four-inch hoop then tried to stop it by lancing it with sixteen-foot poles—a sport they played for hours without stopping or speaking. Others practiced archery shoulder-to-shoulder with whites who fired rifles and Colt pistols, each politely marveling at the other's precision, until the guns outperformed the arrows and a frustrated Mohave finally tore down the shared target in defeat.

"These Indians," wrote Whipple,

> are in as wild a state of nature as any tribe now within the limits of our possessions. They have not had sufficient intercourse with any civilized people to acquire a knowledge of their language and their vices. . . . Nonetheless, they appear to be intelligent, and to have naturally pleasant dispositions. The men are tall, erect, and finely proportioned . . . their eyes are large, shaded by long lashes, and surrounded by circles of blue tint that add to their apparent size. . . . Their bodies and limbs were tinted and oiled so as to appear like well-polished mahogany.[7]

The party's resident draftsman, a perceptive German writer and artist named Baldwin Mollhausen, was struck by their apparent immunity to white or Spanish influences and was convinced that their cultural purity would not last: "The experience of past centuries has shown that the insolence and injustice of the whites, when in close and frequent intercourse with at first innocent savages, will soon stifle any germ of confidence that may be springing up, and transform their friendliness into hostility. The native, who seeing himself trampled upon, revolts against the domination of the white race, is then at once treated like a noxious animal, and the bloody strife never ends till the last free inhabitant of the wilderness has fallen."[8]

Mollhausen was every bit the ethnographer Whipple was, from his ponderings about the reason for the curiously broad space between the Mohaves' toes, to his careful notes on their diet, fashion, agricultural practices, and personalities, to his historically well-founded concern about the tribe's fate. His were some of the most detailed impressions—both visual and verbal—of the tribe. Like Whipple, he was awed by the "horribly beautified" Mohaves who leaned gracefully on their long bows, reporting in his journal that the men, with their "brilliant eyes flashing like diamonds—looked even taller than they were from the plumes of swans', vultures', or woodpeckers' feathers that adorned their heads. Some wore as their sole garment a fur mantle, made of hares' or rats' skins, thrown over their shoulders; but one outshone all the rest of the company, having picked up an old waistcoat that had been thrown or bartered away by some of our people, and now displayed it for the completion of a costume that had hitherto consisted only of paint." He noticed the men caressed and embraced each other affectionately then exchanged "some exceedingly rough joke."[9]

The first person ever to sketch the Mohaves, Mollhausen was less taken with the women, who were shorter and thickset. Despite their "fine black eyes" and cheerful expressions, they could not, he concluded, "be called handsome"—by white standards.[10] They wore long fur cloaks, shell necklaces, and chin tattoos, and painted themselves more elaborately than did the men. As Mollhausen drew them, replicating the red and blue crosshatching on their torsos and the concentric circles on their breasts, they were anxious to make sure he got the lines precisely right.

The women were outspoken, confirming Jedediah Smith's observation that "No Indians I have seen pay as much deference to women as these . . . here they harangue the multitude the same as men."[11] When a lieutenant caned a Mohave across the shoulders for accidentally stepping on his foot in Whipple's camp, an old woman flew into a rage and was soon joined by others who berated and threatened the man with retaliation, implying, said Mollhausen, "that a whole crowd of their warriors should come, and make us disappear from the face of the earth."[12] The Mohave men became silent and slowly crowded around the woman. Finally, the tribe was sent out of the camp, but when they returned the next morning all was forgiven.

The Mohaves were endlessly amused by the hubbub of the Whipple party and their strange instruments. The sight of the white men's beards, now tumbling down their chests after many months of travel, afforded them—especially the women—considerable glee. Some tried to touch them to verify that they were real, but, wrote Mollhausen, "they gave us to understand, in an unmistakable manner, that they did not consider these appendages at all attractive, though we were rather proud of them, as testifying to the length of our journey." When the bearded men rode past them, the women burst into laughter and "put their hands to their mouths, as if the sight of us rather tended to make them sick."[13] Unaccustomed to hairy faces, the women thought the beards made the men look like talking vaginas.[14] Mollhausen, meanwhile, could not determine whether Mohave men, who had little or no facial hair, shaved, singed, or plucked.

One night Mollhausen and a lieutenant named Fitzball revived their boyhood magic tricks for the entranced tribe, and Fitzball was inspired to perform sleight of hand with his false front tooth. He flashed the tooth, secured by a spring, pretended to swallow it by closing his mouth and removing it, then covered his mouth and replaced it. The half-terrified Mohaves invited their friends to see the magic, and Fitzball repeated the performance late into the night, until an old warrior asked him to do it with another tooth. When he refused, the spell was broken and the disillusioned crowd dispersed.

Whipple reported seeing as many as six hundred Indians in a single day in his camp. Few spoke Spanish; most communicated with the whites using hand gestures. Whipple noticed "several sad-looking fellows in the crowd" who were slaves taken in an expedition against the Cocopas, but he saw no white girls, and more significantly, was never approached by the Oatmans, who either remained in their village above the campgrounds or socialized with the others, passing as Mohaves.[15] Either scenario is telling. If they were hidden from the Whipple party, this omission from Olive's biography is glaringly conspicuous: it was not just her first opportunity for escape during her captivity but also one of the more dramatic events of her

FIG. 11. The Whipple party on the Colorado River near the Mohave Villages. Illustration by J. J. Young, based on a sketch by A. H. Campbell.

Mohave life. And if she wasn't hidden, she was in a situation where she roamed freely with Mohaves of all ages, but never sought help from any of the hundred-odd whites in the area. Three years into their captivity, with no knowledge that their brother had survived the Oatman massacre, seventeen-year-old Olive and twelve-year-old Mary Ann had crossed the threshold of assimilation.

Whipple's men continued surveying through the valley and even visited the Mohaves' homes, respecting their requests not to trample their fields along the river. Like Olive, Mollhausen noticed their crops would have done better with an irrigation system, but he was also impressed by the wicker granaries, three to five feet wide, that stood outside their houses, filled with corn, beans, and flour. Where Olive had scolded the tribe for short-sightedness, Mollhausen praised them: "This provident care for the future . . . I had never seen among Indian tribes east of the Rocky Mountains."[16] They had also been able to trade two-foot-wide pumpkins in February because of their practice of wrapping pumpkins and melons and burying them to preserve them. Standing on their low rooftops, the villagers watched the strangers pass then joined them in a train that extended a mile behind them.

On the fifth day, Whipple and his men inflated an India rubber pontoon and made repeated attempts to ford the river. As they struggled, using a pulley system to transport their belongings to an island midway across, a third leader, Homoseh Quahote, arrived to greet them, preceded by a messenger, flanked by a page and an interpreter, and followed by what appeared to be a whole village carrying baskets on their heads. A respected statesman who was over six feet tall, he advanced ceremonially, wearing a blanket around his shoulders and an elaborate black plumed headdress that fell nearly to the ground. He too presented his credentials from Heintzelman, listened to Whipple's description of his expedition, and—in a long and enthusiastic speech—endorsed it.

In all, Whipple would meet five leaders. On his last day in the valley, they came together to inform him they had not only held a national council and approved mapping a road through their country but had also chosen a guide to show his men the best route to the Pacific. It would be the third time the Mohave had helped strangers navigate their trail after Smith, decades earlier, and Francisco Garces, nearly a century before. They asked Whipple to draw up papers certifying the good treatment the Mohaves had given them, to present to subsequent visitors. Furthermore, wrote Whipple, "They wished us to report favorably to our great chief, in order that he might send many more of his people to pass this way, and bring clothing and utensils to trade for the produce of their fields."

When yet another round of trading was proposed, Whipple's men had nothing left to barter. "The Indians," he wrote, "expressed no disappointment, but wandered from fire to fire, laughing, joking, curious but not meddlesome; trying with capital imitative tongue to learn our language, and to teach their own. . . . Every day these Indians have passed with us has been like a holiday fair, and never did people seem to enjoy such occasions more than the Mohaves have done."[17]

In opening their valley to pathfinders and sharing their secret road to the Pacific, the tribe clearly anticipated changes to come—with no idea how devastating they would be. The Mohaves' eagerness to trade was a dark omen of a future that would leave them both bankrupt and deracinated. Cairook, a subchief, and his friend, Irataba—the two men appointed to lead Whipple to the Mohave Road—would be the last great leaders of the tribe.[18] The pair's physical transformation on the road out of the valley foretold their fate poetically. As Mollhausen observed: "A striking and by no means advantageous change had taken place in the appearance of these two since they had left home. When they joined us on the day of our departure from the Colorado, their fine muscular naked forms were fully displayed; but now their powerful limbs were hidden under such a heap of clothes and coverings, that they were scarcely recognizable." Wearing virtually everything their friends had given them before leaving, "they now look[ed] like wandering bundles of old clothes."[19]

After entering the Mohave valley, Mollhausen had asked, in his diary, "How long will it now be before a reason is found or invented for beginning a war of extermination against the hitherto peaceful Indians of the valley of the Colorado?"[20] Sooner than he had probably imagined. Within five years, the only trace of the thriving, unified nation Whipple and Mollhausen had met on the bank of the Colorado would be footprints in the sand.

8

"There Is a Happy Land, Far, Far Away"

> "I plainly saw that grief, or want of food, or both, were slowly and inch by inch, enfeebling and wasting away Mary Ann."
> | OLIVE OATMAN

The Mohaves were famously ferocious warriors, but their conflicts were often instigated by war leaders who steamrolled the pacifist majority of the tribe in their push to battle. They went to war for a variety of reasons: to exact revenge, to take prisoners, to protect their territory, but most often to enhance their nationalistic and spiritual identities, which were intertwined. Because they were secure in their homeland, thousands strong, with their material needs met, they rarely raided or fought for economic reasons. More interested in trophy scalps and captives than plunder, they approached war like a national sport.

Mohave warriors or *kwanamis* (brave men), like doctors, scalpers, shamans, and spies, were born, not trained; they drew their power from mythological dreams that began in childhood, telling them how to both fight and protect themselves in battle. Unlike tribal headmen, whose status was hereditary—and seemingly inferior to that of warriors—*kwanamis* who reported such dreams were tested and cultivated from the age of four or five and trained for warfare between eight and ten. If they showed fortitude and stoicism, they were given a black stripe across their faces and a pair of feathers for their hair and sent to battle in their late teens. Young *kwanamis* were "keyed up" like racehorses, as one Mohave put it, champing at the bit and obsessed with killing, even though war parties only went out once or twice a year.[1]

The Mohaves were friendly with the Yavapais and the Quechans; enemies of the Pimas, the Maricopas, and the Cocopas; and merely tolerant of the Chemehuevis, who in the 1830s had moved into the valley below them on the western side of the river—an area the Mohaves yielded to them because they believed departed spirits lived there, making it dangerous. In the spring of 1854, when the Quechans invited the Mohaves on a retaliatory expedition against the Cocopas, the Mohaves' attitude toward war took a new turn. Irataba, the young *kwanami* who had accompanied Whipple out of the valley a few months earlier, was becoming a pacifist. He knew the army at Fort Yuma was watching them, like the Quechans, and that if they continued their intertribal warfare, soldiers would be sent to their valley to punish them. War with a foe bearing rifles and riding horses was something to reconsider.

Irataba initially resisted the Quechan invitation, saying that although he'd always encouraged his people to fight, he was "quitting." He told his people, "There are four or five of you who are brave and always like fighting; but there is no use in that. . . . Follow what the whites tell you." This was the first of many hugely consequential conciliatory gestures Irataba made toward the white man for the sake of survival. For the moment, however, he relented, privileging his loyalty to his friend, the Quechan leader Pascual (a Spanish rendering of Paskwāole), over his fear of white intervention. "I do not wish to fight; it is bad," he told Pascual, a famous warrior whose scarred body was a monument to his military legacy. "But you wanted me and sent for me."[2]

The Mohave women roundly opposed the attack. "Those of them who had husbands and brothers enlisted in the expedition," wrote Olive, "tried every expedient in their power to dissuade them from it. They accused them of folly and a mere lust of war, and prayed them not thus to expose their own lives and the lives of their dependent ones." They had heard that the Cocopas had allied with surrounding tribes, and they feared defeat. "But go they would," Olive reflected, "and on the day of their departure there was a convocation of nearly the whole tribe, and it was a time of wild, savage excitement and deep mourning."[3]

True to tradition, the women danced around scalps collected in previous battles and wept as the warriors departed. About sixty soldiers left the valley carrying gourd canteens strung with willow fiber, wooden bows nearly as tall as the men themselves, and long wooden clubs carved from mesquite and painted black and red—good for smashing the skulls of enemies felled by arrows. They wore only breechcloths and sandals, their bodies painted red, black, and white, their faces masked in black, their long hair, bound and wrapped, doused in red. They took with them the few well-fed, highly prized horses they owned, trained specifically for battle.

Weeks later they returned, triumphant, having killed three Cocopas and taken two sisters prisoner. The Mohaves had lost no men. Though Olive never wrote about it, she and Mary Ann must have been fascinated to see how these captive sisters were treated when they were adopted for eventual marriage into the tribe through rituals the Oatmans never—at least by Olive's account—experienced. The entire tribe came together to sing in the morning, eat at noon, and in the afternoon dance shoulder-to-shoulder in a revolving circle, after which the prisoners were brought out and walked to the river. A *kohota* rubbed them with soaproot and arrowweed to purify the captives and protect the Mohaves from any illness they carried, led them to the water, and jumped in with them, followed by the rest of the tribe. "Perhaps these young women will bear children" the *kohota* announced. "These children will grow up half Mohave and half Cocopa, and because they belong to both tribes, there may be no more fighting."[4] One sister was given as a wife to an old man and subsequently had two children; the other was not married, and a few years later, when relations between the Mohaves and the Cocopas settled, she was returned.

By now, Olive and Mary Ann were clearly accustomed to Mohave social life; the Mohaves' typical victory party involved both scalp-dancing and, like the harvest celebration, elder-approved socializing and sex. At the celebratory feast, the men sang, and women, painted like warriors, addressed the trophy scalps, which were tied to poles, insulting them and narrating the battles in which the enemies had lost their lives—and their scalps. They also teased and shamed any healthy young men who had stayed home during the battle. The *kohota* gave a speech, encouraging the young people to find partners and multiply. These celebrations often inspired new marriages, tying the ritual of war to the regeneration of the tribe.

The Oatmans soon learned that dreaming was not just the inspiration for war, but served as the mythic foundation of Mohave consciousness. Dreams began in the womb and were caused by the spirit wandering around, having real experiences, while the body was inert. They were not induced by fasting or hallucinogens but rather came spontaneously, in two forms: those that conferred special powers or identity—bravery, leadership, musical talent, running ability, or homosexuality, for example—and everyday dreams. Some people got their dreams from Matavilya, the primary spirit, who was born of the union of earth and sky, or his brother Mastamho, who succeeded him, and created the river and the mountains along it.

Good luck and common knowledge came in dreams, and because information was said to be dreamed, not learned, elderly Mohaves could no longer distinguish between dreamed and tangible experiences. Important dreams were told or sung ceremonially and were open to interpretation, for the purpose of helping listeners individually and for clarifying the future. The ethnographer William J. Wallace theorized that some shared Mohave dream content was induced through suggestion: the imagery and myths that were constantly emphasized during the daytime naturally crept into the Mohaves' night dreams.[5] Conversely, special powers were sometimes attributed retroactively to dreams: a boy who proved to have warrior potential was suspected of having dreamed of it when he was younger. Faked dreams were uncommon because people feared that failed powers would expose the deceit.

Since Olive and Mary Ann's arrival, dreams had served the Mohaves well: the tribe had been on a roll, from the bountiful harvests of 1851–53 to the productive exchange with Whipple in early 1854, and later the same year, the triumph of war with the Cocopas. Now, things were about to change—for the girls *and* for the Mohaves. The harvest of 1855 was bad—fatally so. After a spring drought prevented the banks of the river from overflowing, the crops came up late and the yield was paltry. Aespaneo had given the girls seeds and a thirty-foot-square garden plot, where in previous years they had planted wheat, corn, and melon. "It brought to our minds the extended grain fields that waved about our cottage in Illinois," wrote Olive, along with "the May mornings, when we had gone forth to the plow-fields and followed barefooted in the new-turned furrow." Their labor of love had now turned to tough, necessary work, but the garden had failed. Mesquite mush, ground in a stone pestle, was becoming the tribe's only food, and even that was giving out. By the fall, food was being rationed, and eleven-year-old Mary Ann was faltering. "I plainly saw that grief, or want of food, or both, were slowly and inch by inch, enfeebling and wasting [her] away," wrote Olive.[6]

The Mohaves decided to travel in search of a mesquitelike bush that grew to thirty feet and yielded tasty berries with an orange flavor.[7] Mary Ann started out with Olive on the three-day journey, but was too weak to continue and turned back. The party found the trees and spent two days filling their baskets, but lost their way on their return to their temporary camp one day and wandered around looking for it through the night. People were becoming sick from eating the berries; three died. Their bodies were cremated, their baskets of berries collected, and the party "went howling through the woods in the most dismal manner," according to Olive. When they found their camp the next day, they realized they'd been near it all along. They gathered their belongings and returned to the village.

Back in the valley, Olive found Mary Ann in worse shape than when she had left her. The berries helped, but only temporarily. She spent days searching for blackbird eggs that would give her sister protein; roots took too long to collect and would mean leaving her alone overnight. Soon the girls, along with the rest of the tribe, were going whole days without food, except when Topeka and Aespaneo scraped something up for them. "Had it not been for the wife and daughter of the chief, we could have obtained nothing," wrote Olive. "They seemed really to *feel* for us, and I have no doubt would have done more if in their power."

People—mostly children—were dying. The wailing of mourning rituals filled the night, followed by cremation ceremonies, which for adults included torching the house of the dead along with his or her belongings. Soon Mary Ann was talking about death: she imagined rejoining her parents and sang hymns the family had sung together. "Don't grieve for me," she told her sister. "I have been a care to you all the while. I don't like to leave you all alone, but God is with you."[8]

She asked Olive to sing her favorite hymn with her, which began, "There is a happy land, far, far away," and told her sister she was willing to die.[9] But what Olive described merely as Mary Ann's weakness during this period must have been much more ghastly: people dying of starvation experience hair loss, bloating, and hypothermia, appear aged and withered, and become frantic for food before succumbing to listlessness and depression. Olive said her own cravings were already uncontrollable and observed that others in the tribe had become "reckless and quarrelsome" in their desperation. In her advanced state of malnutrition, Mary Ann could not have, as Olive put it, "s[u]nk away without much pain, and all the time happy."

As Mary Ann slid toward oblivion over the next two days, Aespaneo realized the child was beyond saving. The Mohave mourning ritual occurred before and during, as well as after death, and Aespaneo began her lament for the child. She looked into Mary Ann's face, said Olive, "and wept from the heart and aloud. I never saw a parent seem to feel more keenly over a dying child. She sobbed, she moaned, she howled. And thus bending over and weeping she stood the whole night." Mary Ann died the next day, with Aespaneo and Olive at her side.

Olive wailed like a Mohave over her sister as Aespaneo and Topeka comforted her. When Espaniole prepared to cremate Mary Ann's body, following Mohave custom, instead of burying it as Olive wanted, Olive wandered off to cry privately. Aespaneo later came to her to say that she had argued Olive's case with her husband, who had granted her wish. He gave her two blankets in which to wrap the body and sent two men to dig a grave wherever she wanted it. Olive chose the plot where she and Mary Ann had gardened together. "In this," she said, "they dug a grave about five feet deep, and into it they gently lowered the remains of my last, my only sister, and closed her last resting-place with the sand."

Olive was overcome not just with the heartbreak of losing Mary Ann but also with a more concrete problem: she, too, was starving. She had a burning sensation in her stomach, and she was so weak she could barely walk. "When the excitement of that hour passed, with it seemed to pass my energy and ambition. . . . I found but little strength from the scant rations dealt out to me. I was rapidly drooping, and becoming more and more anxious to shut my eyes to all about me, and sink to a sweet, untroubled sleep beneath that green carpeted valley. This was the only time in which, without any reserve, I really longed to die."

Aespaneo saved her life. Having dug up a stash of cornmeal she had buried, intending to parcel it out until spring, she ground and cooked a gruel and presented it to Olive in a hollow stone. When she had eaten it, Aespaneo brought her more. "I felt a new life and strength given me by this morsel," wrote Olive. "She had the discretion to deny the unnatural cravings that had been kindled by the small quantity she brought first, and dealt a little at a time, until within three days I gained a vigor and cheerfulness I had not felt for weeks." Aespaneo nurtured the girl secretly, because, as Olive put it, "some of her own kin were in a starving condition."[10] She may have realized that she had waited too long to save Mary Ann and was now scrambling to help Olive, or she had recognized from the start that Mary Ann, the younger and more delicate sister, could not be saved.

From there, Olive was able to regain her strength and find her own food. She continued tilling her garden, which Aespaneo watched for her when she went out gathering roots; her Mohave mother also found her a granary in which to store her harvest and made Espaniole promise that it would be protected. Mary Ann's death had left Olive without family, but it had also brought the goodness of her Mohave family into bold relief. Her last tie to the white world now severed, she was a Mohave.

"I saw but little reason to expect anything else than the spending of my years among them," wrote Olive, "and I had no anxiety that they should be many. . . . There were some few for whom I began to feel a degree of attachment." She came to love the valley, and now "time seemed to take a more rapid flight; I hardly could wake up to the reality of so long a captivity among savages, and really imagined myself happy for short periods."[11]

9

Journey to Yuma

"My life was again hung up as upon a single hair."

| OLIVE OATMAN

When Lorenzo left Fort Yuma in June of 1851, none of his extended family in New York or Illinois had come forward to claim him. That September his uncle, Asa Abbott, wrote to entomologist John LeConte in New York, asking about the incident. His confusion about the circumstances of the trauma and his impotence in the face of his in-laws' demise (Mary Ann Oatman was his wife's sister) were clear by the flood of questions he opened: "Why were they traveling alone and where was the rest of the company? . . . Did they make any resistance or were they shot down like dogs? Were they put to death instantaneously or by lingering tortures?" He wanted to know "the name of the tribe that committed this outrage" and asked, "Do you think there will be any chance of recovering the two girls if they are yet alive?"[1]

LeConte responded promptly, addressing each question in turn. He described his encounter with the Oatmans, saying Royce had set out alone because there had been "scarcely any provisions" at the Pima and Maricopa villages, and identified the attackers as the same Indians who had stolen his own horses the night before. He summarized the saga and explained Lorenzo's survival in a few discreet sentences, then he suggested Abbott write to the Boundary Commission for help rescuing the girls. "Had any other officer than

Heintzelman been in command," he added, "the subject would have been vigorously investigated." And he told Abbott about his article in the *San Francisco Herald*, which chronicled the Oatman disaster and "reflect[ed] severely on the conduct of Major Heintzelman."[2]

Despite his concern, Abbott's communications to Lorenzo were thwarted in those pre-pony-express years. The boy would not hear from him until years after the massacre. That fall in San Francisco, Lorenzo worked for a wholesaler until he was forced to quit after hurting his back lifting goods. When Dr. Henry Hewit moved back east to be with his family in Connecticut, Lorenzo was orphaned all over again at sixteen. He was underage, barely literate, and penniless in a half-formed city that the local paper reported was pitted with potholes, saturated with alcoholism, and prone to attacks by desperadoes. In a quixotic moment that highlighted San Francisco's frontier primitivism, the *Daily Alta California* cited the increase in female residents as a sign of impending civilization: "Our city is fast becoming populated with ladies, and we now see a dozen crossing the square where a year ago we saw but one. This is an encouraging sign and gives good promise that California is to be a habitable country."[3] That year, the second governor himself, John McDougall, engaged in a duel in the street four days after his term ended.

After quitting wholesale work, Lorenzo spent two years juggling menial jobs in San Francisco, mining in the gold country to the east, and trying to contact other families from the Brewster wagon train who had settled in California. In the spring of 1854, he moved down to "the Monte" (later called El Monte), the first exclusively white settlement in Los Angeles County, located on the stage road between San Bernardino and Los Angeles. Susan Thompson's family had opened a hotel there called the Willow Grove Inn, and the Richardsons, another Brewster party family who had made it to California in 1852, had settled just a few miles away.

In El Monte Lorenzo saw a letter his uncle Asa had written to the Richardsons, asking if the boy would be traveling back to Illinois.

He responded in language that betrayed his neglected education and in script—scratched out and overwritten—that reflected his literary uncertainty: "I have wroat three leters and not one worde hav I harde from you untill today. . . . I suppose you have hearde of the murder an destruction of my father and his family by the acersed redskins [whom] he would have befriended. It was by merical that I eskaped." He described being struck down and stunned, listening to the screams of his mother and sisters, rolling down the hill and escaping, and then interrupted himself: "I must leave this subject of[f] till mare time."[4]

Though he had earned two hundred dollars from a crop and was not working at the time, Lorenzo declined his uncle's invitation to return to Illinois because he was considering going to school ("It will not doo me eny harte for I canat read my one writing it is spelt so bad and unpraper," he wrote). He was set on finding his sisters, which would involve writing to various authorities in both the government and the military. He asked Abbott to write back immediately with news of his family and friends and expressed a wish to see his "aunt Sarey" and his cousin Charles. "I should like to bee back thre once more to see you all but the lorde nose when we will meat again."[5]

It must have taken amazing courage, given his subliteracy, for Lorenzo to pursue his sisters through a letter-writing campaign, first to authorities at Fort Yuma, then to the California government. In the summer of 1854, Heintzelman had finally extricated himself from Fort Yuma and yielded command to Brevet Major George Henry Thomas, who was more receptive to Lorenzo's inquiries, so the boy returned to the area that fall to question travelers and try to form a party to scour "Apache country" for his sisters. Lorenzo found that "a true sympathy is oftenest found among those who have themselves also suffered," but sympathy didn't translate into action, and he was repeatedly disappointed by men who promised to search with him and then backed out with a "trifling excuse."[6]

The next spring, a German-Mexican named Federico Ronstadt reported to Major Thomas that the Oatman girls were with the Mohaves and that a Quechan Indian named Francisco, well known and liked by the officers at the fort, could provide information on them. Thomas did not pursue it, so Lorenzo wrote to the California legislature asking that a hunt be organized to find the girls, but got no response. He hired a lawyer to investigate his legal resources and in late 1855 joined eight men in a prospecting expedition in the Mohave Desert, in hopes of finding his family. They saw bear "thicker than cattle," he told the Abbotts in a letter, and killed fourteen in two days, but found neither gold nor captives.[7]

In early 1856 a California rancher named Duff Weaver wrote to Lorenzo to say an American woman was living with Mohave Indians and claimed that Fort Yuma's new commander, Martin Burke, had refused an offer to trade her back for a few blankets. Southern California's first newspaper, the *Los Angeles Star*, ran the story, reprinting Weaver's letter and fulminating about the commanding officer's refusal to ransom "two American women from worse than negro slavery." Curiously, although Weaver referred only to "an American woman," the *Star* claimed "the girls" were living and married to chiefs, planting a rumor that would follow Olive for life.[8]

Weaver's charge against Burke was a fortuitous falsehood: it prompted an independent investigation into the Oatmans' whereabouts. The investigating officer, Col. George Nauman, went to Fort Yuma, verified that Burke had never entertained—much less refused—such a proposal, and the two sent runners out to local tribes promising ransoms for the white captives. Word arrived that one of the girls, probably Mary Ann, had died, and Lorenzo, with the support of his neighbors in El Monte, petitioned Governor J. Neely Johnson in Sacramento, asking for help in rescuing Olive. The petition, dated January 2, 1856, referred to the "two sisters taken prisoner, one of which has died since and the other it is believed upon reliable authority is the wife made so by force of the chief of this tribe," and asked for "men or means by which men can be obtained to rescue the unfortunate girls from the custody of these lawless and piratical mohoves [*sic*]."[9] Johnson denied his request, claiming, like Heintzelman before him, that he had neither the authority nor the means to conduct the search, and Lorenzo was directed to the Bureau of Indian Affairs in Washington DC, which ignored his plea.

In late January, Francisco approached the Fort Yuma carpenter, Henry Grinnell, to say he knew where Olive was. Grinnell, a coarse but generous man who was friendly with the Quechans, spontaneously hatched a ransom plan. He seized the *Star* article about the Oatman girls, translating it into Spanish, which Francisco understood, and embellished it, pretending that it said that if the captives were not delivered soon, five million men surrounding the Indian country would find and kill the Indians. "You give me four blankets and some beads, and I will bring her in just twenty days," Francisco promised.[10]

Burke issued a travel pass for Francisco to take with him, demanding the girl's release. But even at that early point in the transaction, there was a hint of doubt about her willingness to return. The pass read:

> Francisco, Yuma Indian,
> bearer of this, goes to the Mohave
> Nation to obtain a white woman
> there; named, SPANTSA.
> it is desirable she should come to this post, or
> send her reasons why she does not wish to come.
> Headquarters Fort Yuma, Cal[a]
> 27th January 1856.
> Martin Burke,
> Lieut. Col., Commanding[11]

"*Or send her reasons why she does not wish to come.*" Burke's caveat may have been inspired by the knowledge that a year earlier when the

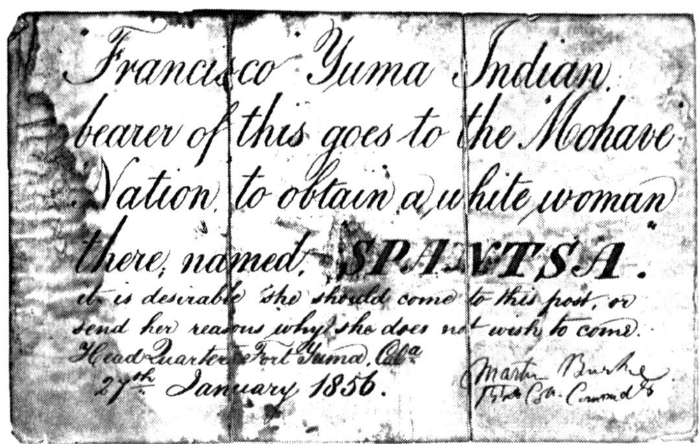
Francisco Yuma Indian.
bearer of this goes to the Mohave
Nation, to obtain a white woman
there, named, SPANTSA.
it is desirable she should come to this post, or
send her reasons why she does not wish to come.
Head Quarters Fort Yuma, Cal.a
27th January 1856.
Martin Burke

FIG. 12. Col. Martin Burke's handwritten travel pass authorizing the Quechan Indian Francisco to retrieve Olive from the Mohave Valley. When Stratton quoted it in *Captivity of the Oatman Girls*, he changed "Spantsa" to "Olivia," probably because in Mohave "Spantsa" meant "rotten vagina" or "sore vagina." Olive Ann Oatman Papers, Center for Archival Collections, Bowling Green State University.

Whipple party had spent a week with the Mohaves, Olive had not presented herself, or by Francisco, who had talked with Espaniole months earlier and may have gleaned that Olive preferred to stay.

Days later, Olive was grinding mesquite outside her hut when a boy approached her to say Francisco was on his way to the Mohave Valley to order her release. At first she thought it was a rumor, but a subchief came to her to confirm it, and within hours Espaniole was calling a meeting. Excitement in the camp mounted as criers spread the news. Olive was taken away by two Indians, and the meetings commenced. "My life was again hung up," she later wrote, "as upon a single hair."[12]

In a marathon council that dragged on for two days, Espaniole refused to return Olive. A Mohave named TokwaOa (Musk Melon) later recalled Espaniole telling Francisco, "I would like to raise this girl. We traveled far to buy her. We like her. And we want to make friends (through her). When those who come by us know how we treat her, they will treat us well too. If the officers want to see her, they had better come here and talk with me."[13] The women, he said, were especially unhappy that she might be taken from them, and told her so.

After a second night of pleading, Francisco gave up and crossed the river to talk with another group of Mohaves, where a leader advised him to offer payment for her. The next day, while Olive was out gathering nuts in a basket on her back, Francisco returned with the second group of Mohaves. At first Espaniole refused to see him, but subsequently called another council, this time with Olive present. She recognized Francisco, having seen him "tarrying" with a headman three months earlier, and now deduced how the whites had found her. Francisco restated his case, this time promising a white horse as ransom, along with blankets and beads, and the talks went on for yet another day and night, punctuated, Olive noted, with passionate eloquence and angry outbursts. The Mohaves could not read the travel pass Francisco presented from Burke, and Olive, who had not seen English writing in five years, struggled to translate it. "I never expect to find so attentive an audience as I did then," she later recalled.

The Mohaves, she said, tried to convince Francisco that Olive was not white, but rather came from "a race much like the Indians, living away to the setting sun." They questioned Francisco's motives, implying that he was trying to take Olive into his own tribe, not back to the whites. Francisco, who until then had been "bold, calm, and determined," according to Olive, now became furious, and challenged them to follow him when he took her.[14] He repeated Grinnell's promise that millions of whites lurking in the surrounding mountains would kill them and all the local Indians if they didn't give her back, which concentrated the minds of the Mohaves, who believed that whites could see through mountains by using binoculars. An elder finally relented, saying, "We raised her so that if anyone wants her back, they can have her."[15] The decision was made at sunrise: Olive would be traded for two horses, blankets, and beads. She responded by bursting into tears.

Espaniole instructed Topeka to travel with Olive, either to ease her journey, to collect her ransom, or both, along with Francisco's brother, two cousins, and Musk Melon, who lived near Olive. Topeka was happy to go, but her brother, a mystery character in the Oatman story who appears, provocatively, only here, was angry, and demanded that she return the beads she had collected while living with the Mohaves, some of which she had been given for her singing, others of which Mary Ann had worn. Some Oatman scholars have theorized that only a lover or husband would so formally demand their return before her departure, but beyond this, Oatman made no reference to leaving a partner behind, and she described her two Mohave brothers as married men. The reaction may have been rooted in a Mohave fear that letting whites take their belongings would bring them bad luck.[16]

Olive later said her release provoked mixed reactions from the rest of the tribe. Some laughed derisively, she wrote, "as if to say: 'O, you feel very finely now, don't you?' Others stood and gazed upon me with a steady, serious look, as if taking more interest in my welfare than ever before." Still others "seemed to stand in wonder as to where I could be going."[17] And some, she said, were genuinely happy for her.

Aespaneo was abject. She cried for a day and a night over the loss of her white daughter, and the decision was no less wrenching for Olive herself: "Every stream and mountain peak and shaded glen I was familiar with," she later wrote, "as with the dooryard of my childhood home."[18] She especially regretted leaving Mary Ann's grave, which had become a shrine for her.

When she learned that Musk Melon would go with her, she asked him to speak Quechan for her at the fort, because she spoke only Mohave.

"You will always follow me?" she asked, referring to the journey.

"Yes, I will go with you," Musk Melon assured her. "If you get sick, I will take care of you; if your feet are sore, I will carry you."[19]

Taking a hyacinth root with her as a reminder of the sisters' garden, she left her Mohave home forever.

The journey lasted ten days. Musk Melon had tied up a little food bag for Olive to carry with her. They traveled south, cooking beans, sleeping in the wild where they could, and staying at Mohave camps where they found them. They crisscrossed the river to shorten the trip, with Topeka carrying the women's blankets over her head. From there they slept at Quechan settlements where they were fed beans, pumpkin, and fish. Musk Melon remembered cooking a "big Colorado salmon" one day: "The fish was cooked soft and we had a little wild seed with it; it made a good supper and we talked, and the Yuma [Quechan] head men talked together and we slept."[20]

The Indians traveled faster than Olive could, so Musk Melon dropped behind to walk with her. When he saw that "the girl was giving out," they floated downriver for a few miles on a rush raft the Quechans had given them. From there, there would be no more settlements. Musk Melon advised Olive to take enough food to last a day and a half. They slept in the wild on their final night, and the next morning, before daylight, Francisco instructed one of his men to run ahead and tell "Carpintero," as Grinnell was known, that they were close, requesting that a calico dress be brought to Olive before she entered the fort. At 9:00 a.m., when they arrived on the eastern bank of the Colorado River, they found a crowd of Quechans and plenty of food but no dress. So they waited.

10

Hell's Outpost

"There was just one thin sheet of sandpaper between Yuma and Hell." | SARAH BOWMAN

Mark Twain called it "the hottest place on earth."[1] A resident lieutenant considered it cool there if the temperature held at one hundred degrees. And legend had it that a soldier who died there had gone to hell and found it so cold by comparison that he returned for blankets.

But in 1856, Fort Yuma was hellish for reasons beyond the heat. It was bedeviled by blinding dust storms and prone to Indian attacks. The barracks were plagued with ants, gnats, and, when the river was high, mosquitoes, and the toilets were open trenches heaped with dirt and lime to squelch the stench. The camp's poorly paid soldiers, who found scorpions in their shoes in the morning and bats in their tents at night, played host to errant bandits and trappers, missionaries and prospectors, scientists and settlers from across the nation, some of whom stumbled into the grounds half-starved, having roasted their own pack mules to survive. Apart from a handful of officers' wives, the only local women were prostitutes, managed by a towering, pistol-packing madam known as "The Great Western." This would be Olive's first taste of civilization after five years among Indians.

Though it had been closed in June of 1851, just after Lorenzo had left for San Francisco, the fort had reopened in early 1852 with bet-

FIG. 13. Fort Yuma, seen from the Arizona side of the Colorado River in 1864. Sarah Bowman (nicknamed "The Great Western") said, "There was just one thin sheet of sandpaper between Yuma and Hell." Illustration by J. Ross Browne.

ter supplies and more soldiers. Its purpose—to protect emigrants from Indians (as well as from their own recklessness)—remained the same. In that respect, the 1851 Oatman tragedy had marked a spectacular failure. But if the legendary episode was a black mark in the fort's annals, Olive's homecoming, five years to the month after her disappearance, was its redemption.

At about 9:00 a.m. on the last day of February, Grinnell learned from a Quechan messenger that Olive and her party had arrived and were waiting for him across the river. He hurried down to the crossing, sped across in Jaeger's ferry, and stepped off to see that Olive already had an audience: a collection of local Quechan Indians, seized with curiosity, had converged on the riverbank with their trademark quivers on their backs, knifes at their hips, and rings in their ears and noses. Wearing only a bark skirt, Olive was sitting on the ground, hiding her face in her hands. Tanned, tattooed, and painted, she was all but unrecognizable as a nineteen-year-old white woman. The straight line of a vertical blue tattoo ascended each of her bare upper arms. Her naturally light-brown hair was as dark as a Mohave's, dyed black with the gum of the mesquite tree.[2] When Grinnell approached her, she cried quietly into her hands but let him lead her to the water, where she washed and changed into the calico dress an officer's wife had sent from the fort. Now, free of face paint and hair dye, and wearing Anglo garb, she was ready—or at least dressed—for her return.

Grinnell called a meeting in his quarters then climbed into a boat with Olive, Musk Melon, Topeka, and Francisco to cross the river. The Quechans swam furiously behind them, intent on witnessing the full spectacle of Olive's ransom. As she ascended the jagged hill to the fort, she was greeted with the shouts and cheers of soldiers and the whoops of local Quechans who had gathered to see the white captive everyone had given up for dead. Cannons boomed. Flags snapped in the wind. And Olive had no idea why she was being applauded. Her anxiety was surely paralyzing: she had left behind a loving, familiar community and was entering a foreign land where—as far as she knew—she had no friends or family, and no idea of where she would live or who would care for her. Francisco and Topeka would return to their respective tribes once she was delivered, and Musk Melon would disappear to spend the coming weeks with Quechans south of Fort Yuma.

Olive was ushered into Grinnell's cabin and seated for a formal interview with Commander Burke. Timid, but also eager to please, she answered questions she clearly did not comprehend with a gentle nod. Burke, a scrupulous interrogator, was careful to record only responses to questions he was certain she understood, even testing her comprehension as they talked. "In answering questions purposely [framed] directly opposite," he wrote in his report, "she invariably says 'Yes' to both."

She gave her name as "Olivino," recalled her father's surname as "Oatman" and said she'd had six siblings, mentioning Lucy and Lorenzo by name. She identified her abductors as Apaches. Asked if they had treated her well, she said, "No. They whipped me." In response to the same question about the Mohaves, she "seemed pleased," noted Burke, and answered, "Very well."

Though she recited the general plot of the massacre, her slippery grasp of significant details indicated how far her pioneer past had receded in her memory. She remembered being eleven instead of fourteen when she was captured, and wrongly stated that Lucy's husband (she was not married) had been killed in the ordeal. Still, she outlined the basic contours of her captivity—one year with the Yavapais, more with the Mohaves—and recalled that she had been traded for blankets, beads, and two horses. She confirmed that she had never left the Mohaves for any reason (even, as Burke probably wanted to know, when the Whipple party had lingered in the Mohave Valley). After Mary Ann's death, she said, "there was not much to eat, but I helped them, and got used to it, and got along with them." "They saved my life," she said.

Burke asked, "What did they give you to eat?"

"Wheat, pumpkins, and fish."

"Mesquite also?"

Olive laughed and answered, "Yes," amused, possibly because gathering Mesquite beans was an arduous task—they were not just handed out.[3]

When Burke finally told her that Lorenzo was alive, she was so stunned that she had to lie down and appeared, for a while, to be unconscious. Burke explained how Lorenzo had escaped and asked Olive whether she could remember how he looked. She gestured that he resembled her, which he did. The commander told her he would notify her brother, now in Los Angeles, who would come see her.

That night, Burke sent word of Olive's arrival to the *Los Angeles Star*, but the news took a week to travel through the desert and make it into print, and even longer to land in Lorenzo's hands. As the news of Olive's return began to trickle out, the press and the public rallied to her cause. The *San Francisco Herald* ran a story about the "young and beautiful American girl," saying she would be cared for at Fort Yuma "until relatives or friends may come forward to relieve the poor girl from her present dependent position" and encouraging philanthropic women to take her in or get her admitted to the "Orphan Asylum."[4] The story, copied by the *Daily Alta California*, the *Evening Bulletin*, and the *California Chronicle*, swept across the country, appearing in newspapers in nine other states, from Iowa and Wisconsin to Georgia and New York.

The San Francisco Sisters of Mercy responded by offering, through the *Herald*, to take Olive. Her Indian leanings were already a concern: the paper hoped someone would try to "wean her from all savage tastes or desire to return to Indian life."[5]

The Collins family, who had traveled with the Oatman train as far as Tucson, convinced a county judge to petition Burke to send her to their home in San Diego, where, the *Daily Alta* projected, "she will shortly be able to resume the position in society which five years of savage bondage has deprived her."[6] And the state legislature passed a bill to grant her fifteen hundred dollars, but when the governor either failed or refused to sign it within ten days, it expired. Knowing none of this, Olive waited for the next two weeks in limbo. For their part, the officers at Fort Yuma pooled their money in a fund for her.

Olive's stay at Fort Yuma must have been unimaginably weird. Though the newspapers later said she was cared for by the wife of Lt. Reuben Twist, her guardian angel was a much earthier character: an Amazonian redhead named Sarah Bowman who ran a combination mess kitchen, boarding house, and brothel across the river. An officer's wife, evidently, was a more respectable caretaker to assign to Olive—at least in print.

A six-foot-tall, forty-four-year-old Irish-American from the South, Bowman was outsized in every way: nicknamed "The Great Western" after the largest of the first steamships to cross the Atlantic in 1838, she had also been dubbed "the heroine of Fort Brown" during the Mexican-American War because she had cared and cooked for soldiers throughout a seven-day siege during which Mexican cannonballs rained down around her.[7] While other women hid in a shelter sewing sandbags to shore up the fort, she had rushed around with bean soup and bandages, feeding and nursing soldiers even as bullets pierced her hat and punctured her bread tray. When the United States won the battle, Bowman was celebrated in newspapers across the country for her calm, courage, and competence. Years later she received a full military funeral.

One soldier found Bowman "modest and womanly notwithstanding her great size." He described her crimson velvet dress, riding skirt, and gold-laced cap, an outfit topped off with pistols and a rifle. "She reminds me of Joan of Arc and the days of chivalry," he said. A man who knew her when she was working as one of the first madams in Texas observed that even the Indians "seemed to hold her in perfect awe, and had a superstition that she was a supernatural being."[8]

Though she was illiterate (if bilingual), Bowman was an enterprising and successful businesswoman. She had worked her way west, kitchen by kitchen, and when the opportunity arose, bedroom by bedroom, until she landed at Fort Yuma, where she now had a full staff and lived with her partner, an upholsterer from Germany. "Among her good qualities," wrote one lieutenant, "she is an admirable 'pimp.' She used to be a splendid looking woman and has done 'good service,' but she is too old for that now."[9]

Bowman could be fierce and foulmouthed, but she was well liked—she had even won over the impossible Heintzelman, barring a few nights when his soldiers returned drunk from her house. She wore a scar on her cheek as souvenir of her service in the Mexican-American War (and claimed she killed the Mexican who cut her), but she was bighearted: she took in as many as five orphans at once, both Mexican and American, which is probably why Olive was put under her protection during at least part of her stay at Fort Yuma. In 1853 she had moved her entire operation across the river into Mexico to prevent her teenaged foster daughter, Nancy, from being hired as a servant to a lieutenant's wife in San Diego.

Bowman's unconventional nature—she was no Victorian lady—may have smoothed Olive's transition back into white America. The Western, as she was called, had had a series of husbands (mostly younger) who, like Mohave spouses, were common law, and, like Olive, she was a survivor with little schooling and no known family. Her legendary maternal touch was no doubt a comfort to Olive, who had now lost two mothers. Likewise, Bowman became attached to Olive in the weeks they spent together and later honored her by taking a crew out to tend to the Oatman family's perpetually disrupted grave. Olive ate and slept at Bowman's (the officers' mess was at the fort proper) and visited with the few military wives in residence, who tried to reacquaint her with the folkways of white women.

Still, Olive's reentry was surely overwhelming. Few women followed their husbands to Yuma (Heintzelman, for one, had called the assignment "an outrage" and left his family in San Diego); consequently there was no female community beyond the brothel to speak of, and the camp was now populated with about 250 men.[10] Because Bowman offered food, lodging, liquor, and women at her adobe house across the river, she controlled the social life of the region—such as it was. She arranged live-in mistresses for soldiers ("It costs almost nothing to keep a woman here. . . . In fact it is a matter of economy," wrote one lieutenant[11]) and threw oyster dinners as well as more formal affairs, including Nancy's wedding to a discharged sergeant from a company in New Mexico—which was followed by a party that went on all night and well into the next day. As a courtesy, Bowman invited two prostitutes to the reception so the men would have dance partners.

Sylvester Mowry, a sex-obsessed lieutenant who had fled Utah after a dangerous liaison with Brigham Young's married daughter-in-law, described army life at Fort Yuma in a letter to a friend: "Our principal occupation at present is drilling, riding, 'rogueing' Squaws and drinking ale—the weather being too hot for whiskey."

He elaborated, "We are surrounded by squaws all day long entirely naked except a little fringe of bark hardly covering their 'alta dick.' Hide is cheaper here than in any place I have ever been. A pound of beads costs $2.50 and you can 'obtain' fifteen or twenty squaws for a tender moment with it."[12]

Mowry, who would become active in mining and politics as one of Arizona's founding fathers, may have sensed the impending doom of the Colorado River tribes. He was the first to interview Olive after Burke, and unlike the newspaper reporters who wanted to know about her personal experiences among the Mohave, Mowry wanted to know about the Indians themselves—beyond their "alta dicks." In a report called "Notes on the Indians of the Colorado," which he compiled that March and submitted to the Smithsonian Institution, he provided, based partly on Olive's descriptions, a brief taxonomy of the Upper Colorado River tribes, detailing their wars, spiritual beliefs, marriage practices, dialects, and hunting and farming traditions. Olive must have regained her English fairly quickly in order to supply the kind of detail Mowry attributes to her in his report—he quotes her saying that some Mohaves practiced a "promiscuous concubinage" that others considered reprehensible.[13] She also betrayed an impressive knowledge of the surrounding tribes and their estimated populations. In a later report to the commissioner of Indian Affairs, he says Olive gave him "much information" about the Yavapais as well.[14]

At Fort Yuma, Olive was quickly immersed in a stagnant culture of military routine, where the soldiers' only diversion from each other—sex—was crassly commercialized, and everyone (Olive included) was merely marking time at what was considered the worst army post in the West. Mowry wrote that "all [the] old officers advise the young ones to resign while they are young enough to do something else."[15] Those with low tolerance deserted. Those who stayed risked the wrath of angry Quechans whom the army had driven from their planting grounds along the Colorado.

The contrast between this benumbed lifestyle and what Olive had left behind was dramatic: she had never known a Mohave to trade sex for money. She had lived in a lovely valley bordered with willow and cottonwood trees, where her people delighted in swimming and sports, group dancing and storytelling. The debased physical conditions at the fort alone must have been appalling to her. To complicate matters, no one there spoke Mohave, so her transition back to English was achieved by total immersion.

Even Yuma's one natural beauty was marred for Olive. Lieutenant Sweeny, who had called the region "about as ineligible a site for a fort as an ice-burg in the Atlantic," conceded that Yuma nights were glorious. "The stars shine like loop-holes into the Heaven of heavens, and [the] moon like the home of calmness, purity and peace. But there is a never-ceasing hum of millions of insects, and the Colorado murmurs like an uneasy Titan, and shines, and whirls its red flood along, like a huge bronze serpent, whose glittering scales reflect the moonbeams."[16] Sweeny didn't mention another source of evening light: the glow of Indian campfires that dotted the vast desert landscape, reminding Olive of her former home. A single pastime carried Olive through her early repatriation: given thread and fabric, she quickly remembered how to sew, and did so in a therapeutic frenzy.

Weeks after Olive's ransom, on a sunny March day in El Monte, California, Lorenzo stood chopping wood—the latest of a series of menial jobs he'd taken since moving down from San Francisco—in a forest a few miles from where he was living with the Thompson family. At the sound of pounding hooves, he looked up to see his friend, Jesse Low, galloping through the woods with a newspaper under his arm. In Los Angeles Jesse had helped Lorenzo in his search for his sisters, where together they had published queries about the girls' status. Near Yuma, the two had gone searching for them on horseback. Low arrived now with the final clue to the Oatman mystery. Without so much as a greeting, he handed Lorenzo the March

8 *Star* article announcing Olive's return: "From Mr. Joseph Fort, of the Pacific Express Company, we learn that Miss Olive Oatman, who was taken prisoner by the Apaches in 1851 . . . has been rescued, and is now at Fort Yuma. Further particulars next week."[17]

Lorenzo was floored. "I now thought I saw a realization," he said, "in part, of my long cherished hopes. I saw no mention of Mary Ann, and at once concluded that the first report obtained by way of Fort Yuma . . . was probably sadly true, that but one was alive."[18] He jumped on a horse and rode straight to the *Star* offices on Main Street in Los Angeles for verification, where the editor showed him Burke's letter asking that the news be printed "with a view that Miss Oatman's friends may be aware of what has occurred."[19] Lorenzo borrowed money and horses from Low and took off for Fort Yuma, desperate to see his sister, yet afraid that there had been a mistake—that the report was wrong or the captive was not Olive; he had been disappointed so many times before.

Ten days later he and Olive were publicly reunited. By then, she had regained much of her English, which promptly failed her in the face of this momentous encounter. "For nearly one hour," Olive said, "neither of us could speak a word—for the history, the most thrilling and unaccountable history of years was crowded into that hour."[20]

Though whites, Mexicans, and Indians alike were said to be teary over the tender reunion, the ferryman L. J. F. Jaeger observed it without sentiment in his diary: "We had a warm day, and Oatman got in from Los Angeles also after his sister . . . and I went up to the fort with him . . . and she did not know him and he did not know her also, so much change in five years."[21] Lorenzo never commented on his reaction to Olive's tattoo.

Most of the men Lorenzo had met at Fort Yuma, the site of his recovery, were gone: Heintzelman had returned to San Diego, Sweeny had moved on to other posts, Dr. Hewit, of course, had left with Lorenzo, and "Dr. Bugs" was now teaching in New York. Jaeger and Grinnell were perhaps the only familiar faces. The landscape had also changed: adobe buildings had sprung up in place of the brush tents that once served as officers' quarters, and the hospital Hewit had battled Heintzelman to build was fully functional. A sutler had set up shop and soldiers now bought their provisions from him. Thanks to the Great Western, the town of Yuma, then called Colorado City, was sprouting on the opposite bank, though it had only about a dozen residents.

Lorenzo spent two days visiting with Olive, rehearsing the past and discussing the future, before taking her back to El Monte. The day they left on a Los Angeles–bound government wagon train, Musk Melon returned from the Indian settlement downriver where he had spent the past few weeks, in hopes of seeing Lorenzo. He arrived when the caravan was pulling out, and called to Olive, who was riding behind the train. When she dismounted to talk to him, Lorenzo grabbed a club and lunged at him.

"Don't!" Olive exclaimed. "He's a nice man. He took good care of me." Her brother backed off, and when she introduced the two men, Lorenzo handed Musk Melon a box of crackers as a peace offering, which he accepted.

Olive turned to her friend, speaking Mohave. "This is the last I shall see of you," she said. "I will tell all about the Mohave and how I lived with them." They shook hands, and Musk Melon watched her disappear into the desert.[22]

Olive would have ample opportunity to tell the world about the tribe. Within a month she was a media darling. In the nascent California print world of the 1850s, fed by articles about phrenology and spiritualism, temperance and bloomers, Pacific Coast fog and the legal "admissibility of Chinese and Negro testimony" against whites, Olive presented a human interest epic with legs.[23] She was often called beautiful. In this era before photojournalism, readers relied largely on verbal descriptions for their visual impressions of the white Indian. "The rescued lady is said to be very fine in appearance with agreeable manners, but has entirely forgotten her native language," wrote the *San Francisco Weekly Chronicle*.[24]

"Her hands, wrists, and arms are largely developed," observed the *San Francisco Herald*. "The hair of the young lady, [is] of light golden color, the Indians dyed it black—using the bark of the mesquite tree. . . . She is more fully developed than many girls of twenty."[25]

The *Star* applauded her "lady-like deportment," "pleasing manners," and "amiable disposition" and said she was "rather a pretty girl" but had been "disfigured by tattooed lines on the chin." Quashing the rumor it had planted in January, it also stated what no one wanted to ask but everyone wanted to know: "She has not been made a wife . . . and her defenseless situation entirely respected during her residence among the Indians."[26] Olive, the paper assured readers, had not been raped. The captive was a lady; she had to be, otherwise she would not merit the attention the media eagerly lavished on her stranger-than-fiction story. But she was no less a freak: one *Star* article described her patience with people who "rush to see her and stare at her, with about as much sense of feeling as they would to a show of wild animals." Still, the writer noted, "she fully realizes that she is an object of curiosity."[27]

In El Monte the Thompsons cared for Olive like a daughter, putting her up in their hotel, the Willow Grove Inn. Ira Thompson was the town's first postmaster; his hotel both housed the post office and served as a station stop on the Overland Butterfield mail route. Eager to resume her abandoned education, Olive spent much of her time in El Monte writing and studying. She was also driven around Los Angeles in Thompson's buggy and saw, for the first time, the proto-urban spread of a burgeoning city, including the extravagant adobe homes that ringed the downtown plaza, the Nuestra Senora la Reina de Los Angeles Catholic Church, built in the thirties when California was still Mexican, and the three-story Bella Union Hotel—the first in the city.

As the local agent for the *Star*, Thompson likely had a hand in arranging Olive's biggest media splash. On April 19, 1856, the *Star* ran a two-column front-page story about her experience, based on a lengthy interview. As the longest early article written on her, it serves as a corrective to the racist, religion-soaked tract that formed the core of her popular biography a year later. In vivid detail, the article describes Olive's "Indian adventures," from the gory massacre to the girls' cruel treatment by the "Apaches" to the famine they faced with the Mohaves, detailing how they were forced to throw away their shoes before the Yavapais ran them into the mountains, dripping blood from their lacerated feet, to the way Olive, when her clothes literally fell off her back two weeks later, "matted together the bark of trees and tied it around her person like the Indians."

Though Olive described the Mohaves as short-sighted farmers and hunters who planted and killed only as much as they needed for the moment, she painted them in otherwise glowing terms. She told the paper about how Espaniole treated her and Mary Ann "in every respect" as his own children. They were not forced to work, "but did pretty much as they pleased." They shared the Mohaves' food and were given land and seeds. Twice Olive mentioned how tenderly Aespaneo cared for her. "She speaks of the Chief's wife in terms of warmest gratitude," the *Star* reported, noting that when Olive left, Aespaneo, "the kind woman who saved her life in the famine, cried a day and a night as if she were losing her own child, then gave her up."

Interestingly, Olive told the *Star* reporter that the Mohaves always said she was free to leave when she wanted to, but that they would not accompany her to the nearest white settlement for fear of retribution for having kept her for so long. Since she did not know the way, she reasoned, she couldn't go. But that didn't explain her disappearance during the Whipple party's stay in Mohave territory. It's doubtful that she would have told her white audience—so appalled by her abduction and thrilled by her return—that she had stayed because she wanted to.

The *Star* story is bookended with strange caveats: it opens by saying that "her faculties have been somewhat impaired by her way of life" and that she was incapable of giving details "unassisted," implying that words were put in her mouth. The piece ends with the provocative comment, "She converses with propriety, but as one acting under strong constraint." Unless the reporter simply mistook timorousness for "strong constraint," Olive may have begun censoring her story already, knowing that not every aspect of Mohave life was suitable for newspaper audiences.

Still, the generosity of the Mohaves impressed at least one reader, who wrote a letter to the editor asking, "Should something not be done in acknowledgment of the Mohave Chief and his noble wife, the benefactors of Olive Oatman? Can anyone read her tale and feel no thrill of gratitude for them?"[28]

Within a week, four northern California papers had snapped up and reprinted the *Star* story; others subsequently conducted their own interviews. But in the gap between what was extracted from her and what she withheld, her emotional profile remained vague. "What were her sensations, during all this time, must be imagined; for she is not, as yet, able to express her thoughts in language," the paper noted. The coverage emphasized her cheery compliance as an interview subject and her frightening adventures as a cultural castaway, but rarely commented on her psychological condition, which was surely shaky. Only private letters and memoirs painted a more nuanced picture. Decades later, Susan Thompson reflected on the time Olive spent at her house in El Monte, calling her "a grieving, unsatisfied woman, who somehow shook one's belief in civilization." And, she said, "more savage than civilized," Olive longed to go back to the Mohaves. Samuel Hughes, who met Olive through Lorenzo, recalled that "she often told me she would like to see some of her old friends, even if they were Indians."[29]

In a letter Olive wrote from El Monte to friends in San Diego, she said, "I feel once more like myself since I have risen from the dead and landed once more in a civilized world. . . . It seems like a dream to me to look back and see what I had ben thrue [*sic*] and just now waking up." The letter, which refers to the "blood," "toil," and "tears" of her captivity, conveys the racking sense of trauma—if not post-traumatic stress—that attended a life of compound emotional fractures. Though Olive's dodgy spelling reflects her broken English, one error resonates with her ambivalence about Indians and her contradictory experiences with the two tribes who harbored her: instead of calling the Yavapais "those fiends," she accidentally wrote "friends."[30]

In early June, Olive's twenty-eight-year-old cousin from Oregon, Harvey Oatman, arrived by steamer in San Pedro to visit the Oatmans in El Monte, presenting family documents to prove his kinship. During a congenial two-week stay, he regaled the siblings with stories of his life homesteading in a budding town called Gassburg, where he and his brother, Harrison, had split a government donation land claim. Neither Oatman had taken to farming, so Harrison had opened a store attached to a saloon and billiard hall, while Harvey ran a hotel directly across from the busy Oregon and California Stage Company.

No doubt Harvey described the Oatman Hotel's regular dances and the spectacular exhibition held there the previous fall, which included a Drummond light demonstration in which burning lime produced a brilliant white light—limelight—that wowed guests, especially when it threw panoramic projections of European sights against the walls. And he probably mentioned the loquacious ("gassy") but quite popular and animated innkeeper's daughter, Kate Clayton—one of the few eligible women in a village dominated by bachelors—who had inspired Gassburg's name.

By the end of the visit, Harvey had convinced his cousins to return with him to Oregon. Ira Thompson was reluctant to give them up; he was suspicious, the *Star* reported, that "an attempt was being made to entrap his ward."[31] Thompson published a letter in the *Star* asking of Harvey, "Where has been his great affection for his cousins for the last three years?" noting that Harvey had told him he had first heard about the Oatman murders in 1853 and knew that Lorenzo, too young to support himself since the massacre, had subsequently traveled to California. "Did he ever spend an hour's time or one dime to advertise for information in regard to his young cousin that he had all reason to suppose was supported at the expense of the county somewhere in this state?"[32]

Harvey had no explanation, but defended himself by saying he had no financial interest in the Oatmans—he'd known them before he'd left Oregon for El Monte—and that no state funds had been promised to them; in fact, he'd spent a lot of money on the steamer journey to Los Angeles, and would spend more on three return fares. He did not, however, mention another possible occasion for his newfound concern for his cousins: earlier that year, his brother, Harrison, had survived a violent Indian attack in the Siskiyou Mountains in Oregon at the start of the Rogue River Indians Wars. Harrison and two companions had been hauling flour across the mountains and had stopped to drink at a spring when they were besieged by Indians. The two other men were killed, and Harrison had run down the side of the mountain for shelter.

One of the dead men, who had looked a lot like Harrison but who was now barely recognizable, having been shot in the head, was carried down the mountain and presented to Harvey for identification—as Harrison. Later that day, Harrison, who was resting on the other side of the mountain, sent a letter to his brother explaining that he had survived. Learning how it felt to lose a family member to Indians may have inspired him to reach out to his orphaned cousins.

In late June, the three Oatmans boarded a steamer called the *Senator*, bound for San Francisco. Olive sat for an interview with the *San Francisco Daily Evening Bulletin*, where her story appeared for the first time in the first person. "My name is Olive Ann Oatman; I

FIG. 14. Olive Oatman, soon after her return. Yale Collection of Western Americana, Beinecke Rare Book and Manuscript Library, Yale University.

FIG. 15. Lorenzo Oatman, soon after Olive's return. Yale Collection of Western Americana, Beinecke Rare Book and Manuscript Library, Yale University.

was born in Whiteside County, Illinois, in 1838," she began, and then skipped straight to the day of the massacre and the two captivities. Again she explained that she and Mary Ann were regarded as slaves by the Yavapais and as kin by the Mohaves, saying that Espaniole "took us as adopted children, and we were treated as members of his family."[33] The Oatman trio then took a river steamer to Sacramento, another ship to Red Bluff, and a stagecoach through Yreka. They crossed the Siskiyou Mountains and entered the Rogue River Valley town of Gassburg, population about one hundred, where Olive and Lorenzo would meet Harrison and his wife, Lucena, Harvey's wife, Lucia, their two boys, and a motley array of homesteaders.

In the end, Thompson need not have worried about Olive's "entrapment" by her cousin: it was the Methodist minister she would meet in Gassburg who would recognize her potential, seize her story, and control her life for nearly a decade.

11

Rewriting History in Gassburg, Oregon

An old, toothless, hump-backed, simpering, graceless wretch—his name is Bigotry. Look out for him. . . . He is abroad still in the forms of ignorance, intemperance, slavery, and blasphemy. | REVEREND ROYAL B. STRATTON, *Church Government*

The march of American civilization . . . will yet, and soon, break upon the barbarity of these numerous tribes, and either elevate them to the unappreciated blessings of a superior state, or wipe them into oblivion. | REVEREND ROYAL B. STRATTON, *Captivity of the Oatman Girls*

There would be no anonymity for Olive Oatman, "the heroine," as a fellow churchgoer called her, in the fledgling town of Gassburg.[1] Founded in 1851, Gassburg (now Phoenix) was a mining village on the trail that connected the fertile Willamette Valley with the California gold fields. Pioneers were drawn to the newly organized Oregon Territory after Congress passed the 1850 Donation Land Claim Act, granting solo settlers 320 acres of farmland and couples twice that, precipitating a flurry of hasty marriages involving children as young as twelve. A year later, when miners struck gold along Jackson Creek in the Rogue River Valley, the influx accelerated. Between 1850 and 1853 alone, the population of Oregon Territory nearly tripled, hitting more than thirty-five thousand.[2]

In its early years, Gassburg was populated by pioneers, many living in the converted wagon trains that had brought them west. Harvey, twenty-five, and Harrison, twenty-three, arrived from Rockland, Illinois, in 1853 with their young wives and Harvey's baby sons. The Oatman brothers took adjoining claims, but neither liked farming, so Harvey traded his plot for land on which he built a livery stable and the town's first hotel, and Harrison opened the first general store, selling supplies to miners. Harrison later become a real estate mogul and one of southern Oregon's most illustrious citizens; Harvey would vanish from the region in 1860, the year his wife died just after giving birth to their fifth child.

By the time Olive came to town in the summer of 1856, Gassburg had the makings of a full-dress, tree-lined downtown, consisting of Harvey's hotel and tavern and Harrison's grocery (attached to a saloon and pool hall), three blacksmith's shops, two stables, a grist mill, and a saw mill. Because Harvey had a wife and young children, and Harrison was living in a rattletrap cabin while he built a proper house, the Oatmans went to stay with the family of Stephen Taylor, a Methodist minister, and his wife Rachel, a teacher. Olive made friends with the young women in town, including the Taylors' daughter, Abigail, and Flora Davenport, who would become the mother of the famous political cartoonist Homer Davenport. Olive and Lorenzo worked at the Oatman Hotel, along with Harrison's wife, Lucena, and Olive likely befriended her cousins' young wives (townspeople called them "the Mrs. Oatmans"), who were close friends with each other.[3]

Like a true Mohave, Olive was a superb swimmer who impressed her girlfriends and their mothers by giving lessons and demonstrations in Bear Creek, a tributary of the Rogue River. She continued sewing, developing a taste for finely tailored clothes—possibly inspired by the six silk dresses she was given, along with many other gifts, en route to Oregon by patrons in California. She studied with Rachel Taylor, who taught her to read and write again. In a letter to relatives in Ohio, Harrison wrote that Olive was "a very intelligent Girl far ahead of the majority wimen [*sic*] of her age."[4]

A customer at the Oatman Hotel recalled, "She had her face, mouth, and chin all tattooed, and her features had a regular Indian cast, and not knowing who she was, [I] would have taken her for a half-breed squaw; her complexion, form, and features had become so by their habits and diet and mode of living."[5] Self-conscious about her tattoo, Olive reflexively covered her chin with her hand whenever she met someone new. This was what "proper" Mohave women did to convey modesty, says Michael Tsosie, but also, according to A. L. Kroeber, something the Mohaves frequently did as a sign of embarrassment, just as the Mohave women had done on seeing facial hair on Whipple's men. Interestingly, a gesture she may have acquired as a Mohave also hid her source of embarrassment as a white.

A miner who knew Olive in Oregon described her in a letter, weeks after her arrival: "She looks cast down but she has not forgot [how] to talk. She was a good scolar [*sic*] and she has not forgot it."[6]

Though he was just a boy when he met her, a local named James Miller remembered Olive as a "beautiful well-formed woman," but claimed she never smiled. "Her youth was destroyed," he said. "She was old beyond her years."

Photographs of the period contradict Miller's perception that she seemed old: she looks plump and girlish. But she was suffering. A Taylor family granddaughter, Elva Wheeler, wrote in her memoirs that Olive paced the floor and wept at night: "The [local] Indian matrons . . . said that her tattoo meant that she belonged to some Indian." Townies also wondered if she'd left a child behind, but, said Wheeler, "she never told."[7]

Olive was clearly grappling with post-traumatic stress. She may have been grieving for her lost Mohave family, struggling with her adjustment to white culture, or both. She had adapted or "acculturated" (in the parlance of anthropology) to the Mohaves at least to the extent that being ripped away from them was emotionally and psychologically painful. But considered in the context of other captives taken at her age and the quality of her relationship with the Mohaves, she had very likely transculturated during her captivity: she *became* a Mohave, adopting the tribe's culture, values, and lifestyle, which made her transition daunting.

Captivity scholars have wrestled with the question of how many of the tens of thousands of captives taken by Indians from the sixteenth to the nineteenth centuries resisted or refused return, and why. One of the few systematic analyses of transculturation ever undertaken involved 641 New England captives seized (by both Indians and the French) between 1605 and 1763. This study concluded that girls aged seven to fifteen were most likely to "take" to their new cultures; 54 percent of girls in the sample group voluntarily stayed with their captors, while only 30 percent of boys did.[8] No studies specific to Southwest tribes or nineteenth-century captives exist; the only certainty is that some captives were absorbed through concerted cultural reconditioning (such as being forbidden to speak their native languages), while others melted into their adopted cultures after long exposure to them.

How does Olive compare to other female captives who partly or fully transculturated? One of the most famous examples, Mary Jemison, was fourteen, Olive's age, when she was captured in Pennsylvania by Shawnees, who killed her family in 1755 during the French and Indian Wars. She was adopted by two Seneca women who had lost a brother in battle, and Mary stayed with the tribe for the rest of her life, marrying twice and bearing eight children. Unlike Olive, she had regular contact with whites during her captivity (and even met other captives), yet she chose to stay. In her story, "A Narrative of the Life of Mrs. Mary Jemison," written when she was eighty, she says she passed through a painful period of longing for her own people before she began to identify as a Seneca, but within four years—the same period during which Olive was with the Mohaves—"I had become so accustomed to their mode of living, habits, and dispositions, that my anxiety to get away . . . had almost subsided.[9] She was, however, a married mother by then. Like Olive, Jemison bonded with the women in her adopted family; she said she loved her Seneca sisters "as I should have loved my own sister had she lived."[10] And like Olive, she was taken by one tribe then adopted (sooner than Olive) by another. "With them was my home," she said, "my family was there, and I had many friends to whom I was warmly attached in consideration of the favors, affection, and friendship with which they had uniformly treated me, from the time of my adoption."[11]

It took another famous captive, Eunice Williams, just three years to transculturate completely, even with a sizable family awaiting her recovery. But she was younger than Olive (seven) when she was adopted by Mohawks near Montreal after an attack on the town of Deerfield, Massachusetts, in 1704. A "planted child" who had lost her English by the time her family tried to redeem her, she refused to rejoin her surviving father and four siblings.

Cynthia Ann Parker's captivity was closer to Oatman's historically and geographically, but not in duration. In 1836 nine-year-old Parker was captured by Comanches in Texas then returned, against her will, when she was thirty-four. The Texas legislature gave her a pension, land, and child support for her baby daughter. (Her son, Quanah Parker, left behind at ten when she was taken from the tribe, became the last Comanche chief.) But she never adjusted to life as a white woman, and her descendants claimed that she died "broken in spirit, a misfit among the white people, and bitter at her enforced captivity"—among whites, that is.[12] Unlike Parker, whose captivity was much longer, Olive was able to transculturate back to white society, but not without serious difficulty.

Above all, Olive's tattoo set her apart from other white captives, marking her forever as different—no matter how she reassimilated otherwise—and her self-consciousness about it may have colored her vision of white life beyond captivity. When a Mexican captive, tattooed on the face like Oatman, was found living with the Comanches in the late eighteenth century, she refused to return to her father, the governor of Chihuahua, even with an offer of a thousand pesos. She claimed that because she was both tattooed and married to a man who treated her well, had become "reconciled" to Comanche life, and believed that she was pregnant, she would be happier staying than going. And stay she did, bearing three children and becoming a white Comanche. With no reason to believe any of her immediate family was alive, Olive had even less incentive to repatriate.

Since no two captives' experiences are identical, Oatman's allegiance to the Mohaves cannot be fully theorized through comparison. Variables beyond age, gender, and length of captivity played into a captive's desire and potential for assimilation. Other factors included the tribe's motivations for taking prisoners, its treatment of captives, the individual whims of the abductors, whether captives had remaining family members, either within or outside the tribe, and whether they married and had children during captivity. Certainly, some Native Americans tortured or murdered prisoners. Mohawks, Senecas, and Comanches all practiced ritual torture, yet Williams, Jemison, and Parker stayed with them.[13] The Mohaves did not share this practice. Though frontier fears about the rape of white women were exaggerated, some western Plains Indians, notably the Sioux, did rape white war captives.[14] But because the Mohaves took captives as adoptees, they were known for treating them well physically. They did not exploit them sexually for fear of disease, or worse, because they thought sex with them could cause insanity. If an older man took one for a wife at his own health risk, it was usually in the context of marriage, which was more a matter of domestic compatibility than sexual conquest.

Considering that Quechans and Cocopas married into the tribe, it is conceivable that as a young adult, by which time Olive looked, acted, and was treated like a Mohave, she may have been wed. A half century after the Oatman massacre, Olive's fellow pioneer, Susan (Thompson) Parrish, claimed Olive had "become the wife of the chief's son and at the time of her rescue, was the mother of two little boys."[15] Compelling as it is, the statement is unreliable: Parrish also claimed Olive lived with the Thomson family for four years (in fact it was for two months) after her ransom.

Olive almost certainly did not marry a Mohave or bear children. According to Barrackman, if she had, it would have been a highly unusual, thus memorable, piece of tribal history. "She never married," he said definitively. "It never was told. If it was we would all know." He added that if Olive had had children, they would have stood out as mixed-race Mohaves who could have been easily traced through the years. Furthermore, though she married after her ransom, Olive never had biological children, which raises the possibility that she could not. Finally, when Musk Melon was interviewed extensively about Oatman a half century later, he said nothing about her husband.

Even if she did not marry into Espaniole's family, Olive clearly bonded with it, and vice versa, as evidenced by Aespaneo's and Topeka's tender treatment of her. Olive also believed that her natural family members, apart from Mary Ann, were dead, therefore she had little reason to resist the embrace of a new family. She had lost her language (the Mohaves probably forbade her and Mary Ann to speak English, otherwise she would have spoken better English on her return), which pushed her that much farther from the matrix of her native culture. "It is plain," wrote Kroeber, one of the first anthropologists to study her case, "that by 1856 Olive was pretty much acculturated to Mohave living."[16] The fact that she told the *Los Angeles Star* that she would have been permitted to visit whites in the region, had she wanted to, reinforces the likelihood that Olive, like Jemison, Parker, and Williams, stayed voluntarily. Because of the heavy traffic among Quechan runners between the Mohave Valley and Fort Yuma, she certainly knew an army post was not far, and she could have floated down the river to it or, says Tsosie, sent a message through a Quechan or even local Mexicans, many of whom, unlike the Mohaves, spoke English. Oatman's postransom interview with

Mowry proves she was well versed in local geography and the locations and populations of tribes along the river.

Though she was welcomed by yet another family on her return from the desert, Olive was clearly not at home in Oregon. Still, she and Lorenzo seemed to enjoy themselves with cousin Harry. A letter he wrote them in October of 1857, after they moved away the following year, offers a glimpse not only of the warmth that developed between them during their stay but also of Harry's flamboyant personality. Calling them "Len n Olive," he apologizes for a miscommunication that ruffled Olive's feathers, writing, "Let us not accuse each other. . . . But let us express the same feelings in our writing as was made in confidence while we were together." He describes the chaotic life he leads while his wife is away visiting a friend as he finishes building their house, where Olive and Lorenzo had spent time with him:

> If you were outside of the old Logg cabin peeking through the crake you would behold Harry in such a fix as he was never seen before. You would see him at the old pine table penning away to you with the dishes all piled up and on the table with a pot in one place and a frying pan in another and the beds turned topsey turvey and living a batchelors life all alone. . . . I like to forgot to tell you how I do the house worke. You know about the amount of crockery that we had in the House (or had) when you left. . . . Lucena had them all put away nicely and clean in the cupboard (as she always has) and I take one plate one cup and saucer and knife and fork and use it all day then I pile the dirty dishes upon the end of the table the next morning . . . and so on through the weeke and when Sunday comes I have a days work before me washing dishes and making Beds and Sweeping out the Batchelor's cabbin. I have no time through the week to do the house work.[17]

Harry closes on a more serious note, with an aside to Olive: "I'm afraid you will think I am sliting [*sic*] you because I don't write to you individually . . . But if you knew what my feelings were you would never entertain such a thought of one moment. I will not attempt to discribe [*sic*] my feelings for you with the pen any further than I love you as devotedly as ever a brother loved an only sister. Remember me as your friend and well wisher and be a good girl until I see you and ever afterwards, Coz Harrison."

The letter also runs through the town news, referring to "all . . . your friends," indicating the Oatmans had a solid social circle. There were dances at the two hot spots in town: the Oatman Hotel and the newly built Samuel Colver House, where lectures and traveling shows were also hosted on the open second floor. Colver had emigrated from Ohio with his wife, his brother Hiram and *his* wife in 1850, becoming the first permanent residents of Gassburg; their parents later followed. Nicknamed "Uncle Sam," Colver was an early abolitionist, a prohibitionist, an advocate for women's rights, and a fierce agnostic who loved a good debate. Sam Colver's aging father was a stubborn Universalist, and the Colver household attracted people with unorthodox views from all over. A minister named Moses Williams made repeated efforts to convert them, harrumphing in his diary, "They all seem to be totally ignorant of the nature of piety and of the Plan of Redemption."[18] Colver's wife, Huldah, was an exception. A religious woman, she welcomed preachers into her home, and her husband had no objection—they only made for stimulating conversation.

The 1850s was a tumultuous time in the development of Oregon's dawning statehood—something Oregonians voted against to avoid the heavy taxation. The territory, organized in 1848 and admitted to the Union in 1859, sought to ban blacks from the state. Many of its founders had come from the South and were weary of racial conflict. Though the majority were abolitionists, the early pioneer Jesse Applegate contended that "a much larger number of them hated free negroes worse than even the slaves."[19] Oregon was the only state admitted to the Union with a black exclusion clause; it went on to pass legislation against other minorities and to institute an anti-miscegenation statute in its effort to ensure the state would attract only "the best elements." With blacks outlawed, the harassment of Chinese and Hawaiians followed. Local Indians, of course, were considered homegrown undesirables.

It's hard to imagine what Olive made of the settlers' attitude toward Indians as she navigated a town newly built at the expense of local tribes. Emigrants had seized eight thousand square miles of land from the Rogue River Indians, who were either killed in attacks or sent to reservations, first in nearby Talent, then to the Grand Ronde Reservation on the northern Oregon coast. The Oatman massacre was well known in southern Oregon: legend had it that in 1853, Harrison was invited—as an act of revenge for the Oatman murders—to drive a wagon out from beneath an Indian being hanged for killing several white men. Harrison's near death in an Indian attack as he trundled flour across the Siskiyou Mountains for his store marked the beginnings of the Rogue River Indian Wars of 1855–56, which pitted miners and settlers against Indians who had long farmed and hunted in the region. And he became an Indian fighter. In 1866, as a lieutenant at Fort Klamath, he led an attack on a tribe near Lake Albert, Oregon, killing thirteen men and capturing thirty women and four children.[20] By contrast, Samuel Colver was sympathetic: he was an Indian agent for the government and had spent much of 1853–54 on the nearby Fort Lane Reservation, teaching Indians farming, advocating for them, and sometimes paying their expenses.

Though her cousins were not religious, Olive soon became a churchgoer. Either at the Colver house, a pit stop for traveling ministers, or through Taylor's Methodist ministry, she met a young reverend named Royal Byron Stratton who would change her life. Tall, fine-boned, and silver-tongued, Stratton was a New Yorker who went west and found gold not in the California mountains or the Rogue River Valley but in the Oatmans. He would publish their sensational story, both funding the siblings' aborted educations and enriching the coffers of the newly bicoastal Methodist Church.

Raised in Potsdam, New York, Stratton was ordained in the Black River Conference of the Methodist Episcopal Church in 1846, when he was just twenty. With his wife and four-year-old son, he arrived in California, fittingly, on the steamer *Oregon* (by way of Panama) in November of 1851—about the same time the Mohaves were visiting the Yavapais and proposing to take the Oatmans. Stationed first in Sacramento, then in San Francisco, he took the pulpit in 1854 at a three-year-old log cabin that would become the Benson Methodist Episcopal Church, in Yreka, California, a booming mining town just below the Oregon border. Both scholarly and evangelical, Stratton commanded "large and attentive" congregations. According to one church history, "Many traditions of his eloquence lingered long in the minds of the early settlers."[21]

Itinerancy was intrinsic to nineteenth-century Methodism, especially in the sprawling expanse of the Pacific Northwest, where a Bible was useless without a saddlebag. Stratton's preaching frequently took him to the Rogue River region, where he met the famous Oatmans. When Lorenzo asked him to write the Oatman story with an emphasis on his sisters' captivity, he agreed, and the two survivors began traveling back and forth between Gassburg and Yreka, about fifty miles, to deliver their testimony. Their book, called *Life Among the Indians: Being an Interesting Narrative of the Captivity of the Oatman Girls*, would consist of first-person narration by both Olive and Lorenzo, with an introduction and interstitial commentary by Stratton. Though Olive starred, it was Stratton's production: even a brief look at Olive's and Lorenzo's letters confirms that the book's passages attributed to the Oatmans, neither of whom had the literary skills to write their own stories, are heavily ventriloquized.

More important though, Stratton omitted, exaggerated, and fabricated information in order to deliver a title that was at once pious and titillating for his publisher, Whitton, Towne and Company, an

FIG. 16. The Reverend Royal Byron Stratton. Courtesy of First Congregational Church in Worcester, Massachusetts.

arm of the Methodist Book Concern, which was trying to boost book sales in order to fund less lucrative church projects. His selective storytelling created a collage effect: there was what he knew and told, what he knew and did not tell, and what, perhaps, Olive never revealed, which cannot be reclaimed or reconstructed. Stratton even acknowledged the omissions in his conclusion: "Much of that dreadful period is unwritten, and will remain forever unwritten." But what *was* written sounded a clear refrain of white supremacy: "We have confidence that every reader will share with us the feelings of gratitude to Almighty God for the blessings of civilization, and a superior social life, with which we cease to pen this record of degradation, the barbarity, the superstition, the squalidness, that curse the uncounted thousands who people the caverns and wilds that divide the Eastern from the Western inheritance of our mother republic."[22]

His account differed significantly from what Olive said in her first interviews (both at Fort Yuma and in early newspaper articles), from what the *Olive Branch* revealed about Royce and the journey west, and from what Musk Melon later recalled about Olive's life and status as a Mohave. First, Stratton removed all references to Mormons from the story, possibly in light of American antipathy to Mormonism in the wake of Joseph Smith's lynching, and in keeping with his own Methodist agenda. There was no question that the Oatmans' trip was, at least initially, a religious quest, but as Stratton had it, cold Illinois winters aggravated the pain of Royce's injured back and drove him west: "He became convinced that if he would live to bless and educate his family, or would enjoy even tolerable health, he must immediately seek a climate free from the sudden extreme changes so common to the region in which he had spent the past few years." The pain, however, did not stop him from riding around Iowa and Illinois in the winter of 1850, drumming up converts for the Bashan journey. Stratton said the Oatmans joined a party of people heading for the northern Gulf of California, "to form there a colony of the Anglo-Saxon people," without saying they were Brewsterites or even Latter-Day Saints. He even listed the six families who were "most active in projecting the movement," vaporizing the Brewsters from history.[23]

Though purged of its Mormon particulars, the book is shot through with religious sentiment intended to remind readers that faith carried the girls through their ordeal and elevated them above "an untutored and demoralized tribe of savages." In one heartless evangelical aside, Olive writes off Aespaneo's intervention during the drought as evidence of divine—not human—beneficence. "It was the hand of God," she wrote, "and I would do violence . . . to the strong determination I then made to acknowledge all His benefits—if I should neglect this opportunity to give a public, grateful record of my sense of His goodness." As for the Mohaves, she concluded that the incident proved that "kindness is not always a stranger to the untutored and untamed bosom. I saw in this, that their savageness is as much a fruit of their ignorance as for any want of susceptibility to feel the throbbings of true humanity."[24] In other words, the book assured readers, even "subhumans" can be kind. The repetition of key words like "untutored" and "throbbing," in passages by both Stratton and Olive, reveal his unmistakable hand in her prose. One of the reverend's pet verbs, "kindle," appears throughout the book and in one of his later sermons.[25]

Stratton also filled the Oatman story with racist slurs in language Olive never used (at least in describing the Mohaves) in early accounts of her experience. While it's understandable that Olive might call the Yavapais who killed her family "lumps of a degraded humanity," her descriptions of the Mohaves clash not only with her initial statements that they treated her well but also with others' historical impressions of them. The same tribe that struck early Anglo visitors as stunning and dynamic, who bathed daily, some of whom were said to routinely run a hundred miles at a stretch, she called "filthy looking" and "lazy."[26] The psychoanalyst George Devereux observed that among the Mohaves, "unemotional people are believed to be insensitive and lacking in human feelings," and reported that they valued sharing and expressing emotions.[27] But in the book, they are "unfeeling idlers." And while other white visitors to the Mohave Valley characterized the tribe as good-natured and generous, Olive accused them of "stupid, barbarous inhumanity."[28]

Stratton's meddling caused Olive to contradict herself within the text, on one hand disparaging the Mohaves as a tribe, on the other, calling Topeka "mild" and "sympathizing," depicting Espaniole as gentle and accommodating, especially when it came to Mary Ann's burial, and declaring that Aespaneo saved her life.[29] The three Mohaves she knew best apparently counted for nothing against the generalizations the book made about them in print. Furthermore, Stratton was an abolitionist who saw no conflict between moralizing about the emancipation of blacks in his sermons and championing the suppression of Indians in his book.

Stratton's most dramatic modifications seem designed to sink any suggestion that the Oatmans stayed with the Mohaves by choice. His conspicuous tinkering, however, only enhances the possibility. He began by shuffling the chronology, placing Mary Ann's death in 1853 instead of 1855, the year Olive had assigned it in her interview with Commander Burke at Fort Yuma. She had told a friend the same thing when she arrived in Oregon.[30] Mary Ann supposedly starved during a famine, but the Mohaves experienced anything *but* famine that year: the tribe could not have traded so much produce to the Whipple surveyors the following February if their yield had been poor. In June of 1853 Lieutenant Sweeny even remarked in his journal at Fort Yuma, "The Colorado is very high and the Indians are all planting."[31]

Stratton may have rolled back Mary Ann's death for dramatic pacing—to spotlight Olive, the surviving heroine, early on and heighten the tragedy of her plight by isolating her. But more likely, he did it to fill the gap left by the omission of a major event in her life as a Mohave: the arrival of the Whipple party in early 1854. "I managed to drag myself along to March of 1854," Olive writes of the period following Mary Ann's alleged 1853 death, eliding Whipple's arrival in February.[32] Better for Olive to be seen tending to her dying sister that year than spending weeks in the vicinity of hundreds of white men who could have saved her.

Having concealed Olive's one opportunity for escape, Stratton segues into a passage illustrating the futility—and folly—of fleeing. Olive's account of the Mohave war expedition against the Cocopas in 1854 — which did happen — includes a subplot involving a captive crucified for attempting to flee the Mohaves — which almost certainly did not take place. A Mohave who later described the Cocopa battle reported the fate of the two captives taken in it, both of whom were living around the turn of the century when he reprised it, making the Cocopa killing implausible. There are no other accounts of Mohave crucifixions and, according to at least one anthropologist, Mohave captives were typically treated well enough (since their very purpose was to increase the fold) that they did not try to escape. When she was interviewed by the *Los Angeles Star*, Olive did, however, recount the killing of two Cocopa war prisoners *after* the battle, which may have inspired the crucifixion story. Their dead bodies were hung on what the reporter called first a crucifix, then a pole, which the tribe danced around as they threw arrows at the bodies.

Stratton used the story to craft a parable about Olive's captivity, adding an extra dash of suspense by stating that before the Mohaves went to war, they agreed that if any Mohaves were killed, the same number of their captives, Olive included, would be slain "in the most torturing manner."[33] This was also not Mohave war protocol. As Kroeber rightly asked, "Why would a white girl be killed in 'revenge' for losses inflicted by the Cocopa?"[34]

The crucifixion scene unfurls one of the goriest and most emotionally wrenching episodes in the book. The captive, Nowereha, a young mother who has left a baby and husband behind, wanders around in despair, "insane" and insomniac, until she escapes and faces recapture four days later. Stratton devotes three pages to her getaway, in which she eludes the Mohaves despite a massive search, swims "several miles" in the river, and travels 130 miles on foot before a Quechan finds her. In exalting the superhuman Nowereha, whom Olive calls "resolved and of unconquerable determination," the passage unwittingly accentuates Olive's comparative paralysis as a captive.[35]

Once reclaimed, Nowereha is nailed to a wooden cross with wooden spikes driven through her palms and ankles, and crowned with thorns, in a jarringly New Testament martyrdom—especially for a tribe that didn't take to missionaries and would not likely have heard the biblical story. But it features a native flourish: Olive is forced to stand with other Cocopa captives and watch as the Mohaves circle around Nowereha, shooting poison arrows into her "quivering flesh": "She hung in this dreadful condition for over two hours ere I was certain she was dead, all the while bleeding and sighing, her body mangled in the most shocking manner. When she would cry aloud they would stuff rags in her mouth, and thus silence her. When they were quite sure she was dead . . . they took her body to a funeral pyre and burned it."[36]

The Mohaves used neither poison arrows nor wooden nails. ("I do not think it would have occurred to a people of Mohave technology," wrote Kroeber, "that anything could be 'driven' into a log.")[37] Furthermore, the episode paints a peculiar picture of Indian barbarity by casting the Mohaves as savages martyring a Cocopa Christ figure. Stratton's scrambled semiotics are further confused by his selective bigotry: even this wicked tale includes a compassionate gesture by Aespaneo, who gives Nowereha corn to make a cake she hides in her dress before running away. It is tempting to imagine Stratton and Olive arguing in Yreka throughout the winter of 1856 as they negotiated the book's opposing quotas of Indian slander and praise. Stratton, of course, had the advantage: Olive knew he controlled the book's production and understood that too much sympathy for the devil would reflect badly on her, reducing her chances of "resuming her position in society," as the *Daily Alta* had put it. Olive was again a captive—this time of her ghostwriter.

The crucifixion passage provided strategic value along with dramatic tension: it liberated Olive from the burden of planning her own exit, explaining why she remained for years with the Mohaves.

"I had before this thought since I had come to know of the vicinity of the whites," wrote Olive, "that I would get some knowledge of the way to their abodes by means of the occasional visits the Mohaves made to them, and make my escape. But this scene discouraged me, however, and each day I found myself, not without hope it is true, but settling down into such contentment as I could with my lot. . . . To escape seemed impossible, and to make an unsuccessful attempt would be worse than death."[38]

Stratton altered other details as well. In the travel pass Francisco carried to the Mohaves, Olive is identified as "Spantsa," which Stratton changed to "Olivia" in the book, presumably after learning the nickname's explicit meaning.[39] He removed the renowned but disreputable Great Western from the narrative and neglected to mention that army deserters protected Lorenzo and the Wilder-Kelly party on their way to Fort Yuma. He inflated the number of Indians who attacked LeConte, the Cocopas captured by the Mohaves, and the distances Olive traveled in her captivity. The pound of beef the Oatman girls were given for their journey to the Mohave Valley shrinks to "a small piece of meat." Protesting a bit too much, he writes, "If there is any one who shall be disposed to regard the reality as being overdrawn, we have only to say that every fact has been dictated by word of mouth from the surviving members of that once happy family."[40]

On February 1, 1857, Stratton signed the preface and finished the book. Lorenzo borrowed money to pay for a press run of five thousand copies, and the German-born artists Charles and Arthur Nahl were hired to illustrate it. Charles, an illustrator and genre painter who was one of California's best-known artists, had a taste for drama well suited to Stratton's. The Oatman girls appear bare-breasted, facing forward, in every depiction of their life with the Mohaves, including at the moment of Mary Ann's death. Their native attire was evidently a pleasant aesthetic shock. The tattoos, however, were not; the Nahls erased them from their visual narrative entirely.

Nonetheless, Olive's tattoo played an important role in the book: it appears on the face of the returned captive, where it registers as a mark of permanent violation, unlike her Mohave wardrobe, which signaled only temporary membership. Olive's portrait, with her tattoo drawn in finer, more delicate lines than those of the actual tattoo, served as the coda to *Life Among the Indians*. The blue tattoo was the flourish that would make it a stand-alone story, supplying visual evidence of Olive's ordeal and its irreversible impact.

FIG. 17. The Oatman girls appear bare breasted, facing forward, in every drawing of them as captives in *Captivity of the Oatman Girls*, including at the moment of Mary Ann's death. Illustration by Charles and Arthur Nahl.

FIG. 18. Returning to consciousness after the massacre, Lorenzo looks back at the looted wagon. Illustration by Charles and Arthur Nahl, from *Captivity of the Oatman Girls*.

FIG. 19. Olive's arrival at Fort Yuma. Her Mohave sister, Topeka, at left, carried the blankets the two women slept on during the ten-day journey from the Mohave villages. In the second edition, Olive appeared in her bark skirt in this illustration. Illustration by Charles and Arthur Nahl, from *Captivity of the Oatman Girls*.

12

Captive Audiences

> To the degree that the captive resists taking on the attributes of her captors, she represents the impermeable, defensible borders of the white, Anglo nation. | CHRISTOPHER CASTIGLIA, *Bound and Determined*

Life Among the Indians sold out within three weeks of its publication in April of 1857. A second printing of six thousand followed, with changes and additions: a new title, *Captivity of the Oatman Girls*, shifted the focus from culture-crossing to white victimization, dramatized most vividly by a new engraving of Olive arriving at Fort Yuma, this time in a dress instead of her bark skirt.[1] Olive's tattooed face became the frontispiece and a weepy poem in four stanzas served as an epilogue. Called "Stanzas to Olive Oatman" and written by a forgotten California scribe named Montbar, it cast Olive as a national symbol, conflating her personal trial with the nation's collective history:

> In captive chains whole races have been led,
> But never yet upon one heart did fall
> Misfortune's hand so heavy. Thy young head
> Has born a nation's griefs, its woes, and all
> The serried sorrows which earth's histories call
> The hand of God . . .[2]

Stratton added forty-eight pages to the second edition, expanding the preface with what he claimed was material about Indian customs and Southwest geography that had been cut from the first. Stung by early reviews in the *San Francisco Bulletin*, the *San Francisco Herald*, and the *Golden Era* that called his subject interesting but his writing poor, he mounted a three-pronged defense of the book in his new preface. Reviewers, he charged, tend to write based on a quick look at a book's preface; this title's brisk sales, however, were inspired by readers who had read thoroughly and responded flatteringly. Second, in his eleven years of public speaking, he had always worked from a carefully written manuscript, with no complaints. Finally, even if it was poorly written, he hedged, the book wasn't intended as a literary performance.

Stratton's fustian, which seeped into Olive and Lorenzo's narratives, was the book's weakness (apart from its factual errors and inconsistent spellings), and the new preface highlighted it hilariously. In a paragraph larded with meandering dependent clauses, the author argues that he has used nothing but "the plainest matter-of-fact style." The book, he writes, "is not dependent on an exorbitant fictitiousness of expression for enlisting the attention or interest of the sober reader."[3] Yet he editorializes freely, edging Olive and Lorenzo aside to rail against the Indians.

Though he claimed to have no literary ambition, Stratton was working a well-established literary genre as old as the nation itself—one with which he, like most readers of his era, was familiar. Captivity literature sprang from the culture clash between colonists and Indians in the New World and the eastern wars and westward migration that followed. Ministers quickly became mediators for returned captives who wanted to tell their stories, presented as parables of moral, religious, and, for women, feminine correctness as early as the seventeenth century. The narratives—nearly two thousand were published by 1880—loosely followed a standard formula: the captive begins life in a happy family setting, often on a farm, is attacked, abducted, and taken into an alien culture and suffers nobly until escape or rescue. The texts are peppered with religious asides and spiritual meditations, if not scripture itself, and culminate with the captive's redemption. They were endlessly entertaining, both for the cultural exotica they described and for the tremendous sense of schadenfreude they imparted. "Our American ancestors," wrote historian R. W. G. Vail, "did not believe in play-acting or the corrupting influence of the novel, so they limited themselves to true tales of horror in the form of deathbed confessions, stories of shipwreck, piracy, plague, and disaster, and of Indian captivity and torture."[4]

By the time Stratton met Olive, women's captivity literature had snowballed into what captivity scholar Kathryn Zabelle Derounian-Stodola calls "the first American literary form dominated by women's experiences as captives, storytellers, writers, and readers."[5] During the westward migration, it was one of the only vehicles of expression for middle-class women in particular. Its beauty, whether it took the form of memoir or fiction (to which it was first adapted in the early eighteenth century), lay in its passive aggression: it featured female protagonists pushed out of their proper sphere and propelled into lives of independence and self-assertion. "Because the heroine is a captive, taken against her will," writes Christopher Castiglia, "she can enter the wilderness without blame. The captivity romances thereby both express and veil the daring of women authors."[6]

Indeed, the first full-length, stand-alone captivity tale published, *A True History of the Captivity and Restoration of Mrs. Mary Rowlandson* (1682), was also the first American best seller. By the time Stratton was writing Olive's story, Rowlandson's narrative was considered a classic; it had also served as a model for many other captivity stories. Stratton appears not only to have read it, but also to have cribbed from it. In describing her eleven-week captivity among Narragansett Indians in 1675, Rowlandson, a preacher's wife, defended her honor by saying that "not one of them ever offered the least abuse of unchastity to me, in word or action."[7] Stratton quotes Olive as saying that the Indians "never offered the least unchaste abuse to me."[8] In each book, the line was pivotal: the captive's chastity hinged on it, and the acknowledgement of a survivor's unspoiled virtue was essential to many women's captivity tales. Stratton, like most of the minister editors who preceded him, worked from a well-thumbed cultural script.

As Lorrayne Carroll explains in *Rhetorical Drag: Gender, Impersonation, Captivity, and the Writing of History*, a book about male editors who hijacked captivity narratives, men often appropriated women captives' voices in order to establish how their stories "should be understood within the historical vision of the impersonator."[9] Stratton's fantasy was a heady blend of racial superiority, religious authority, and territorial entitlement, which required tempering the powerful feelings Olive surely felt about the Mohaves after four formative years among them. In the captivity genre, ambivalence was not an option. Though early reviews of the book emphasized Oatman's personal misfortune, at least one reviewer had clearly registered Stratton's message: "The reader will rise from its perusal with a feeling prompting him to seize the musket and go at once and chastise those inhuman wretches among whom Olive has spent five years," he wrote in Sacramento's *Democratic State Journal*. "The American people ought to go and give them a whipping.[10]

The release of the second edition followed a frenzy of anticipation in the Northwest. One review stated that readers had been searching for it for weeks; another said it had been "anxiously" awaited for months.[11] It was heavily advertised in the *San Francisco Evening Bulletin* in the summer of 1857, where readers were told the new edition was already half-exhausted and were reminded that the first print run had sold out in three weeks.

Captivity of the Oatman Girls was published at a perfect moment for success—particularly for a female audience. It appeared at the height of the industrial revolution, when women were reading more because of increased education for girls, lower birthrates, and lighter domestic workloads, thanks to new technology. Middle-class women were becoming voracious readers not only because they were better schooled but also because they were trapped: their domestic responsibilities were reduced by manufacturing, yet they were confined to the home. The captivity story presented a tantalizing alternative to enforced domesticity. As Castiglia writes, "[It] offered American women a female picaresque, an adventure story set, unlike most early American women's literature, outside the home. In the American 'wilderness,' white women could demonstrate skills and attitudes of which their home cultures thought them incapable."[12]

This was also a period when women were finding their own voices in literature, another vehicle for escape and projection. (One of the first significant novels by an American woman, Catharine Maria Sedgwick's *Hope Leslie*, published in 1827, even featured a white captive who married an Indian.) But while women's experiences were increasingly valorized in new fiction by women, the sentimental novel had for over half a century emphasized earnestness, melodrama, and feminine duty, and Stratton tailored the Oatman saga to its specifications in order to downplay the transgressive nature of her story. His voice both penetrates Olive's (and to a lesser extent Lorenzo's) and interrupts it to tweak and fetishize tragic moments. The narrative rarely lingers on Olive's physical endurance or emotional forbearance, but rather frames and savors scenes of feminine helplessness. After Lorenzo's description of the massacre, for example, Stratton interjects a passage that begins and, never finding its verb, doesn't quite end, even three pages later: "The mind instinctively pauses, and, suspended between wonder and horror, dwells with most intense interest upon a scene like the one presented above. . . . Two timid girls . . . trembling with fear, swaying and reeling under a wild storm of a catastrophe bursting upon them when they had been lulled into the belief that their danger-thronged path had been well-nigh passed, and the fury of which exceeded all that the most excited imagination could have painted, these two girls, eye-witnesses to a brutal, bloody affray . . ."[13]

Stratton also bursts on the scene just after Mary Ann's death to milk more pathos from it: "Precious girl! sweet flower! nipped in the bud by untimely and rude blasts. Yet the fragrance of the ripe virtues that budded and blossomed upon so tender and frail a stalk shall not die."[14]

Historian June Namias identifies three archetypes for female protagonists of captivity stories, each reflecting dominant attitudes about women during particular periods: (1) the Survivor, of the colonial era, who adapts and endures; (2) the Amazon, of the mid-eighteenth to early nineteenth centuries, who fights back and escapes; and (3) the Frail Flower, spanning 1820–70, who doubts her own courage and fails to transcend the trauma of her captivity. Stratton casts Mary Ann as the latter, and attempts to do the same with Olive, but her sheer endurance and chronic ambivalence toward the Mohaves, gradually shading into acceptance, make her a survivor, seemingly against Stratton's will. He labors to cast her as a sentimental heroine, if not to satisfy his florid literary impulses then to cash in on a highly salable genre. But he can't completely mask Olive's genuine resourcefulness and adaptability.

Stratton's commercial sensibility, however, was dead-on. In July, with the second edition selling apace, he arranged for a simultaneous printing in Chicago by the publisher Charles Scott and Company, and the Oatman phenomenon began to flourish, spreading its literary tendrils east and sprouting up in other media in the west: a play dramatizing Olive's captivity opened in Sacramento that summer and played in San Francisco that fall. Written by C. E. Bingham and titled "The Captivity and Massacre of the Oatman Family by the Apache and Mohave Indians," it ran with the rumor that Olive had married a Mohave and starred Junius Brutus Booth Jr. (the older brother of John Wilkes Booth) as an Indian married to Olive, who was played by Booth's wife, Harriet Mace. The script did not survive, and if the general tenor of Booth's career is any indication, the play flopped. But it probably helped book sales, which accelerated around the time of the play's run.

After illustrating *Life Among the Indians*, Charles Nahl improvised his own version of the legendary incident in a small painting called *Massacre of the Oatman Family* (c. 1856) that was much more caricatured than his renderings for *Life Among the Indians*. In it the attackers have dark skin, bug-eyes, and European features and wear their hair either in high ponytails or cut to the shoulder—styles foreign to the "Apaches" Olive described, coiffed in the salon of Nahl's imagination.

The captivity genre never boomed in painting as it did in literature. Nahl's interpretation harkens back to the first painting of a captive drama, John Vanderlyn's famous 1804 *Murder of Jane McCrea*, which shows a pair of Indians poised, hatchets in hand, to kill a creamy white female, or John Mix Stanley's *Osage Scalp Dance* of 1845, in which Indians surround a young mother who begs her colossal captors for her life, her bare-bottomed baby at her side.[15] Like these artists, Nahl depicts the villains at the moment of the attack, but in a reversal emblematic of the changing status of Native Americans, he shows the Oatmans both dominating and outnumbering the natives eleven to six. This Oatman family features two anonymous bearded men (one wielding an ax, the other a rifle), an extra boy, and no hint of five-year-old Charity Ann. The action radiates out from one central figure, who appears to be Mary Ann (not the heroine, Olive) holding her felled younger brother in her arms in front of the wagon. Above her, Lucy teeters at the edge of the prairie schooner as a gleeful Indian tries to pull her down, and to her left, Olive appears to be scratching the face of an Indian who staggers backward before her.

Showing the Oatman attack as Nahl would have liked it, the painting was the first of many fictionalized adaptations that would appear over the next century. It also expressed a national sentiment that had

FIG. 20. The massacre scene from *Captivity of the Oatman Girls* as illustrated by Charles and Arthur Nahl.

FIG. 21. Charles Nahl's second depiction of the Oatman massacre. This small wash on paper work was much more caricatured than the drawing the Nahls made for Stratton. Here, the Oatman party outnumbers the Yavapais eleven to six.

come to ground three years earlier on the staircase of the U.S. Capitol: Horatio Greenough's sculpture *Rescue* (1836–53), a bookend to Luigi Persico's portrait of Columbus on the opposite side, showed an enormous, helmeted white settler overpowering a gangly Indian after rescuing his pioneer wife and children, who cowered nearby. The piece, Greenough explained, "endeavored to convey the idea of the triumph of the whites over the savage tribes, at the same time that it illustrates the dangers of peopling the country."[16] So while *Murder of Jane McCrea* had crystallized Americans' worst fears, *Rescue*—and Nahl's *Massacre of the Oatman Family* after it—inverted the power structure, and allayed them.[17]

In early 1857, Stratton and his family moved to Santa Clara, California, fifty miles south of San Francisco, where he joined the Visiting Committee of Methodist-affiliated University of the Pacific and fathered a second son, named Edward. Flush with the payout from book sales, Olive and Lorenzo followed him that summer to attend the three-year-old preparatory school at the university, along with Stratton's ten-year-old son, Albert. With forty-four other women in the Female Collegiate Institute, Olive studied painting, embroidery, music, history, poetry, and religion, as well as "hair work," including "weaving into intricate floral patterns locks of the hair of one's relatives and friends."[18] The university, which emphasized "self-reliance in intellect as well as in morals," was ahead of its time in admitting women at the college level, but male and female students were taught separately, and women were allowed visits from men only at the suggestion of a parent or guardian. They were also forbidden from going out alone without a relative or teacher. Less than two years earlier, Olive had been wandering around shirtless and barefoot in the Arizona desert, sleeping in the sand, and foraging for food; the supervised "freedom" of campus life must have chafed by comparison.[19]

She and Lorenzo finished one term and started another in Janu-

FIG. 22. Olive Oatman in San José, probably 1857.
Courtesy of History San José.

ary of 1858, but by then the ever-resourceful Stratton had hatched an idea that both curtailed their education and sealed Olive's celebrity: they would take the book to New York. Inspired, he said, by western readers who encouraged him to sell it in other parts of the country, Stratton arranged for a third edition to be published by Carlton and Porter, the Methodist Book Concern's New York publishing house. A friend of Olive's quipped, "The purpose was to improve the fortunes of the minister, if not of the Oatmans as well."[20] Thomas Carlton, who had recently turned the flagging publishing house around, was better known for boosting profits than spreading the gospel, and he saw the commercial potential of the Oatman story. He would publish twenty-six thousand copies of the third edition.

The Oatmans docked in late March then rode for the first time on a steam-powered train to stay with their great uncle, Moses Sperry, in Chili, a town near Rochester, where they stayed for two months. Both the *Rochester American* and the *New York Times* announced their arrival in Chili. Stratton took his family to settle in Albany and began an intense publicity campaign for the book, starting by arranging for a brief notice in the *Methodist Quarterly Review*.

In early April Lorenzo wrote to the Abbotts in Illinois, telling them about the move, the train ride ("we took the cars"), and the book (out in three weeks):

> Olive is here with me. . . . As soon as our book is out for sale we intend to travel out west. So you may look for us fore long without fail. . . . I should like very much to go out [to Illinois] imediatly but I think it is best to make a start with our book in this county first & it will require some time and as we intend to make a business of it we shall hav to attend to it an get it in sirculation here then go west. . . . It seems now there is a very good prospect of once more seeing the olde stomping ground and I believ that it will look to me like good olde home. I think that I shall enjoy

very well when we get there looking over the olde place where we have spent many happy hours yet there will be a gloomy shade hover[ing] over the thought for those that were there will not be with us now. A chang has taken place. Fate with is mighty hand has wealded its sway and its colde chilling blast has the vitles of happenings in my heart and happy hours of days gone by seems like sweet visions of a dream.[21]

Spurred, perhaps, by their recent classes, their publishing success, or Stratton's influence, each Oatman included a bit of poetry for their aunt and uncle. Lorenzo (borrowing Stratton's signature word, "throbbing") wrote:

Since early youth my wayward
Path has been ore shadowed
With chiling blasts
But hope still twines round
My throbing heart—that brighter
Sunclad hours may on my lot be cast.

Olive chimed in:

I cannot! How can I
express to you here;
of the sorrow and grief
That still linger near;
It seams to have molded
and fashioned my heart,
and casts a dark cloud
Ore my bright hopes of youth.

Sperry, a well-known farmer and probate judge in Monroe County, New York, introduced the Oatmans to his two brothers

FIG. 23. Promotional photo of Olive taken in Rochester, New York, ca. 1858. The hash marks in her dress mimic the tattoo pattern on her chin and hint at the traditional Mohave arm tattoos she also wore, but never showed in public. In other photos from this session, Olive's tattoos appear to be concealed by powder or makeup. Courtesy of the Arizona Historical Society, Tucson. AHS no. 1927.

and took Olive to see the Bloomfield Congregational Church, where her grandparents, Joy and Mary Ann Sperry, had been married, as well as to the site of her mother's birth. Afterward, the mention of Olive's visit to her mother's birthplace elicited "tears and *sobs*," Sperry wrote in a letter to Asa Abbott. "We all feel interested in the wellfare [*sic*] of Olive. She is an interesting girl and with proper education will make her way through the world with [a] mark."[22] A relative of Sperry's offered to take her in and pay for her schooling at an academy in East Bloomfield, an idea Sperry endorsed. In anticipation of the book's East Coast publication, Sperry took Olive to Rochester to have her photo taken professionally. The surviving photos from the session show Olive wearing a dress with hash marks on the hem and sleeve that mimic the tattoo marks on her chin, standing with her hand on an upholstered chair, in various poses, including some in which her tattoo appears to be concealed by makeup.

Olive and Lorenzo traveled back to Manhattan to promote the book, which went on sale in April for a dollar a copy. With fifty-nine added pages, the third edition was the slickest yet: it was printed on better paper; the engravings were recut; three new illustrations were added, including a portrait of Lorenzo; and the red cloth cover featured elegant gilt detail—a new indulgence for the Book Concern. Stratton's new preface announced that the added pages were "chiefly of the peculiar traditions and superstitions of the tribes," but they more accurately reflected the superstitions whirling around in his own mind.[23] The conclusion of the third edition crescendos in a tirade against Native Americans, including the delusional claims that the Indian system of government was one of "absolute monarchy," that Indian women regularly approached Olive to tell her they lived in "constant fear," and that Indian men sometimes threatened to go live with the whites. "They are human, but live like brutes," Stratton rants. "They seem totally destitute of all those noble and generous traits of life which distinguish and honor civilized people. In indolence and supineness they seem content to pass their days without ambition, save of war and conquest. . . . In their social state, the more they are studied the more do they become an object of disgust and loathing."[24]

The third edition, like the others, flew off the shelves. That week, the *New York Times* ran an article on the Oatmans, describing Olive as "a modest, intelligent young woman [who] has evidently suffered from the hardships she has been compelled to undergo. . . . Her chin bears the 'Chief's mark,' a species of tattooing, set in fine parallel lines, running downwards from the lower lip." The writer coyly observed, "This savage embellishment does not materially enhance the personal charms of the lady, but it is an indelible evidence of the scenes she has undergone." Lorenzo was deemed "a fair specimen of a Western man." With its emphasis on Olive's appearance and experiences, and the title "Six Years' Captivity Among the Indians—Narrative of Miss Olive Oatman," the article foretold the evolution of the Oatman story: it belonged to Olive.[25]

But Stratton still thought it was his. He booked himself a lecture at the Trinity Methodist Episcopal Church on Thirty-fourth Street on May 10 and placed an ad for it in the *New York Tribune* the day before. The presentation, titled "Lo! The Poor Captive!" promised "a new and thrilling work more startling than any romance, yet very true." Stratton would discuss "the Indians of California and the Southwest" and Olive and Lorenzo would be present to recite "some incidents of murder and starvation they witnessed."[26] At the lecture, Stratton claimed his information came from seven years of travel among tribes along the Pacific, something that may have come as a surprise to the Methodists, who had sent him west to harvest settlers' souls, not to carouse with savages.

Eager to see their mother's sister, Sarah Sperry Abbott, and visit their home town, Olive and Lorenzo combined a trip to Illinois with a promotional tour. They stopped in Cleveland to arrange for book sales then traveled to Chicago, Hemlo, and Morrison, Illinois, where they were reunited with the Abbotts and met their three young children, only two of whom were born before the Oatmans left for California almost a decade earlier. The Abbotts were well accustomed to houseguests of a different sort: their farm was a stop on the Underground Railroad, and they had fed and hidden many runaway slaves.

The Oatmans walked past the one-room schoolhouse where they'd studied before going west and spent time with old friends. After the visit, Sarah told her sister in Utah that Olive was "an intelligent girl for one that has not had better advantages," and noted that Lorenzo was a lot like his father in looks and manner. Probably as a result of the attack, he was also, she said, prone to spasms and cramps at night. Olive's reunion with Sarah was important: her thirty-six-year-old aunt would be her comfort, confidante, and surrogate mother in the coming decades. Olive later told Sarah's children, "She has always been kind and thoughtful towards me and she seems nearer to me than any of my kin-folks of the olde generation for she is next to my own dear mother."[27] Likewise Sarah, who mothered six boys and a girl, who died at three, bonded with her sister's only surviving daughter.

When Olive returned to the East Coast in January of 1859, Lorenzo stayed behind to sell the book locally, work on the farm, and court Edna Canfield, an eighteen-year-old servant working next door who had caught his fancy. She was the eldest of thirteen children and, like Lorenzo, an orphan. Lorenzo would visit Olive in New York the following year, but in the summer of 1860, finished with the business of selling the Oatman story, he married Edna and they moved to a farm in Minnesota. He skipped town without telling Stratton, who wrote an agitated letter to the Abbotts in 1861, asking: "1. Where is Lorenzo 2. When did he leave and where did he start for. 3. What did he do with all his books. I paid for getting out the books. He has had 1500 and not paid one cent. Did he leave any books in that region. Did he leave an agent and who. I do not like to trouble you but if you will write you will oblige me so much."[28]

Having borrowed $150 from Abbott during his stay in Illinois, Lorenzo repaid his uncle with a horse cart and two hundred copies of *The Captivity of the Oatman Girls*, and he did something he was by now well accustomed to: he started over.

In early 1859 Olive moved in with Stratton and his family in Albany, where the reverend was busy promoting the book, whose success had outpaced his expectations. When he left California, the Methodist ministry had assigned him a position (again, as an itinerant preacher) in Oroville for 1858, indicating he had planned to return that year. When he didn't, the church reported in its minutes, "By refusing to do work given him by the constituted authority of the church, [he] invaded the integrity of our itinerant system and furnished an example mischievous in its influence."[29] Though he was not formally dismissed from the California Conference, he was now considered a local elder, not an active preacher.

No matter—the reverend was on a winning streak. The book was selling steadily, with co-publishers in his hometown of Potsdam, New York, and in Cleveland, Ohio. Stratton was planning more lectures and using his church connections to do so, in one case landing a blurb for his lecture broadside from the famous—and later infamous—reverend Henry Ward Beecher, who called it "more exciting and entertaining than any romance of the land. May God Bless the brother and sister who survive, to give the public this book, and for their benefit may it have a wide sale."[30] Olive, too, was lecturing as early as February of 1859, when she and Stratton appeared in Rome, New York. He discussed the "Traits, Customs and Prospects" of the Indians, "and the True Position our People and Government should assume towards them"; she described her "horrid and merciless captivity."[31]

At some point, Stratton saw that audiences were more interested in hearing Olive than hearing her editor; the lecture broadside for their Rome appearance reversed the lineup Stratton had established in New York City: now she was the featured speaker, "accompanied

FIVE YEARS AMONG THE INDIANS!

Miss Olive A. Oatman,

Whose Portrait is here given, and who has spent nearly six years in a horrid and merciless captivity among the APACHEE and MOHAVE TRIBES, will give some Incidents of her Sufferings and adventures

At ....

On .... 1859.

Commencing at 8 o'clock P. M.

The Public were informed of the tragical fate of the OATMAN FAMILY in 1851.

Miss OATMAN will give a brief, simple statement of the whole affair; her own and her Sister's Captivity by the Apachees, their sale in 1852 to the Mohaves, the circumstances of her Sister's death, Brother's escape after being left for dead, &c., Also a brief statement of the

TRAITS OF THE INDIANS, COUNTRY, &C.,

in that far South West.

She has given the narration to large audiences in New York City, Rochester, and Herkimer and St. Lawrence Counties, and numerous notices might be given showing it has been received with great interest.

The N. Y. *Tribune* says—"Her story is one of facts, and is more replete with romance than any novel." The *Times* says—"Her preservation and escape is a miracle, the audience listened with breathless interest, and all were deeply affected."

☞ THEIR BOOK, narrating the entire of their perils and sufferings, will be for sale at the Lecture.

ADMISSION, CENTS.

Children under 12 years of age, cents.

Heath & Seaver—Palladium Power Press—Malone.

FIG. 24. Lecture handbill. The two surviving broadsides advertising Olive's lectures both presented her as an ethnographic authority and played up the sensationalism of her story. Reproduced by permission of the American Antiquarian Society.

by" Stratton, and the handbill specified she was lecturing to make money for her education. Olive soon became the public face of the book, not just because she was the captive, but also because she was tattooed. Nearly thirty years before tattooed circus women began appearing in dime museums and sideshows, Olive was presenting a kind of educational freak show in churches and schools in New York, Indiana, Ohio, Illinois, and Michigan.

Though she did have at least one relative offering to pay for her housing and education, Olive knew she couldn't rely on family charity forever, and with a tattooed chin and a questionable Indian history, her prospects in the marriage market were slim. The lecture circuit would support her. Emboldened by her initial joint appearances with Stratton, she took the podium to tell her story alone. No longer covering her tattoo in embarrassment as she had in Oregon, she now referenced it in her lectures, exploiting it as a commodity. "I have had pretty good success so far in the lecturing business since I came here," she wrote to Sarah Abbott. "And I expect to give several more." And she did, spending parts of the next six years on the road.

When she took the stage in the late 1850s, Olive became the first American woman to show her tattooed body publicly for profit.[32] At the time, tattoos were virtually unseen in the United States. In the 1840s and '50s, when the first tattooed man to exhibit himself in America, James F. O'Connell, appeared in public, children reportedly screamed in horror and ministers warned pregnant women not to look at him lest their babies turn out like him. Audiences and reviewers were more discreet about Olive's tattoos, but her lecture broadsides played up the drama of her story, promising a mouthful. One, titled "Five Years Among Wild Savages," read, "Miss Oatman will describe interesting incidents in the Journey Across the Plains, the Horrid and Brutal Murder of her Father and Family, and being compelled to witness the bloody deed with her own eyes, she will give a history of her Wonderful Adventures, Extreme Sufferings, and Hair-Breadth Escapes; also, will portray the Manners and Customs of the Savage Indians[,] Character and resources of the vast tract of country she has traversed, and describe her extraordinary and miraculous manner of escape."

O'Connell entertained in circuses and vaudeville shows through the 1850s, distributing a thirty-one-page booklet that claimed he had been shipwrecked in the Caroline Islands, tattooed by beautiful maidens, and forced to marry the last woman who marked him. Olive's story resonated with his: the tattooing, inflicted by "natives," was coerced, and the violation had sexual as well as cultural connotations. Like O'Connell (who probably had been tattooed in Micronesia, but not by force), Olive could have cashed in as a sideshow or at least a dime-store attraction, and she certainly fit one definition of a freak: "an ambiguous being . . . who is considered simultaneously and compulsively fascinating and repulsive, enticing and sickening."[33] But freaks did not typically tell their own stories—their autobiographical broadsides were usually fictionalized and scripted for them—nor did they invite legitimate, book-length biographies. Olive's story, no matter how contaminated by Stratton, was her own. While her lecture handbills amplified the sensationalism of her exceptional double life, they also insisted on her ethnographic authority. Two surviving templates for her appearances (each with a blank for dates and locations) feature her name and proclaim her five years among Indians; one promises information on "Manners and Customs of the Savage Indians"; another, "Traits of the Indians, Country & C."

The lectures themselves were shrewdly designed marketing tools in which Olive withheld key scenes, like the actual attack or her reunion with Lorenzo, and then directed listeners to her book for particulars. Considering the high number of Oatman photos still in circulation—one recently sold on eBay for over two thousand dollars—she almost certainly sold photos as well as books at these events. Because she was appearing at a time when "proper" women shrank from public view, Olive opened with a preamble of modesty, explaining that she was orating out of duty, not desire: "Ladies and Gentleman, I appear before you at this time, not as a public lecturer but as a Narrator of events. . . . Neither the position of public speaking nor the facts that I am about to relate are in harmony with my own feelings, for my nature intuitively shrinks from both. But I yeald to what I conceive to be the opening of providence & the sterne voice of duty."[34]

In her sole surviving written lecture, which may have been a template for all of them, she establishes the theme of white superiority straightaway by saying her story "leads the anxious enquirer through the wooliest and wildest reagions of the 'great west' and brings into view the rudest barbarism & the highest civilization." She recounts her ordeal much as the book does, sometimes lifting lines directly from it. But the lecture also shows evidence of tampering, probably by Stratton: in a passage describing the aftermath of the massacre, Olive says that she and Mary Ann stood "all night" as the Indians plundered the family's wagon, but the words "all night" are crossed out and replaced with "nearly one hour." The former probably seemed more dramatic initially, but conflicted with the Yavapais' frantic haste to get the girls back to their camp without being discovered. In the lecture, unlike the book, the Indians spit at the girls when they arrive in their camp, Nowereha becomes Nowercha, and grown men—white and red—cry when she and Lorenzo are reunited.[35]

A few of the changed lines contradict the book, notably where Olive says Mary Ann was ten when she died, which would locate her death in the fourth, not second, year of their captivity, confirming the historical evidence that Mary Ann died after the arrival of the Whipple party. But the main change is Olive's emphasis on having been a slave to the Mohaves, as well as to the Yavapais, and her claim that her tattoo was applied to all slaves, white or Indian, so

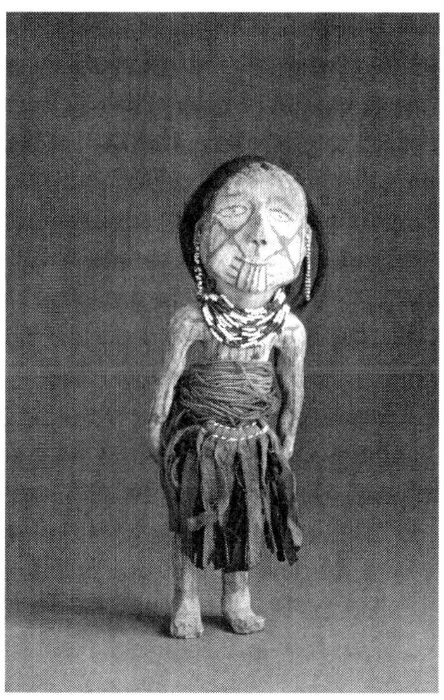

FIG. 25. Mohave female figure, 1880–1910. In *Captivity of the Oatman Girls*, Olive claimed she wore a slave tattoo that was different from other Mohave women's tattoos, but this ceramic figurine exhibiting traditional Mohave fashion, including a beaded necklace, simulated bark skirt, and body paint, features a tattoo identical to Olive's. School for Advanced Research, Catalog no. SAR.1994-4-5. Photograph by Jennifer Day.

they could be recognized if they escaped. "They give them the tribe's slave marks so that in case they desert to any other tribe they can be recognized at once. You perceive I have the mark indelibly placed upon my chin," she said, with no mention that *most* Mohave women wore chin tattoos.[36] The book, too, claimed that the girls received designs specific to "their own captives."[37] But the very pattern Olive wore appears on a ceramic figurine of the late nineteenth or early twentieth century that displays traditional Mohave face painting, tattoo, beads, and clothing.[38] The distortion, like Nahl's erasure of the tattoo in the book, removes from the story the possibility that the tattoo made her Mohave. And it neglects a larger truth: the Mohaves did not tattoo their captives; they tattooed their own.

By presenting her inscribed body as evidence of her captivity—literally making a spectacle of herself—Olive pushed the boundaries of feminine propriety in appearances that could only be validated by her victimhood. Still, Michael Tsosie notes, after years with the uninhibited Mohaves, her body image was probably very different from that of other white women, which may have been what enabled her to present herself publicly in the first place. Her carefully controlled exhibitionism offered a striking contrast to another famous captive body making its debut in New York around the same time. A marble sculpture called *The White Captive*, said to have been inspired by Oatman, was a sensation in the New York art world in the 1859–60 season.[39]

Albany artist Erastus Dow Palmer began work on the piece in 1857, soon after Stratton's arrival in Albany, and may have known Stratton and Olive personally. His sculpture, which shows a naked pubescent girl, referenced Hiram Powers's *The Greek Slave* of 1844 in its classical simplicity. "It represents the young daughter of the pioneer in Indian Bondage," wrote Palmer, "standing and bound with bark thongs at the wrist to a truncated tree . . . her only garment, the night-dress (as if she had been taken from her home during the previous night) is torn from her and lies upon the ground at her feet."[40] Palmer intended it to convey the effect—or lack thereof—of Indian savagery on a Christian girl. As a reviewer for the *New York Post* put it, "Virgin purity and Christian Faith assert themselves in her soul, and chasten the agony they cannot wholly subdue; accordingly, while keen distress marks her expression, an inward comfort, an elevated faith, combines with and sublimates the fear and pain."[41]

The pure form of *The White Captive*'s body reflected the unsullied condition of her Christian soul; she was, as one writer put it, "clad in purity" and stood for "all beauty, moral and ideal, in the divine perfections of the human form."[42] Not so for Oatman, whose body was scarred by her experience and whose story was the unthinkable next chapter to *The White Captive*'s. Though Olive hadn't willingly transgressed, her Christian faith had not prevented her from surrendering to savagery, and the tattoo—the indelible mark of the Indian—was every bit as damning, physically and culturally, as rape or miscegenation.

As Joy Kasson writes in *Marble Queens and Captives*, "The nudity of *The White Captive* did not pass unremarked, even though ten years had elapsed since the success of [Powers's] *The Greek Slave* made nude sculpture more widely accepted by American audiences."[43] But it was still a subject of discussion and, for some, debate. One reviewer's comparison between the voracious Indians who exploited innocents and the prurient audiences who leered at *The White Captive* could easily have been applied to Oatman at the podium, peddling a book in which she appears bare-breasted and addressing listeners who gaped at her marred face: "We feel we are almost as ruthless as her savage captors in continuing to look at her while she suffers so much."[44]

Visual spectacle, however, was not the only reason audiences lined up to hear Olive's lectures; she was a spellbinding speaker. The *New York Times* reported on an early appearance: "The audience listened with breathless interest, and all were deeply affected." By the end of 1859 alone, she had lectured in New York City and upstate, as well as in Toledo, Ohio, and Evansville, Illinois, to large audiences. A review in the *Terre Haute News* said, "The lecture was of a sad but deeply affecting and interesting nature. . . . Her whole discourse was stirring romance. She will have crowds to hear her wherever she goes."[45] Even when she returned to Rochester in 1865 at the close of her lecture career, she packed the house: "Her pathetic story, surpassing in interest the most thrilling romance, was told with an unaffected simplicity and grace and a touching pathos that went to every heart and drew tears from eyes unused to weep. Miss Oatman evinces much dramatic power in the grouping of incidents. . . . No one can listen to her without feeling the deepest sympathy for her misfortune, and the most profound respect for the depth of womanly tenderness and heroism, and the nobility of the soul, which could survive five long years of barbarous captivity and shine with so bright a lustre."[46]

The juxtaposition of "womanly tenderness" with "heroism" was significant at a time when feminine virtue was becoming the last bulwark against the advances of modern womanhood. Just a decade before Olive began lecturing, the first wave of feminism had hit the streets, propelled by the Seneca Falls Conference of 1848, and the very first women were becoming doctors and activists. The maverick journalist Margaret Fuller's influential *Woman in the Nineteenth Century* (1845) argued for legal, educational, and economic equality for women. The New York State Legislature ratified the cause when it passed the Married Women's Property Act of 1848, declaring that a husband could no longer claim ownership of whatever property his wife brought to a marriage. Women were breaking the confines of domestic life and inching toward public agency.

As if in response to these developments, Olive told audiences, "You have pleasant homes[,] kind parents & affectionate brothers & sisters . . . and perhaps the luxuries of Christian society. I once had all these; & having experienced in frightful contrast, the other extreme, I think I know now how to appreciate the word Home & had I one should know how to enjoy it."[47]

Public speaking itself was a freedom women had barely tested. The Seneca Falls Conference was chaired by a man, confirming women's—even feminists'—tentative feelings about it, and anticipating the larger culture's resistance to it. Elizabeth Cady Stanton prefaced her talk at the conference by saying, "I should feel exceedingly diffident to appear before you at this time, having never before spoken in public," and insisted, like Oatman after her, that "duty" had driven her to it.[48] Even Horace Mann, the education reformer who helped pave the way for women's entry into the professions, carped, "When a woman . . . appears on the forum and makes public speeches she unsexes herself."[49]

Like other early women speakers, Olive blunted the effect of this transgression by campaigning for women's domesticity while she lived the life of a professional, traveling alone, appearing publicly and getting paid to tell her story and show her body. Nonetheless, her enormous fortitude as a captive was an irrepressible element of her appeal; it demonstrated the innate potential of even the most humdrum pioneer girl, showing the kind of feminine capability feminists had begun to promote. As the *Evansville Enquirer* reported, "Her story . . . is instructive in showing what privations human nature can endure, and the energy and resources, trials and difficulties will develop even in delicate and sensitive girls."[50]

Olive never attended Bloomfield Academy as Moses Sperry had hoped she would, but rather stayed in Albany, where in 1861 she attended the Albany Normal School, a two-year teacher training college attended largely by men. She lived with the Stratton family in a newly built, brick row house, blocks from the Arbor Hill Methodist Church where Stratton had become pastor. The reverend was rebuilding his career: he was appointed chaplain in a New York regiment of volunteers at the start of the Civil War, and when he returned, he preached with passion. His 1862 sermon *Church Government, Its True Place and Use* was pointedly abolitionist, though his excoriation of bigotry did not apply to Indians. A year later, he preached the rightness of "rooting out" the red man and plowing over his land.[51] The Arbor Hill sermon also challenged the methods of the church government, generating a flurry of publicity that caused him to resign and take a new job: in 1864 he was hired at the Congregational Methodist Episcopal Church in Great Barrington, Massachusetts.

Around the time Stratton moved to Great Barrington, Olive moved back upstate to East Bloomfield. In the early years of the Civil War, she continued to lecture and make other celebrity appearances. She visited the Old Ladies Home in New York City, where she bought a needlepoint bookmark in the shape of a Latin cross. She shopped in Boston. She visited the Abbotts in 1863. And in 1864, she learned that the Mohave leader who had orchestrated her adoption into the tribe was coming east. After a chain of events on the Colorado that Olive could never have imagined during her life as a Mohave, Irataba, now a Mohave diplomat and leader revered by whites, was in the city after a visit with President Lincoln in Washington. She bought herself a ticket to see him.

13

"We Met as Friends, Giving the Left Hand in Friendship"

> In little more than a decade, from the middle of the 1840s to the middle of the 1850s, the United States burst through the bounds—both of territory and policy—that formerly limited its sway among the Indians west of the Mississippi. In the wake of a successful war with Mexico, the admission of Texas to the Union, and the movement of thousands of its citizens across the plains, mountains, and deserts to the Pacific Ocean, the concept of a permanent boundary separating whites and Indians was dissolved. . . . While not shorn by their conquerors of all their legal rights, the Indian nations were deprived in practice of many of these powers and rights. The greatest real estate transaction in history, effected through wars, treaties, and mass population movement, had been accomplished. | Wilcomb Washburn, *The Indian in America*

During the years Olive traveled the lecture circuit describing her life among the Mohave, the very foundations of the Mohave life she had known were crumbling. In 1857, just a year after she had left, the tribe had joined the Quechans in a disastrous attack on the Pimas and the Maricopas. In what has been called the last major Indian battle in North America, the Mohaves, who considered the death of ten men in battle to be high, lost sixty of about two hundred warriors. The Quechan warrior Francisco, who had finessed Olive's return to Fort Yuma, also died fighting.

Soon after, the diminished tribe also began seeing greater transnational traffic. Lt. Joseph C. Ives, a member of the Whipple expedition, returned to the Mohave Valley in 1858 to test the navigability of the Colorado on a steamboat called *Explorer*, built in Philadelphia and shipped west. Ives remembered Irataba fondly and sought him out as a guide, recalling how Irataba had led Whipple out of the valley in 1854. Ives had trouble finding him at first, probably because his conversation with the Mohaves required translation from English to Spanish to Quechan to Mohave. His comments were sometimes received by the Mohaves, Ives wrote, "with an astonishment and bewilderment that the original sense does not at all warrant." But one day, camped on a riverbank in the Mohave Valley, he noticed an Indian who had been sitting nearby for a long time. "At last I observed that he was constantly regarding me with a half-smiling, half embarrassed air, and, looking at him more intently, discovered that it was my old friend Irataba," wrote Ives. "He had been too modest to introduce himself. He was delighted at being recognized, and at the cordial greeting he received."[1]

Spotting him on the other side of the river, Ives summoned Cairook, the tribal leader who, with Irataba, had walked Whipple out of the valley in 1854. Cairook crossed over, standing regally atop a raft guided by four swimmers and trailed by Mohave sightseers. At six and a half feet tall, he was a man, noted Ives, "with a magnificent figure and a fine open face," who laughed uproariously in recounting his adventures with Whipple. Ives marveled at the isolation of the Mohaves, their scant exposure to whites, and their lack of interest in Euro-American inventions. "In most respects," he wrote, "they think us their inferiors." Only firearms and the steamboat's whistle impressed them. When he showed them a compass, they found it pitiable that the men needed a device for finding their way. Daguerreotypes unnerved them. ("Very bad," they muttered.) When some musicians in the party played them a few bars, they disapproved and showed Ives how to do it properly, chanting, he said, in a "discordant, monotonous tone, and after making some of the most unearthly noises that I ever listened to, regarded us with an air of satisfied triumph."

In soliciting the Mohaves' permission to navigate the river, Ives brought out a map and attempted to show them the extent of the United States and the number of people who lived there. "The statements," he reported, "were received simply as a piece of absurd gasconade, and had the same effect of the visits of some of the chiefs of the northwestern Indians to the Atlantic cities, which have resulted in destroying the influence of the unfortunate ambassadors, by stamping them forever, in the estimation of their own tribes, as egregious liars."[2] Ives had predicted, to some extent, what would soon happen to Irataba.

After securing approval for the river trip, Ives took Irataba and (for part of the way) Cairook on the steamboat with him. But the Mohaves' genial response to him was soon tempered with wariness. They were being invaded—geographically and psychologically—from two sides that year, making them uneasy about whites in their territory. The Mormons, who were in open conflict with the U.S. government under Brigham Young's leadership, had started a colony in San Bernardino, over two hundred miles west, and were busy scouting the region with an eye to planting a string of settlements between the new colony and Utah, to be supplied via the river. They entered the valley from the north during the Ives expedition and told the Mohaves that Ives was plotting against the Indians to get their land. (They also tried to baptize Cairook, who, said Ives, was "disgusted" when they attempted to dip his head in the water.[3]) Meanwhile, a captain at Fort Yuma who had gotten wind of Ives's plans was offended that he'd been passed over as the first navigator of the Colorado River and launched his own exploratory river journey a week before Ives could get started. When he met and befriended the Mohaves, he warned them that the Mormon-U.S. conflict could end in warfare, and they assured him that if it did, they would support the government.

Mindful, now, that the river that had defined and united them now opened them to attack, the Mohaves saw their allegiances and hospitality tested. And then a new threat materialized: in August of 1858, three months after Ives left, the first California-bound pioneers to enter the valley emerged on a newly opened emigrant route called Beale's Wagon Road. They camped on the east bank of the river, cut down cottonwood trees to make a raft, and sent their animals ranging over Mohave croplands. After Sitgreaves and Whipple, Edward Beale had been the third modern explorer the Mohaves received in their valley when he had come to clear a route to California a year earlier.[4] Because of his presumptuousness, he had met a decidedly cool welcome on his arrival. As one Mohave put it, he "came right in and looked like he owned the place, and didn't bother to talk to anybody, or ask if he might cross [the river] or anything. . . . He acted as though he owned the whole world."[5] Now the pioneers following his route seemed to do the same. Though the Mohaves had given the emigrants permission to cross the river to get to California, they secretly believed the party intended to settle on their land. The angered tribe joined the Hualapais in an attack, killing eight emigrants, prompting the U.S. Army to crack down on the Indians.

In December, when fifty soldiers arrived to build a fort at the site of the attack, hundreds of Mohaves promptly assaulted them. The cavalry fired on them, killing about a dozen Mohaves. In February, five hundred more men appeared. The Mohaves, who had never harbored any substantial fear of whites, partly because they'd never seen them in any great numbers before, were sobered by the sheer volume of soldiers, and deferred to them. Col. William Hoffman called a meeting with six Mohave leaders, including Cairook (who had led the attack) and Irataba (who condemned it and had been at Fort Yuma when it happened). Using the Quechan leader and Mohave ally Pascual as a translator, Hoffman insisted that the tribe allow white men into the valley and permit the construction of the fort on the river. He also demanded ten hostages as insurance against subsequent violence, and Cairook volunteered. A Mohave who later described the incident recalled, "Our people loved their head man and said, 'I'm a nephew. Take me instead. Don't take him.' Another nephew said, 'I'm another nephew, take me.' . . . The others said 'take me. Take me.' And he had nine volunteers and he said, 'That's enough.'"[6]

The prisoners, Cairook and Musk Melon among them, were locked up—something unprecedented for them—from early May until late June, when temperatures ranged from 100 to 118 degrees. Irataba visited several times, on one occasion trying to free the men by making a galvanic speech to a lieutenant powerless to release them, recalling how well Cairook had served both Whipple and Ives—each envoys of the federal government—during their travels through the valley. He returned home, disconsolate over his failure. The inmates suffered, shut in, with the Colorado River roaring within view of the prison door. A *Daily Alta* correspondent at Fort Yuma reported, "A soldier told me that, one day while he was on guard, one of the hostages asked him to cut his throat. . . . The general feeling here is that the Indians never did comprehend that they were to be kept incarcerated to insure the good behavior of the rest of the nation."[7]

On June 21 they snapped. Cairook told the other men, "You're all young. I'm years ahead of you . . . when it's lunch time, all the guards go to their lunch except for that one up there. I'll go up and hold him while you men dive into the water."[8] When they were let outside for air, Cairook pinioned the guard while the others ran for the river. He was bayoneted through the abdomen and shot in the head. Two others were shot and killed; the six survivors floated down the river to safety.

In the coming years, Irataba emerged—from the perspective of the federal government—as the leader and spokesperson not only of the Mohaves, but of all the Colorado River tribes. He was inclined to peace as a means of survival, even if it meant making concessions to

Americans — and opposing other *kwanamis* who advocated militant resistance to government activity in their region. He made multiple trips to Los Angeles and, unlike his brethren, had first-hand knowledge of the pervasive white presence beyond the Mohave Valley. "Irataba was a man six feet four inches tall, of very powerful frame, but very gentle and kind in demeanor, and a staunch friend of the whites," wrote Edward Carlson, a soldier at Fort Mohave, who knew him in the 1860s. "He seemed to have great influence over neighboring tribes, and acted in disputed questions as a kind of supreme judge."[9]

In 1864 Irataba was invited to Washington to meet President Lincoln, mainly so that Lincoln could convey to the influential Mohave leader the formidable power and vast reach of the federal government and to drive home the folly of opposing it. Escorted by a prospector and scout named John Moss, who both initiated and secured approval for the visit, he made the most of his adventure, sailing first to San Francisco, staying at the Occidental Hotel, and creating a sensation as he paraded down Jackson Street in Anglo garb. The press tracked his movements, describing his massive build, strong jaw, black suit, and felt sombrero, noting that "in all his interviews he maintained the stoical and impassable bearing so peculiar to the red man of the forest."[10] The duo sailed to Panama then New York, where Irataba's reputation preceded him.

Little was written about Irataba's meeting with "Abee," as Irataba called Lincoln (except that the president gave him a silver-headed cane), but the press spilled plenty of ink on his public movements and physical appearance, with an awe comparable to that of the slack-jawed explorers catching their first glimpses of the Mohaves in their homeland a decade or more earlier. The *New York Times* called him "a splendid specimen of physical development. He is about fifty years of age, six feet two in height, and very muscular." *Harper's Weekly* declared him "the finest specimen of the unadulterated aboriginal on this continent," remarking on his "magnificent bodily presence"

FIG. 26. Irataba, "Chief of the Mohaves," in New York, 1864. The engraving accompanied a *Harper's Weekly* article that read, "He is the chief of the Mohaves—the great tribe of the Colorado Valley—and is the finest specimen of the unadulterated aboriginal on this continent."

and reporting, "The only thing that has yet excited an expression of wonder in his travels was the sight of a school of whales on his way to San Francisco." Even back in Los Angeles, the *Tri Weekly News* announced, "The 'big injun' has arrived in New York and is being lionized."[11]

And so, when the leader of the same tribe that Olive publicly accused of enslaving her arrived in New York that February, she went to shake his hand and speak his language. She took the train to meet him at the palatial Metropolitan Hotel on Broadway and Prince streets, which employed freed slaves and offered modern luxuries like steam heat, speaking tubes, spring mattresses, and bathrooms on every floor. Mrs. Lincoln herself had stayed there two years earlier and the P. T. Barnum midgets Tom Thumb and Lavinia Warren, his tiny wife, had thrown their wedding reception in the hotel's elegant parlor the previous year, standing on a grand piano to receive two thousand guests, Barnum himself among them.

For her own survival, Olive had publicly chosen between binaries.

She was an Indian hater happy to be back in the bosom of Anglo culture, not an Indian lover yearning for her lost tribe. But her meeting with Irataba, and her account if it, crystallized her warring impulses. She described it in her subsequent lectures with a confounding mix of affection and condescension: "It was a singular coincidence, that after the laps of 8 years the wild savage & the released captive should again *meet*; not among the mountain solitudes of the Paciffic slope; amid the filth & degradation of an unmitigated barbarism; but in the metropolis of the highest civilization; not in the wigwam; but in the beautiful adorned reception room at the Matrepolitan. We met as friends giving the left hand in friendship, which is held as a sacred pledge, among some tribes."

She spoke with him in Mohave, asking lots of questions about the tribe, and learned, she said, of the Mohaves' desire to become "sivalized." Irataba told her that Topeka still hoped she would return. "The picture of sadness is upon her countinance," she wrote, "& she goes too & from her daily labors, *alone and lonely*. May *God bless* the poor forest *Girl*."[12] Just as she marginalized Aespaneo, whose life-saving was reduced to an act of God in her book, she diminished Topeka, her guardian and soul sister, in her lectures, characterizing her as a wounded creature pining for the returned white girl (Topeka did, after all, have her siblings and a whole tribe of peers to keep her company), without revealing her own feelings of loss. But perhaps now that Irataba was being touted as a peacemaker and even a celebrity, her public expression of interest in his tribe was safer than it had been in the early years of her repatriation.

Irataba returned to San Francisco overland, in a blaze of glory, bearing medals, gifts, and photos signed by congressmen and their wives. He reached Arizona a month after he had predicted, leaving the tribe—and his family—convinced he had been murdered by whites. They had no vocabulary for the sort of epic journey he had made—one Mohave called it "going over the ferry" for lack of a phrase to describe a marathon voyage involving steamers, stagecoaches, and railroads. The whole tribe appeared at the ferry terminal to meet him, where he emerged wearing a major general's uniform, a hat with an ostrich plume that touched his shoulder, a Japanese sword swinging from his belt, and his shoes—which hurt his feet—strung around his neck. That night he made a speech, describing the wonders he had witnessed and telling the Mohaves, as one spectator recorded it, "that the Mohave must never go to war with the whites, as they were too numerous and had too many guns."[13] Irataba had seen too much.

But his account backfired. As Ives had anticipated, some of his people simply did not believe what he described. More important, others, led by the chieftain Homoseh Quahote, disagreed that peace was the key to surviving white encroachment in their land. In 1865, half the tribe, including the Oach clan into which Olive had been adopted, followed Irataba to a reservation near Parker, Arizona. The others stayed with Homoseh Quahote near Needles, California, at the newly established Colorado River Indian Reservation. The Mohaves and other newly disrupted tribes clashed over how to handle white incursions into the area. To this day, the tribe is divided not just geographically but also politically.

The Mohave homeland was literally wiped off the grid. Area maps printed after 1859 no longer identified the site of the Mohave villages; instead, the region, dubbed Fort Mohave, was distinguished by a military post, erected, on Beale's recommendation and under Hoffman's command, to protect westward-bound emigrants from the Mohave Indians. Mollhausen's words had come true: "The native, who seeing himself trampled upon, revolts against the domination of the white race, is then at once treated like a noxious animal, and the bloody strife never ends till the last free inhabitant of the wilderness has fallen."[14]

14

Olive Fairchild, Texan

> The handsome woman always wore a dark veil around Sherman to hide her secret. But the secret she hid made her a legend in Arizona, not Texas. | *SHERMAN DEMOCRAT*, July 4, 1976

Like most nineteenth-century women, Olive's movements were determined by the men in her life, and the women she befriended tended to fall away from her with each relocation. Her father took her west, Stratton took her east, and when she married John Brant Fairchild, a farmer and rancher from Michigan, she made her home in Texas.

She met Fairchild in late 1864 after lecturing in a church in Farmington, Michigan, just outside of Detroit. His mother and sisters had taken him to see her presentation then invited Olive home to visit. Born in New York to Canadian parents, Fairchild had lost a brother in an Indian battle in Sonora, Mexico, while driving cattle from Missouri to Arizona in 1854. The attack, not far from the site of the Oatman massacre, occurred while Olive was with the Mohaves, and may have played into his attraction to and sympathy for her. Having driven cattle from Los Angeles to northern California during the 1850s, Fairchild had surely heard about Olive's captivity long before he met her. When he invited her back to Michigan in July of 1865, he proposed. They were married in Rochester in November and returned to live on his farm in Michigan. Olive later called this the happiest period of her life.

If Stratton had controlled the telling of Olive's Indian history, Fairchild appointed himself its censor. Before the wedding, he bought and burned every copy of the Oatman book he could find, possibly out of shame about his wife's dark past and her public life. He may simply have wanted to protect her; it probably didn't take long for him to learn that the wounds of her traumatic past were still tender. The Oatman story had served its purpose—notably bringing Fairchild and Oatman together; but it did not reflect well on the society wife Fairchild envisioned for himself as a wealthy businessman. By then, rumors had begun circulating that Olive had left Mohave children behind. In 1863 a Nevada man claimed that he had adopted five Indian orphans in 1858 when he was an agent for the Butterfield Stage Company at Oatman Flat, the newly named site of the Oatman massacre. "One," he said, "was a beautiful, light-haired, blue-eyed girl, supposed to have been a child of the unfortunate Olive Oatman." Four of the five children, including the girl, allegedly died from severe diarrhea after being fed only meat.[1]

Olive's closest relative, Sarah Abbott, was happy with the marriage, and told her sister in Utah that Olive had "done well in getting a husband."[2] Indeed, Fairchild came from a large and impressive family. His father was a civil engineer and he had three sisters and two brothers, a lawyer and a doctor. Having made money herding and selling cattle, Fairchild had also learned how to invest it. On his return to Michigan from the West, he had become a successful money broker.

Now financially secure, with her book behind her, Olive severed her relationship with Stratton without bothering to tell him about her new husband, much less invite him to the wedding. Her break from Stratton may have resulted from Fairchild's attempt to suppress her past, but it could have been provoked by Stratton himself, who was spiraling into madness. After his 1864 appointment to the First Congregational Church in Great Barrington, he was recognized as one of the best preachers the church had ever had. When he preached the Sunday after Lincoln's 1865 assassination, there was reportedly not a dry eye in the pulpit. But his reputation suffered when a female parishioner charged that during his year as an army chaplain he had gambled, bribed an official, and committed adultery. The allegation divided the church, and when Stratton's accuser refused to testify publicly against him, charges were brought against her. The case, though never resolved, stirred enough controversy that a petition demanding Stratton's resignation began circulating around the town. He resigned in 1866.

High profile and protracted as it was, the Great Barrington scandal did not destroy Stratton's career; in early 1867 he was hired at Old South Church in Worcester, Massachusetts. Now nearing forty, he and Lucia had a third son, Samuel. The timing was poignant: the following year the couple learned that their elder son, Albert, who had returned to California to become a schoolteacher, had committed suicide at twenty. From there, Stratton's life began to unravel. As the church later reported, "serious disability, more or less impairing his usefulness, led to his dismissal" in 1872.[3] A family vacation in Germany didn't help. Soon after their return, a guardian was appointed to Stratton, who was designated "insane" and "incapable of taking care of himself," then committed to a mental institution.[4]

Olive was seemingly oblivious to the reverend's decline. In 1872 the Fairchilds moved to Sherman, Texas, where they settled permanently. A boom town at the junction of several stagecoach lines, Sherman was on a growth spurt in the 1870s, sprouting five flour mills, a huge grain elevator, a steam-powered cracker factory, two secondary schools, and a college. With two other men, Fairchild's contribution was the City Bank of Sherman, which made him rich. A friend later remembered the Fairchilds as a "romantic" couple—who didn't socialize. John was handsome, distinguished, and phlegmatic. People called him "Major Fairchild" for no apparent reason. Olive was shy and reclusive. She wore a dark veil when she went into town and walked, said a friend, "with great dignity." Everyone knew she had

FIG. 27. The Fairchild home in Sherman, Texas. Olive threw "lawn parties" here for her daughter, Mamie, every summer. Special Collections, University of Arizona Library, Papers of Edward J. Pettid.

been an Indian captive. She was considered warm to those who knew her, but one friend observed that the "sadness of her early experiences never quite lifted." Another said that "the great suffering of her early life set her apart from the world."[5] She did charity work, taking in and caring for children from the local orphanage, and in 1873 the couple adopted a three-week-old baby girl, Mary Elizabeth (the combined names of the Fairchilds' respective mothers), whom they called Mamie. Once a Mormon child then a Methodist mouthpiece for Stratton, Olive, like her husband, was now a practicing Episcopalian and had her daughter confirmed in the Episcopal Church. The family lived in an impressive two-story Victorian home, with a well-manicured lawn, flower gardens, and a servant.

Lorenzo hadn't done as well. Farming in Minnesota had been hardscrabble and, worse, Edna and Lorenzo's two young sons had died of scarlet fever. "You cannot imagine how lonely we are here this winter with no little darling boy to cheer us in our lonely hours," Edna wrote in a heart-breaking letter to Sarah Abbott, pleading for a visit. "Here I must sit alone & think if you or some of my sisters were near they would see me quite often."[6]

Olive and Lorenzo corresponded sporadically, each claiming the other didn't keep in touch. A letter to Sarah Abbott from Harrison's wife, Lucena, confirmed that both were to blame: "I think [Lorenzo] is some[thing] like Olive: rather neglectful about writing to friends."[7]

While Lorenzo was struggling to make a living, Olive was battling debilitating eye trouble, headaches, and welling depression. When Mamie was just six, Olive had spent a month in bed because of eye pain and could only see out of one eye for short periods. In 1881, she spent nearly three months, most of them in bed, at a state-of-the-art medical spa in St. Catharines, a resort area known as the Saratoga of Canada, twelve miles from Niagara Falls. Founded by Theophilus Mack, a renowned surgeon and physician who specialized in "women's diseases," the Springbank Hotel and Bathing Establishment was as much a sanatorium as a hotel, featuring mineral cures and Turkish baths. Drawing special waters from artesian wells, Mack used water, steam, and electricity to cure rheumatism and "other obstinate diseases."[8]

During Olive's stay at the Springbank, Fairchild wrote to Asa Abbott to tell him she was at a "medical institution," encouraging him to write her there.[9] He was open about Olive's condition without naming it. But did it have a name? Her treatment suggested she had been diagnosed with what the nineteenth-century neurologist Weir Mitchell called "neurasthenia," caused by a depletion of the central nervous system's energy reserves, brought on by the stresses of modern life, with symptoms ranging from weakness and fatigue to headaches and depression. During the last two decades of the century, Mitchell became famous for his rest cure, a medical antidote for cultural and psychological conditions that spanned "hysteria," postpartum depression, and anxiety. The treatment drew patients, mostly upper-class women ground down by domestic responsibilities, out of their homes and into a regimen of mental and physical inactivity and seclusion, sometimes for months at a time.[10]

But some men, too, suffered from neurasthenia. Mitchell's prescription for them was exactly the opposite of the rest cure: they warranted a break from routine—and a trip west. The doctor recommended sleeping beneath the stars, getting food from "the earth," and pursuing "some form of return to barbarism."[11] It sounded a lot like the life of a Mohave. Paradoxically, the "cure" for men's neurasthenia may well have been the root cause of Olive's. Unlike the typical female neurasthenic, who was deemed overwhelmed by the pace of modern living, Olive may simply have been unable to adjust to a life of leisure after growing up among the unconstrained Mohaves and spending her early adulthood as a traveling celebrity. In Texas she personified Thorstein Veblen's ornamental woman, moneyed and idle, volunteering and running a household. If the effect of this unvaried existence drove many average women to despair, Olive's history would only have heightened her vulnerability to it, and any number of factors could have exacerbated it: menopause, biochemical depression, or the ripple effects of post-traumatic stress.

Olive's troubles would ultimately become chronic and multivalent. In 1882, at forty-five, she was agonizing over her mother's death and yearning for female companionship. As an afterthought to a letter to Sarah Abbott, she scrawled on the envelope, "I long to have my dear mother back. Her memory is so dear to me—all gentleness + goodness. I never felt the kneed [*sic*] of a mother. I do . . . so long for a long confidential talk with you." Her confession that she had never, until then, needed a mother indicated that something in her had slipped. Now nine, Mamie was exactly the age Mary Ann had been when her family was massacred and Olive became her only guardian. When Mamie cried, did Olive hear Mary Ann's voice as the Yavapais marched her barefoot through the desert?

Then again, Olive's condition may not have been unique; her loneliness was echoed by other women in her family who had been scattered wide by westward migration. In the 1860s Harrison's wife, Lucena, had written Sarah Abbott from Oregon, pining for Harvey's wife, Lucia, who had died in childbirth. After her death, Harvey had disappeared into the mountains, leaving his five children to be fostered out to another family. One of Sarah Abbott's sisters was off in Utah; the other, Olive's mother, was long dead. Edna Oatman suffered the loss of her and Lorenzo's sons with no one to comfort her. As for Olive, her birth sisters were dead and Topeka was locked away in the past. She had lost touch with her close friend from Phoenix, Abi Colver, whom she addressed as "my friend and sister" when she sent her a promotional photo before leaving Rochester, asking her to write.[12] Olive's melancholy may in part have been the burden of the far-flung pioneer woman who had finally arrived—alone.

In the 1880s Olive's Indian past was publicly revived, retrofitted, and trivialized in what must have been a troubling turn of events. Nora Hildebrandt, the first female tattooed attraction in America, debuted at a dime museum in New York in 1882, wearing 365 tattoos and brandishing a backstory seemingly inspired by Oatman: Hildebrandt claimed to have been captured, with her tattooist father, by Indians, and forcibly tattooed by him at their insistence.[13] Unlike Oatman, who had abstract tribal tattoos, Hildebrandt wore decorative popular imagery—birds, scrolls, and flowers indeed rendered by her father, Martin Hildebrandt, a pioneering shop tattooist in New York. Beyond the wild Indians and the compulsory tattoos, her story posed a prickly parallel to Oatman's; Olive's father *had* ultimately caused her to be tattooed—by recklessly marching her into the desert without protection.

The most famous of the early tattooed circus women, Irene Woodward, who followed on Hildebrandt's heels, also implicated her pioneer father, somewhat incestuously, in her marking. He had suppos-

FIG. 28. Olive Fairchild at forty-two, with her tattoos concealed. Courtesy of Dorothy Abbott Fields.

edly tattooed her as a child to keep track of her in the wilds of Texas, and (unlike most early tattooed ladies) she claimed to have liked it: "At first the father implanted a few stars in the child's fair skin. Then a picture was indelibly portrayed by the father's hand," her broadside read. Delighted, Woodward urged him to continue. "It was an occupation that filled many idle hours, and work continued until the skin was lost in a mass of tattooing that covered the girl's entire body."[14] Both Hildebrandt and Woodward depicted themselves as motherless children; their tattoos represented just one of the primitive things that could happen to a girl in the Wild West without the civilizing influence of a mother — things that *had* happened to Oatman.

The tattooed captive became a common circus theme throughout the 1880s and '90s. Other attractions used similar fictions to cast themselves as victims of "redskins," rather than self-made freaks who, after the invention of the tattoo machine in 1891, could get a full body suit in a matter of weeks. Their stories turned, provocatively, on the notion that people of color could transform whites into people of color—ethnically and decoratively, as a means of exploitation and degradation. The opening of the transcontinental railroad in 1869 allowed circuses to crisscross the country, and many now did so with tattooed ladies who appeared with or without broadsides trumpeting their sensational histories, whose skin shows were titillating for more than just the artworks their skimpy outfits exposed. Olive's fading tattoo had now been overlaid with associations no lady hoped to abide.

Perhaps the only thing worse than becoming an unwilling member of a subculture of circus freaks was being reported to have died in an insane asylum—a rumor (planted by the writer E. J. Conklin in his 1878 Arizona travelogue *Picturesque Arizona*) that trailed Olive for a lifetime—and beyond. The prominent historian Hubert Howe Bancroft perpetuated it in books published in 1882 and 1889 and it was even revived in the preface to a 1935 edition of *The Captivity of the Oatman Girls*, decades after Oatman's death.[15] Friends of the Fairchilds in Sherman were aghast at first hearing it and Fairchild tried his best to correct it. Olive's reaction to it was never recorded. The rumor carried a morbid irony: in 1875, forty-eight-year-old Stratton had indeed died in an asylum, having been institutionalized for two years, during which time, said his obituary, "he gradually sank away, his death being attributed to a paralysis of the brain."[16] Try as she had, Olive had not completely broken her ties with her ghostwriter; Stratton had appropriated her tragedy in life then imparted his own to her in death.

Unlike Olive, Lorenzo had maintained his affection for Stratton through the years and named his son, Royal Fairchild Oatman, after him in 1883, eight years after Stratton's death. "Roy" was the couple's only surviving child of four; their third boy had been thrown from a wagon and killed over a decade earlier. From their childhoods as orphans to their adulthoods as mourning parents, the two seemed doomed to a life of serial tragedy, but around this time they found their financial and geographical footing. Having abandoned farming, Lorenzo and Edna moved to Montana, where they ran a boarding house, then moved to Red Cloud, Nebraska, to buy and run a series of hotels, including the Royal Hotel, whose restaurant was a favorite haunt of Willa Cather. Lorenzo's correspondence with Olive was still spotty. In 1889 she said she hadn't heard from him in over two years, and tisked, "I don't know why he does so, unless he thinks it's cute to be odd. He used to want to be like old Lorenzo Dow [an eccentric minister for whom he was named]. But I think for such oddities, the day is past. Edna writes when she can, poor woman. She has always worked too hard. Mamie and I both write to her occasionally."

In the fall of 1888, Harrison Oatman and his seventeen-year-old daughter, Lucina, came visiting. Now a successful and well-known real-estate broker, Harry and his family had moved to Portland. His trip east, which started at Coney Island and ended in Texas, was written up in the *Morning Oregonian*. He told the paper he approved of Texas's strong democratic tendencies, but concluded there was no place like Oregon. Harvey had resurfaced in Arizona during the 1860s, threatening to rebury the Oatmans and provide a new marker for the graves, but soon disappeared; he never stayed in one place—or one marriage—for long, and the family ultimately lost track of him.

Though Olive's health troubles persisted throughout the 1880s, she managed to function not only as a wife and mother but also doing what she called "my work" in charity. Mamie attended the newly founded St. Joseph's Academy, and Olive threw a lawn party for her every summer. When her daughter turned sixteen, Olive wrote with pride to Sarah Abbott, "Mamie is doing nicely in school and is doing good work in her music. I think, looking with a mamma's eye, she plays beautifully. We gave her a birthday last Friday. Just to think she is 16 years old and will soon think she is grown, I presume."[17] Olive sounded busy—often her letter-writing was interrupted by visitors. But soon after, in a letter to Sarah, written in perfect penmanship, Mamie wrote that she and her mother had hoped to go to Detroit that summer after six years without a visit, noting, "Mama has not been feeling very well but I think she has been too busy visiting."

They made the trip after all, spending months with the Fairchild family in Detroit instead of returning to Illinois, where Asa Abbott had died that spring. When Mamie finished school in the early '90s, she continued to live at home, assisting her mother, who was now having heart trouble.

Though the book was long out of print, the Oatman story was still making the rounds. In 1893, the *Arizona Republican* reprised it, this time assigning Lorenzo as well as Olive tattoos and claiming that a "half-breed" working at a meat market in Phoenix was rumored to be one of Olive's three lost sons.[18] Five years later the same paper ran another mangled version of the story, in which Olive and Lorenzo were the captives, and Lorenzo was said to have become a Methodist minister who had lectured on the topic over the past ten years. The source of the account was a man who claimed to have been the first to discover the Oatman bodies after the massacre. In the 1890s, Lorenzo was asked to recount the details of the drama and wrote it

FIG. 29. Sarah and Asa Abbott, Olive's maternal aunt and uncle. Courtesy of Edward Abbott.

out on hotel stationery for posterity, himself botching or forgetting some of the facts, which had grown hazy with age.

The Oatman story wasn't the last of the women's captivity narratives. Sarah Wakefield's 1864 *Six Weeks in the Sioux Teepees: A Narrative of Indian Captivity*, was an interesting follow-up to *The Captivity of the Oatman Girls* because Wakefield said about the Sioux—forcefully, unapologetically, and without the interference of a male editor—what Oatman only implied about the Mohaves: that they treated her well, that Chaska, her Sioux protector during the six-week Dakota War of 1862, should be rewarded "in heaven" and that she had no regret for defending him afterward, even though she was derided for it. "I should have done the same," she wrote, "for the blackest negro that Africa ever produced; I loved not the man, but his kindly acts."[19]

Wakefield's story also confirms the social attitudes that likely prevented Oatman from expressing her powerful feelings for the Mohaves after four formative years among them: having claimed that she came to "love and respect" the Indians "as if they were whites," and after defending Chaska, who had protected her and her children during her captivity, Wakefield was vilified as an "Indian lover," and Chaska, who had surrendered, was hanged.[20]

In 1866 Cynthia Parker's eponymous story of her Comanche "captivity" was written by James T. DeShields. The book was published a few years before Parker starved herself to death, having failed to reassimilate after her forced return to white culture after twenty-four years; the book barely tapped the depths of Parker's sadness. But where the text failed, the frontispiece succeeded: a photo of Parker shows a bronzed, careworn woman nursing a baby, her hair cropped short as a Comanche expression of mourning.

One of the most sensational captivity stories was published a little more than three hundred years after Mary Rowlandson's pioneering colonial classic. The plotline of Emeline Fuller's 1892 *Left by the Indians* was not unlike Oatman's, though Fuller was held captive to wild nature, not savage Indians. After a string of Indian raids on the Oregon Trail in 1860, Fuller was orphaned at thirteen and led a baby and four children into the wilderness with scattered members of other families. Like Oatman's, her narrative was written—and probably embellished—by a minister. But for sheer horror, Fuller's ordeal outstripped every woman's Indian massacre tale before it: she had eaten the flesh of her own siblings to survive.

Oatman was neither as heroic as Mary Jemison, the most famous acculturated captive, during her captivity, nor as devastated as Parker on her repatriation. She was not a vindicator like Hannah Dustan, who escaped her captivity by axing—and *scalping*—ten Abenaki Indians before stealing away into the cool Canadian night in 1697. The triumph of Oatman's story was in what she achieved both as a captive and on her return. She assimilated twice: first, as a Mohave, where the evidence is overwhelming that she was fully adopted into the tribe and that she ultimately considered herself a member. She was taken at a vulnerable age, had no known family to return to, and bonded with the family that both rescued her from the Yavapais and gave her their clan name. She submitted to a ritual tattoo, bore a nickname that confirmed her insider status, and declined to escape when the Whipple party appeared in the valley or through the many Quechan runners or local Mexicans who could have carried a message to Fort Yuma for her. By the time Francisco came looking for her, Olive had become a Mohave, and almost certainly didn't want to go "home."

Her second, perhaps more difficult, assimilation occurred after her ransom, when she was plucked from her tribe against her will. Willing ransomees did not cry on their return, pace the floor in tears at night afterward, or rush to shake the hands of their former oppressors years later. But there was simply no running back to the Mohaves from Los Angeles, or from Oregon, and the social and financial rewards Oatman reaped for turning her back on the Mohaves were tangible and immediate, while the risks of declaring herself an Indian lover were tremendous. In an act of self-preservation, she was able to cross back over and make herself a life first as a public figure, then as a working woman helping orphans, and finally as a mother, giving her own orphan child the unconditional love her mother, and Aespaneo, and Sarah Abbott, in turn, had given her.

In her later years, Olive's failing health was evident in her spidery handwriting and her frequent references to punishing headaches. "I have been so very nervous and my general health has been poor," she wrote to the elderly Sarah Abbott in 1898, the year Olive turned sixty. Two years later, her confidante and surrogate mother died. The following year, sixty-five-year-old Lorenzo, who was busy building a ten-thousand-dollar brick luxury hotel in Red Cloud, fell ill and also died. A front-page, two-column obituary in the *Red Cloud Chief* called him "one of the best known hotel men in the val-

FIG. 30. Lorenzo Oatman in Nebraska. Courtesy of Dorothy Abbott Fields.

FIG. 31. John Fairchild. Sharlot Hall Museum photo, Prescott, Arizona.

ley," and quickly segued into a partial retelling of the Oatman saga, promising the full story later. The next day, the paper ran a six-column "sketch" of Oatman, predicting that his "name will go down in history as one of a very few," and offering an account of the Oatman massacre largely in his own words, adapted from *The Captivity of the Oatman Girls*."[21] The town of Red Cloud shut its doors on the day of his funeral.

Olive became increasingly reclusive in her later years and, unlike Lorenzo, never discussed her family's past. "I used to sit by the fire, when a child, watching Mrs. Fairchild and admiring her kind and gentle ways," wrote a Fairchild family friend. "Her sweet face was surrounded by beautiful white hair like a halo. The tattoo had faded to a pale blue, and of course I was so used to seeing it I didn't even notice it anymore."[22] In 1903, she died of a heart attack. Her obituaries—one in the *Sherman Daily Register* the day after her death, another in the *Sherman Weekly Democrat* five days later—suggested that her husband was still censoring her story: they made no mention of the Oatman massacre.[23]

Ever Olive's protector, Fairchild, who feared the Mohaves would come to reclaim their lost daughter after her death, had her coffin sealed in iron and marked her grave at Sherman's West Hill Cemetery with a thick granite tombstone. But in a touching concession to her true identity, he inscribed it with her birth name—and claimed her as his own:

Olive A. Oatman
Wife of J. B. Fairchild
1837–1903

Five years later, after a day at the office, Fairchild died in bed at seventy-seven. Mamie moved to Detroit, married in 1908, and later that year gave birth to a daughter—her only child—who lived for just a few days. Her name was Olive.

EPILOGUE

Oatman's Literary Half-Life

> To be American is to be unfinished. And although that state is powerful and creative, it carries with it nightmares all its own. | PHILIP J. DELORIA, *Playing Indian*

Olive's legacy, like her Mohave ethnicity, would be more notional than genealogical. She had slipped into another skin and passed as a Mohave, then she peeled away her Indian self and resumed her whiteness, leaving no genetic trace in either realm.[1] Still, a fertile afterlife awaited her: she would be reborn, again and again—in newspaper articles, short stories, and novels—well into the twenty-first century.

In the decades after Oatman's death, a series of yarn-spinners worked themselves into her legend, claiming to have saved her, or at least to have known her. The most bizarre example involved a wealthy Mohave in Arizona named John Oatman, who said he was Olive's grandson. His story hit the papers when his wife sued him for divorce in 1922, alleging that he ate "dog dinners," frightened her by painting himself with phosphorous and doing ghost dances, and carried on with an albino Yavapai. He had reportedly lost an eye in an explosion in a gold mine, along with part of his scalp and lower jaw. He thus wore a wig and dentures, and he had taken to removing his glass eye and "scalping" himself to scare the children of the tribe. By comparison, his countercharges were hopelessly bland: he said his wife wore mud in her hair and cooked boring meals.[2]

On slow news days, newspaper editors pulled the Oatman drama out of storage and ran it as a novelty item, often in the Southwest, sometimes in multiple parts. The first such story appeared in the *Syracuse Herald* in 1913 with a tenuous tie-in to the Oatmans' relatives in the area; as recently as 2007 an Oatman article ran in the *San Pedro Valley News Sun*—for no reason at all. By 1909 the Stratton book was back in print and has been published continually ever since, targeting popular audiences and, in recent decades, scholarly, romance, and young readers.[3] Since the 1970s, feminist academics have revisited the story in their explorations of women-in-captivity literature and examinations of the female body in nineteenth-century writing.

But when it was fictionalized, as it was within fifteen years after the Stratton book was published, the Oatman experience acquired rich new subtexts, revealing as much about the historical mindset of its appropriators as the dramatic plight of the captive. In 1872 the Baja California native Maria Amparo Ruiz de Burton used Oatman as the basis for Lola Medina, the heroine of her satirical novel, *Who Would Have Thought It?*[4] Ruiz de Burton, a Mexican of European descent, was a newspaper correspondent living in San Francisco when the Oatman ransom story broke in 1856. Like Olive, Lola is a white Indian captive traded from the Apaches to the Mohaves and recovered near the Gila and the Colorado rivers by a man who takes her—and the riches her mother left her before she died—to live in New England with his family.

Lola, too, carries the physical imprint of her tribe back to "civilization." Because the Mohaves have dyed her skin to make her blend in, her foster mother, Jemima Norval, assumes the girl is black and tells her to sleep with the servants. "Drop her hand Mattie!" Jemima exclaims when she sees her daughter examining the girl's white palm. "You don't know what disease she might have!" Referencing a spate of sex scandals involving ministers in the 1860s and 1870s and culminating in the indictment of Henry Ward Beecher, the novel even features a smooth-talking, Strattonesque clergyman who has an eye on Lola's inheritance—and her virginity.[5] The novel ingeniously knits together themes of class, race, religion, and gender, with a final flourish: written during feminism's first wave (and published the year the first woman, Victoria Woodhull, ran for president), it satirizes the sentimental novel. Dr. Norval, Lola's rescuer, tells his wife that Lola "is only ten years old, but her history is already more romantic than that of half of the heroines of your trashy novels."[6]

Set during the Civil War, *Who Would Have Thought It?* ridicules the racist double standard of abolitionist Northerners, exposes the gold rush venality that made a mockery of Puritan values (Lola's new family happily accepts her fortune but not her ethnicity), and dramatizes the racial dualism—white against not—that flourished after the Mexican-American War. When one abolitionist character is told that California "natives" are of Spanish descent, and should not be confused with "wild" Indians, she responds, "To me they are all alike—Indians, Mexicans, or Californians—they are all horrid. But . . . as soon as we take their lands from them they will never be heard of anymore, and then the Americans, with God's help, will have all the land that was righteously acquired through a just war."[7] Like Royal Stratton, she sees no disconnect between her abolitionist views and her intolerance of Southwesterners.

Lola's captivity and blurred ethnicity, like Oatman's, is the result of American expansionism, specifically in Mexico, where each was captured. And for each girl, whiteness is its own reward: only after Lola's European ancestry is revealed can she reclaim her Anglo status and, by book's end, marry her foster brother, a colonel in the Union army. But unlike Oatman's ethnicity, permanently tainted because of both her tattoo and her veiled sexual history, Lola's is merely indeterminate, mirroring the muddled status of Southwestern Mexicans who became U.S. citizens after the war.

When the Oatman story was adapted for the popular Western television series *Death Valley Days* during the cold war–civil rights era of the mid-1960s, it was no longer a parable of shifting borders and confused identity, but rather one of segregation, aired the year after the 1964 Civil Rights Act was passed. With the frontier tamed, whatever threat Western "natives" may have posed to whites had expired, and the broader perils of race mixing had replaced it. Spooning a hefty dollop of geopolitical self-satisfaction onto a thin slice of Western lore, the 1965 script oozes machismo and white superiority. The plot is a prefeminist exercise in family values, where the social order hinges on racial separatism, which the Mohaves threaten to disturb. Since this Oatman encore features a sexually pristine and culturally redeemable heroine (here, Olive's only meaningful relationship is with her Mohave father), her tattoo—the central symbol of her cultural violation—disappears from the narrative.

Titled "The Lawless Have Laws," the adaptation was part of the *Death Valley Days* series hosted, appropriately enough, by Ronald Reagan, who also played Martin Burke, the colonel who first received Olive at Fort Yuma, reimagined here as her rescuer. In the introduction, Reagan selects and leafs through a book (the script specifies that it is Stratton's), and addresses the viewer: "There's a town on the Arizona side of the Colorado River, near Lake Mead, called Oatman. Quite possibly you never heard of it. But back in the 1850s, Oatman was a name that sent a chill of horror across the still-wild West." Calling it "one of the strangest dramas in western history," Reagan summarizes the massacre with general accuracy, but the show itself culminates in a purely fictional rescue operation.[8] And though the white characters go by their real names (Lorenzo's is inexplicably spelled "Loranzo"), the Mohave characters are fabricated.

The episode opens with Burke and Loranzo riding into Death Valley to save Olive, played by Shary Marshall, a TV actress who had appeared on *Gunsmoke*, *The Fugitive*, and *The Untouchables*. Loranzo plays an angry and buffoonish sissy to Burke's "desert toughened" commander, who diminishes him at every turn. ("I find it real hard to shed tears for you, son, considering what your sister's put up with," Burke scoffs when Loranzo complains about the desert heat.[9]) When the two men meet an elder named Nakoda in Mohave country, Burke tries to negotiate for the blue-eyed captive, but the old man refuses to acknowledge her existence. "What's the problem, Chief?" Burke taunts him. "If you're telling the truth, and she's not here, you've got nothing to lose. . . . If she is, [then] it's a choice between letting her go, and having your people hunted and killed like the Apaches."[10]

In an ensuing scuffle, the Mohaves take the upper hand, tying the two white men to posts while Olive and Nakoda tenderly confirm their bond: having no wife or child, Nakoda had bought Olive as a slave five years earlier and raised her as his daughter, but since he isn't her biological father, he wants to let her go. "You've given me a father's love," she says. "Until I knew you, I thought all Indians were lawless savages. . . . You've taught me that isn't true. You live by a law you'd break, for me."[11]

The exchange offers the show's only real moment of cultural slippage: in playing her love for the Mohave father she knows against her loyalty to the white brother she doesn't, Olive acknowledges that tribal kinship could trump blood ties. But the prospect vanishes when a rogue warrior named Chibichah vows to kill the captive men, buy Olive, and take her away. She agrees to marry him in order to spare Loranzo and Burke, in short, opting to become an *involuntary* Mohave (who *will* be violated) to save her blood brother. As the "sadistic" Chibichah swings her up onto his horse, Nakoda trains a gun on him, exposes Olive's ploy, then frees her. "Tell your people," he tells Burke, "there is law for the Indians, too. . . . Give love. . . . Love is given."[12] In an Irataba-like flourish, he also instructs his own people not to fight the whites before Burke and Loranzo walk the freed captive "home."

Though "The Lawless Have Laws" grants the Mohaves a modicum of integrity through Nakoda, its segregationist subtext undermines its surface tolerance. Unlike Ruiz de Burton's Indians and Mexicans of the nineteenth century, the racial Others in this context are permitted their difference and even their dignity by whites—as long as they keep to themselves. The episode touches on and dispenses with the postsegregationist anxiety that was mined with more nuance and ambivalence in John Ford's film *The Searchers*, released in 1956 and set in the Southwest in roughly the same period. *The Searchers* also follows a captive-rescue plotline, but admits the inevitability of race mixing, two years after the 1954 *Brown v. Board of Education* decision, as Barbara Mortimer explains in *Hollywood's Frontier Captives*. In Ford's hands, the white captive (played by Natalie Wood) resists return. An assortment of adoptive relationships are characterized as more enduring than blood ties, and the male lead (John Wayne) is portrayed as a relic of a bygone era who vacillates between a desire to retrieve his white Comanche niece and his impulse to kill her for having crossed over.[13] Where *The Searchers* probes the tensions of evolving race relations, "The Lawless Have Laws" stubbornly denies them.

When Oatman was reborn in the postfeminist 1980s, Elmore Leonard seized on the one glaring but perpetually sublimated theme of her ordeal—her sexuality, and for the first time, she was unabashedly eroticized. In his 1982 short story, "The Tonto Woman," Leonard pulls her out of the background, where she had hovered in previous adaptations, gives her a strong—sometimes angry—voice, and makes her desirable *because* of her tattoo. (Olive's tattooed face even appears on the cover of his 1998 collection, *The Tonto Woman and Other Western Stories*.) Leonard modified the details of her history by marrying her off before her abduction, giving her twelve (not five) years with the Indians (first with the Mohaves, then the Apaches) and making her husband a cold, rich rancher who forces her, on her return, to live alone in the desert instead of on his ranch with him. ("Unclean from living among the red niggers," explains a local cattleman.) Held captive by a white man who won't discuss her, much less touch her, Sarah Isham's story begins here, when a Mexican horse thief named Ruben Vega watches her bathe, "bare to her gray skirt, her upper body pale white, glistening wet in the afternoon sunlight."[14]

In this Oatman iteration, Sarah's tattoo is a sexual magnet as well as a cultural touchstone whose meaning she subverts in the interest of her own self-definition: she asks the Mohaves to tattoo not just her chin, but also her cheeks. "I told them if you're going to do it, do it all the way. Not like a blue dribble," she tells Vega, who immediately falls under her spell. A fellow outsider, he affirms her sexual power and individuality by touching the tattoos, and says, "You're in there, aren't you? Behind these little bars. They don't seem like much. Not enough to hold you."

Vega takes her into town and holds her hand in a restaurant, telling her he could look at her and touch her and love her for the rest of his life. "You're the loveliest woman I ever met. And the strongest." But his goal is to free her, not to take her. "Are you ready?" he asks. "I think the man coming is your husband."

When Sarah's husband approaches, itching for a fight, Vega invites him to sit down, adding wryly, "I'll introduce you to your wife." The couple wrangles over their stunted marriage, which Sarah threatens to abandon when he offers to move her into the house. Vega excuses himself to prepare for a trip south, telling her, "You'll do alright, whatever you decide. Just keep in mind there's no one else in the world like you."[15] Unlike the white men—historical and fictional—who rescue Oatman from Indian captivity and attempt to restore her to her former social station, Vega redeems Sarah's self-worth, leaving her to choose where her freedom will take her.

Fifteen years after Leonard refracted Oatman through the prism of male desire, she reappeared as a romantic heroine in Elizabeth Grayson's *So Wide the Sky* (1997), expressing her own yearnings in a compelling Western romance novel chock full of period detail, if bloated by bodice-ripper rhetoric. In an author's note, Grayson explains that her protagonist, Cassie Morgan, was directly inspired by Oatman, whose photo she had seen in Time-Life's *Old West* series. A

Kiowa captive for nine years, Cassie is returned to the whites with a tattoo on her cheek — a circle with radiating lines — and marries her childhood sweetheart, now a cold and bigoted cavalry captain turned off by her free spirit and strong will, not to mention her skin art. By contrast, a handsome half-Indian scout named Hunter Jalbert identifies with her Otherness and wins her heart. Like Vega in "The Tonto Woman," Hunter declares his love by touching the tattoo: "'This makes you special. . . . It makes you beautiful. It makes you mine,'" he says, first caressing and then kissing the mark. Cassie, Grayson writes, "had finally found someone who saw her for herself."[16]

By linking their heroines with minority lovers, both Leonard and Grayson acknowledge the racial implications of Oatman's tattoo. Their white savage is an ethnic Other, thus — it takes one to know one — only a brown-skinned man (and even better, a hybrid such as Hunter) can really understand her and vice versa. When Hunter suggests that whites and Indians can find a way to live in harmony, Cassie startles him by asking, "Have the white and Indian parts inside you found a way to make their peace?"[17] Though Cassie is validated by a man, as Oatman is in virtually every reworking of her story, she finally speaks for herself, something Stratton (for the most part) and Fairchild denied Olive. Leonard grants Sarah a more three-dimensional personality through a few deft and funny conversational exchanges, but Grayson lets Cassie luxuriate in cultural acceptance and sexual fulfillment, allowing her a relationship of equals in what amounts to a sentimental novel retrofitted for the '90s.

So Wide the Sky stands on a historical continuum of books and stories about marked women who, beginning with Hester Prynne, redefine the symbols of their transgression. "Outlawed from society," wrote Hawthorne in *The Scarlet Letter*, Hester refused to discard the "A" that branded her as an adulterer because its meaning had changed. Like Olive's and Cassie's marks, "The scarlet letter was her passport into regions where other women dared not tread." Even the contemptuous townspeople ultimately accept the scarlet letter's new symbolism: "They said it meant Able; so strong was Hester Prynne, with a woman's strength."[18]

Wendy Lawton's *Ransom's Mark* (2003), one of four children's books published about Oatman in the past decade, also features a heroine who revises the meaning of her mark, this time as "a sign of God's love and deliverance." Lawton treats the Mohaves respectfully, portraying them as Oatman's saviors (because they bought her from the hostile Yavapais), then theorizes the tattoo as a down payment on her Christian soul. The tattoo, she writes, "has become the ransom's mark—the remembrance of the price that had been paid for her by the Mohave and their promise of protection." But she also liked to think of it as "the remembrance of the ransom price Christ had paid for her with His own life and His promise of protection."[19] With a good squint, Lawton seems to say, you can see a cross in the hash marks on Oatman's chin. The Mohaves didn't save her—God did. In foregrounding the salvational aspect of the story, Lawton returns the captivity tale to its infancy, reprising its Puritan premise. As Vaughan and Clark explain in *Puritans Among the Indians: Accounts of Captivity and Redemption, 1676–1724*, "Captivity was God's punishment, redemption was His mercy."[20]

Refigured variously as a disfranchised Mexican (Ruiz de Burton), a rehabilitated white Indian (*Death Valley Days*), a sexual creature shedding her chrysalis of repression (Leonard), an Indian lover (Grayson), and a saved soul (Lawton), Oatman has shape-shifted through three centuries, morphed by the cultural fantasies and geopolitical preoccupations of her interpreters. In literature as in life, she is always a lone woman trafficked among men and delivered back to the Anglos, though her redemption, significantly, no longer turns on her reabsorption into exclusively white romantic relationships. Topeka and Aespaneo are typically dismissed from the narratives, whose appeal seems to lie in the spectacle of Olive's return to society and the conundrum of her emotional isolation within it, orphaned and maladjusted.

Indeed, unlike the best-known female captives, Oatman was not a mother struggling to protect or reunite her family (like Rowlandson, Dustan, and Wakefield) nor did she become a mother during her captivity (like Jemison and Parker). Try as her contemporaries did to confer maternal status on her through the suggestion that she left Mohave children behind, in the end she was a loner whose story embroidered the classic *male* American themes of frontier adventure and individual survival. And though Ruiz de Burton gave her a father to return to in *Who Would Have Thought It?* her twentieth-century incarnations center on her status as a white woman who is not only culturally but also emotionally unmoored. In these versions, she is a fascinating case study in feminine self-reliance.

Still, the limits of her reinvention reveal a remarkable ethnocultural blind spot. In every Oatman reprisal, even the historically sensitive ones, American Indians are interchangeable: Kiowas, Apaches, or Mohaves, their sole purpose is to reflect her whiteness as she negotiates her way back into Anglo life. Thus, the Mohave nation—mighty as it was—fades without distinction into a hazy vision of generic Indians, and the one story that has not been written becomes as telling as those that have: who will return Oatman to her tribe? When will her Mohave persona be fleshed out and validated, and how would her life have unfolded if she had reclaimed her adopted family?

As a national symbol, Oatman remains similarly unfinished. She evokes the multiethnic American future as powerfully as she recalls its territorial past. In *Playing Indian*, an analysis of white Americans who have dressed as Indians throughout history, Philip Deloria observes that our national identity was born of a cultural cleavage—British versus American—at a time when the only *authentic* Americans were Indians. They were both the "us" we first encountered and the "them" we overcame. "There was, quite simply, no way to conceive an American identity without Indians," writes Deloria.

"At the same time, there was no way to make a complete identity while they remained."[21] The arrival of Africans and mainland Europeans further complicated the project of national self-definition. In 1892 Ellis Island opened its doors to the greatest influx of immigrants in American history; more than 40 percent of Americans can trace their heritage through it.[22] We are "the Nation of many nations," Whitman wrote in "Song of Myself," a poem in which the physical self incarnates national *selves*, much as Oatman did.[23] And yet Oatman was an American without a country: her family left the United States to establish a new "nation" under Brewster, she spent her adolescence with a tribe with its own fully formed national identity, and long after she was "repatriated," she remained marked as an outsider.

Today, with the myth of the Western frontier long exhausted, America's current preoccupation with brown-skinned terrorists abroad has supplanted our historical fear of red-skinned terrorists within. In an effort to fortify ourselves, we have shored up our borders, tightened immigration policy, and embraced political isolationism even as we struggle to contain a rising tide of diversity. Yet our own ethnic boundaries are often blurred beyond recognition. When our first biracial president, Barack Obama, declared his candidacy he was considered either too black or too white, depending on who was looking. About 40 percent of the so-called millennial generation, born in the United States after 1981, are black, Latino, Asian, or racially mixed.[24] The country has seen a growing influx of adopted Asian babies, and Latinos have replaced blacks as the largest minority in America, with 10 percent of Mexico's population now living in the United States. In short, our whiteness is fading.

Gazing out from the pages of history, Oatman is a poster girl for our inherently split and perpetually multiplying national identity. If her legend once illustrated the dangers of frontier Americans colliding with the ethnic unknown, it is now a parable about what mixed-race America has ineluctably become. She is a white woman of color, a foreigner in her own country, a beautiful freak whose blue tattoo denotes the shaky fault lines between civilization and savagery. Cassie Morgan's query is a fitting epigraph for her unsettled—and unsettling—portrait: "Have the white and Indian parts inside you found a way to make their peace?"

POSTSCRIPT

Letter from Farmington

Since *The Blue Tattoo* was published in 2009, dozens of readers have contacted me to respond to, elaborate on, and, occasionally, challenge elements of it. They include an Apache historian who suggested the Indians who met and shot at Olive on her journey "home" with the Yavapais were too far west to be Comanches; a doctor who theorized that Olive's inability to bear children was probably the result of her malnourishment during the famine that killed Mary Ann; and an Oatman descendent in Oregon who reported that the Colver House, where Olive attended dances, burned to the ground the year before the book came out.

But when a librarian at the LDS Church History Library and Archives in Salt Lake City sent me the letter transcribed below, she changed the story, providing a happy postscript to a painful saga. Writing to her aunt, Sarah Abbott, Olive describes meeting and marrying John Fairchild, in a document that yields many gifts. It's a luxuriously long sample of Olive's prose (untouched by Stratton), whose narrative structure and dramatic pacing may explain why audiences found her to be a dynamic speaker: She hints at "news" in the second paragraph, challenges her aunt to guess it in the third, and tosses off a reference to "my dear husband" before formally declaring, "I was married last Nov. 9th to Mr. John B. Fairchild of this place + came to my new home the last of the same month after spending two weeks visiting his people."

The letter from Farmington offers an unusually intimate glimpse of Oatman; she's funny, promising that Sarah will see her "handkerchief flying" from the train when she passes Illinois en route to Missouri to join Fairchild, and playful, asking about her cousins' emerging "whiskers" and threatening to take her aunt by "force" for a visit. She describes a week in the life of her lecture schedule, which was probably even busier than surviving handbills and newspaper accounts reveal (she mentions back-to-back dates in Michigan, followed by a trip through the state, where she met "hundreds" of people). Sadly, it also shows that the eye trouble she suffered in middle age was already afflicting her in her twenties. Her reference to the "sorrowful" and "greavous" things she witnessed as a teenager, as well as her mention of the "sore eyes" that had kept her "confined" for six weeks, conjure a poignant metaphor: what she saw as a child seems to have damaged her very ability to see, for life.

That said, the letter would be worth reprinting if only for this comment about her wedding day: "I was that day the happy wife of one wholly worthy of me." Olive was *choosing* a husband, not settling for someone who would take her ("disfigured by tattooed lines on the chin," as the *Star* had described her). She was clearly in love with Fairchild, who had all the "qualifications" she wanted in a spouse: He was a resourceful businessman and a committed family man, and he had three sisters who embraced her at a time when her correspondence with Lorenzo had stalled out and she had lost touch with her Gassburg "friend and sister," Abi Colver.

One of the frustrations of researching *The Blue Tattoo* was the discovery that Olive's relationship with Fairchild was so poorly documented. The letter from Farmington illuminates its beginnings, confirming the couple's mutual attraction and the good times that led to their wedding, launching what Olive calls the "happiest period of my life." Equally significant, it shows Olive in the process of building the one family she would never lose.

A note on the transcription: I've adjusted some of Olive's punctuation for clarity, updating nineteenth-century conventions that might confuse contemporary readers. Where she used an underscore symbol to indicate a period, comma, or line break, I've inserted them. Where she neglected to punctuate sentences that conclude at the end of a written line, I've provided periods. And where she used an equal sign to signal a broken word at the end of a line, I've closed the word. I've also retained her misspellings and her somewhat random capitalizations.

||||
||||

P.S. The enclosed is a piece of my Bridal dress + the cloth is a piece of my traveling suit. I have not been to the P.O. but will go this afternoon + mail this—
July 20
With my love

Farmington Michigan, July 15th, 1866

My Dear Aunt Sarah Abbott
I scarcely know where to begin or what to say first to my dear Aunt after neglecting to write her in so long a time + acknowledge the receipt of her last letter which was received by me at this place. The excuse I have to offer for not answering it then is, that I was then suffering with sore eyes + was closely confined to my room for 6 or eight weeks, but then since that time you will say, I might have written, yes I might have done so I know but for that one thing that I have been scholded for so many times "neglect."

I have thought of you so many many hundred times during the last eight months still have not written. + then if you have not taken the (Rochester Daily) paper I have some news to tell you that will be interesting to you perhaps. First is that I am well, + the friends in Rochester so far as I know. I heard however some two or three weeks ago that Aunt Fanny [Amelia?] James['s] wife was no more. She died sometime in May last. Uncle James is in very feeble health + very childish minded, + hardly knows his own children. The remainder of the sperrys are usually well I believe. You not being acquainted with your numerous cousins, it will not be of interest to you to write conserning them. Only they will get married.

There has been quite a change taken place with me + conserning my future destiny since I last wrote to you. Can you guess? I think you can, for I gave you warning in my last. In earliest child-hood I was happy—for I knew no better—but so many years has been so sorrowful + greavous for me to endure. Stil the God of right protected me + shielded me til the present time + during this my happiest period in my life he is the same Father + Protector.

Did I say happiest period of my life? yes, it is even so. the "Dark Clouds" show silver linings, + could you see my dear Husband, you would say I aught to be happy. I was married last Nov. 9th to Mr. John B. Fairchild of this place + came to my new home the last of the same month after spending two weeks visiting his people. My new home was a beautiful place Called Maple Farm, + one side of the farm ran within stones throw of the principal street of Farmington, a town larger than Morrison + only 19 miles from the City of Detroit. I have three sisters-in-law (young ladies) two Brothers + Father + mother. One of my Brothers is a lawyer + Practising in the city of Niles, this state, the other is a Doctor + Practising in Farmington, but I presume you are anxious to know something more about the one that interests me the most + how I came to get a quainted & C & C. Wal, you remember that I was lecturing in this state a year ago last winter + I came to Farmington + I was introduced to a Gentleman who they said had been in California + went by the name of John B. Fairchild (this hapened at the church the evening of the lecture) + He + his sisters invited me to come + take dinner + tea at their house (as it was Sunday). But I was previously engaged + promised to spend an hour or so in the evening

+ did so + the call was so pleasant that I staid all night + the next morning had to start for Northville as I was to lecture there that night (Monday) + so Mr. Fairchild wanted permission to drive me over himself to N. so we went in company of his sister + we had a jolly good time + they returned home + I went on through the state meeting hundreds of others with pleasing addresses + smiling faces, but somehow I thought none was more interesting to me than Mr. F.'s, but I thought I never should see him again, of coars. But it was not long before I had letters from him + his sisters too inviting me to spend the warm month of July at "The Maple Farm."

I then did not think that I could spare the time but it so happened that my health was not good enough to lecture + was resting at Memphis + Romeo [Michigan]—with friends— + they insisted on my coming out here + spend a few weeks at least so I thought I would come + I did + I never enjoyed myself more than I did then. The family were all so kind a[nd] pleasant.

During which time I became very much interested in him [inserted: J.B.F] + I will presume to say he did in me + made up my mind that in him were all the qalifications that I had so often pictured to myself I would like to see in [a] man.

Before leavetaking of Maple Farm I was betrothed to Mr. Fairchild + our wedding day was to take place on the 9th of November, + I returned to Rochester + made some addition to my wardrobe + was married in the First Baptist Church in R. at half past 9. A.M. at the appointed day, + I was that day the happy wife of one wholly worthy of me.

Mr. Fairchild has been to California three times by overland route, buying Texican + Mexican cattle + driving them in to Cala during the years of 52, + 56, + 7. He went to Cala when a mear boy in 49, + since that time has accumulated considerable money, but at two different times lost every cent he had, but accumulated a little again, + during the year of 58 came back to Mich. to look more particular after the wants of the family + bought the Maple Farm, for to make a home for them. Previous to this He had sent them means from Cala + kept his three sisters + youngest Brothers in school at the Academe at Ypsilanti + since sent him to the law school at Detroit. He did not intend to stay on the farm himself, but by some means or other he kept staying + overseeing things + staid 7-years, but thought each year he would return to Cala.

So last March He had an offer for the place + as Father was getting to old to see to the place himself + Mr. Fairchild did not want to stay on the Farm He concluded to sell it, which he did, + Father, Mother + sisters were nicely located in the Village of Farmington.

My Husband saw, he thought, a chance of making money by going down to Texas + drive some cattle to a Northern Market + so he started the 6th day of Apr. in Company with Mr. [Leo?] Kator. They intended they would be gone between four or five months. They have already been gone three months + over. I hear from him as often as is possible + the last letter was written at Ft. Gibson Indian Territory. They had from six to eight hundred head of cattle + were coming as fast as they could towards home or I should say Mo., as that is where they may sell their cattle + they may ship them through to Chicago.

They did not know what they would do when they last wrote. There has been a law passed prohibiting Texican cattle being driven through Kansas + Mo. I learned but do not know how they will get along with that.

They have been delaid on account of swollen streams during their trip so far + they say it rains all the time.

They some thought that they would, after they got into Mo., stop some four or six weeks to let their cattle [rest?] + if so Mr. F. said he would send for me + if I go at all it will be with in four or five weeks from now—so if you will look out some fine morning when the cars pass you may see my handkerchief flying.

Where we will locate now it is hard to tel for I cannot imagine where it will be, but it will be somewhere + as soon as he gets back from this trip. During the time he has been away I have been staying with Mrs. Kator to keep her company + have been very busy preparing for housekeeping canning cherries + making jells, quilting + everything I can + get in readiness + then, O, then dear Aunt will you not come + see me. You must for I will go out after you + take you by main force, + then after you have been with me three months Uncle Asa will come after you providing he will stay another month. We would be most happy to see you both. We sold everything but about 200-Sheep, + I have 127 fleeces of wool for sale + hope to get about 60, or 70 cts a-lb. for it. We sold the farm for twelve thousand five hundred + now as I pass by it it looks so pleasant I almost wish we had not sold. But Mr. Fairchild says wherever he locates again he wants to stay for good, + I say Amen to that. And now do you not say to yourself that you think I have written a nough for once—I think so too— + if you will only write me one equally as long I will be ever so much obliged. How are all the dear cousins.

Charles I presume is with you + Morton I presume is a young man grown (have they got to the point of putting cream on their faces to make their whiskers grow?)

I don't presume I would know one of the children. They have grown so.

How is Uncle Asa's health this summer? + how are the crops in Illinois? All kinds + everything, poor [undecipherable] Mich. Write me all about the friends how they are doing + what they are doing—for you do not know how glad I am to hear of them + more particular of your own family.

You speak of Brother Lorenzo's good health + Sister Edna also—I am glad to hear that + hope they will be prosperous in every good undertaking + when [crossed out: they get at that period when they think they can + would take pleasure in so doing I shall be most happy to hear from them] as I think I have said a nough + written a nough on this subject to remain silent til I hear from them.

no better — but so many years has been
so sorrowful & grievous for me to endure
Still the God of right protected me & shield-
-ed me til the present time & during this
my happiest period in my life he is
the same Father & Protector.

Did I say happiest period of my life
yes, it is even so — the Dark clouds
show silver linings — & could you see
my dear Husband, you would say
I ought to be happy. I was married
last Nov — 9th to Mr John B. Fair=
=child of this place & came to my new
home the last of the same month
after spending two weeks visiting
his people. My new home was a
beautiful place Called Maple
Farm. & one side of the farm was within
stones throw of the principal street of
Farmington, a town larger than
Monson & only 17 miles from
the City of Detroit. I have three
Sisters-in-law (young ladies) two Brothers

FIG. 32. A page from Olive Oatman's 1866 letter to Sarah Abbott. Courtesy of the Church Archives, The Church of Jesus Christ of Latter-day Saints.

If I had my Husband's photograph I would enclose it in this but have not a good one so you must wait til he returns. Do write me very soon + let me get it inside of four weeks, will you?

Give much love to each member of your family and receiving a share for yourself. I remain your ever affectionate

Niece,

Olive A. Fairchild

P.S. Address me at this place

Farmington, Mich.

Notes

PROLOGUE

Epigraph. Lossing, "Extreme Western Tribes," 23.

1 Parker, Arizona–area Mohaves spell the name with an *h*, while in the Needles area a *j* is preferred. The choice of *Mohave* for this book is arbitrary.

2 Stratton, *Captivity*, 205.

3 Oren Arnold, "The Wild West's Favorite Indian Story," *Galveston Daily News*, May 21, 1943.

4 Llewellyn Barrackman, interview with the author, Needles CA, February 26, 2005.

5 Corle, *Desert Country*, 122.

6 Charles F. Morgan, "Omaha Veteran Traveled with the Pathfinder in 1845," *Sunday World Herald*, magazine sec., January, 12, 1913.

7 Morton J. A. McDonald, "This Man There When Marshall Found Gold / Adventurous Is Career of W. H. Jonson / Rescues Olive Oatman from Cruel Apaches," *Oakland Tribune*, April 28, 1918.

8 Devereux, "Psychology of Feminine Genital Bleeding," 237.

9 Even accounting for Mohave intermarriage with whites or into other tribes, today only 2,600 people claim Mohave ancestry. Michael Tsosie, interview with the author, March 3 and 14, 2007.

10 Sides, *Blood and Thunder*, 248; Hine and Faragher, *American West*, 199–200; McWilliams, *Southern California*, 43; Hurtado, *Indian Survival*, 135.

11 Didion, *Slouching Towards Bethlehem*, 172.

QUICKSAND

Epigraph. Browne, "A Tour Through Arizona," 697.

1 At the time, Fort Yuma was called Camp Calhoun. In March of 1851 the name was changed to Camp Yuma or Fort Yuma.

2 Maloney, "Some Olive Oatman Documents," 109.

3 Stratton, *Captivity*, 74.

4 Stratton, *Captivity*, 79.

5 In 1846 Lt. Col. Philip St. George Cooke had upgraded it to lead five hundred Mormon volunteers (the Mormon Battalion) from Albuquerque to San Diego during the Mexican War. Faulk, *Destiny Road*, 7.

6 S. Hughes, "Murder at Oatman's Flat," 3.

7 O. Oatman, "Narrative," 21.

8 Stratton, *Captivity*, 87.

9 Olive's account of the distance and duration of the trip varied from 100 to 250 miles, over one to four days. In *The Oatman Massacre: A Tale of Desert Captivity and Survival* (78–86), Brian McGinty makes a convincing case for a sixty-mile journey, based on the distance between the site of the attacks and the location of the Western Yavapais.

INDIAN COUNTRY

Epigraph. Thomas Hart Benton quoted in Gohres, "San Diego History," 1.

1 Stratton, *Captivity*, 118.

2 Stratton, *Captivity*, 116–17.

3 Stratton, *Captivity*, 124–25.

4 Stratton, *Captivity*, 127.

5 Sides, *Blood and Thunder*, 243, 247.

6 Stratton, *Captivity*, 129; O. Oatman, "Narrative," 13.

7 Stratton, *Captivity*, 133–34.

8 O. Oatman, "Narrative," 32.

"HOW LITTLE WE THOUGHT WHAT WAS BEFORE US"

Epigraph. Campfire song taken from Martin, *Yuma Crossing*, 127.

1 Vogel, "James Colin Brewster," 125; Denton, *Faith and Betrayal*, 27.

2 "Notice," *Times and Seasons* (Nauvoo IL), December 1, 1842, 32.

3 Denton, *Faith and Betrayal*, 29.

4 *Olive Branch*, January 1849, 103–4.

5 *Book of Mormon*, 456, 21, 154, 253, 154, 333, 403.

6 *Olive Branch*, September 1849, 37; *Olive Branch*, August 1848, 25; *Olive Branch*, March 1850, 130.

7 *Olive Branch*, March 1849, 137–38.

8 *Olive Branch*, January 1850, 111–12, 138.

9 *Olive Branch*, September 1849, 108, 66.

10 *Olive Branch*, March 1850, 131–32.
11 Denton, *Faith and Betrayal*, 26.
12 Remini, *Joseph Smith*, 178; Corle, *Desert Country*, 151.
13 Sperry, "Pioneer Journal," 139–40.
14 Krakauer, *Under the Banner of Heaven*, 192.
15 *Olive Branch*, November 1850, 61.
16 McGinty, *Oatman Massacre*, 39–40; *Olive Branch*, October 1850, 151.
17 McGinty, *Oatman Massacre*, 41; Vogel, "James Colin Brewster," 132.
18 *Olive Branch*, July 30, 1850, 37.
19 Faulk, *Destiny Road*, 82.
20 Root, *Following the Pot of Gold*, 1–2.
21 O. Oatman, "Narrative," 2.
22 Martin, *Yuma Crossing*, 127.
23 Faulk, *Destiny Road*, 70; Wagner, "Road to California."
24 Wyllis, *Arizona*, 129–33; Faulk, *Destiny Road*, 77.
25 Root, *Following the Pot of Gold*, 3.
26 O. Oatman, "Narrative," 2–3.
27 Russell, *Land of Enchantment*, 14, 25; Denton, *Faith and Betrayal*, 97.
28 Root, *Following the Pot of Gold*, 4–5.
29 O. Oatman, "Narrative," 3.
30 McGinty, *Oatman Massacre*, 45.
31 *Olive Branch*, April 1851, 141.
32 Greene, *Kansas Region*, 58–60.
33 *Olive Branch*, October 1850, 38.
34 Root, *Following the Pot of Gold*, 3–4.
35 Dary, *Oregon Trail*, 218.
36 Pettid, "The Oatman Story," 19–20. The Reverend Edward J. Pettid wrote a book about the Oatman massacre in the 1960s, but it was never published and most of his research notes have since been lost. His article "The Oatman Story" appeared in *Arizona Highways* in November 1968. Pettid fabricated details for purposes of scene-setting where he lacked information, but his use of original sources (I have cross-referenced his with mine) is otherwise reliable. I have also quoted from his original interviews with people who knew Oatman and her family in Sherman, Texas, and used details from his quotes from her scrapbook, whose existence various relatives have confirmed but which, too, is now lost.
37 Stratton, *Captivity*, 46–7.

38 *Olive Branch*, March 1851, 149.

39 Greene, *Kansas Region*, 60.

40 O. Oatman, "Narrative," 5.

41 *Olive Branch*, September 1851, 17.

42 *Olive Branch*, May 1851, 151.

43 "The Brewster Branch of the Mormons," *Republican Compiler* (Gettysburg PA), April 19, 1852. Brewster ultimately made it to California—but lost his religion in the Golden State. Joseph Smith's 1900 *History of the Church* noted, "The last we heard of James C. Brewster he was lecturing in California [on] spiritualism" (78). By 1856 Brewster had returned to Illinois, where he worked as a farm laborer and as a schoolteacher. He fought and was partially disabled in the Civil War, then he lived in Minnesota and Louisiana but had no further association with the Mormons. He died in 1909, at sixty-one, at the National Home for Disabled and Volunteer Soldiers, in Milwaukee, Wisconsin. Vitale, "Whatever Happened to James Colin Brewster," 11–14.

44 Faulk, *Destiny Road*, 199. Today, Interstates 10 and 8 follow the trail from El Paso to San Diego.

45 O. Oatman, "Narrative," 6; Root, *Following the Pot of Gold*, 3–4.

46 *Olive Branch*, September 1851, 17.

47 Root, *Following the Pot of Gold*, 6.

48 *Olive Branch*, September 1851, 18.

49 Root, *Following the Pot of Gold*, 8.

50 Gohres, "San Diego History," 1; Trafzer and Hyer, *Exterminate Them!* 62; Richards, *California Gold Rush*, 57.

51 Stratton, *Captivity*, 62; O. Oatman, "Narrative," 8.

A YEAR WITH THE YAVAPAIS

Epigraph. Browne, *Adventures in the Apache Country*, 16.

1 The term was so broad as to be almost generic. In his 1874 book *The Native Races of the Pacific States*, historian Hubert Howe Bancroft included as Apaches tribes of New Mexico, northwestern Texas, northern Mexico, and Arizona—fourteen tribes, from the Yavapais to the Navajos (591). Cultural similarities between the Yavapais and the Apaches, their neighbors to the east, also probably contributed to the confusion between the tribes: they were both hunter-gatherers who inhabited similar landscapes. Only

some Apaches had Yavapai blood. Kroeber and Kroeber, "Olive Oatman's First Account," 314n10; Kroeber and Fontana, *Massacre on the Gila*, 28.

2 Braatz, *Surviving Conquest*, 63; McGinty, *Oatman Massacre*, 81–83; Timothy Braatz, e-mail correspondence with the author, July 15, 2006; Gifford, "Northeastern and Western Yavapai," 247–48.

3 Tuttle, "River Colorado," 5; Martin, *Yuma Crossing*, 158.

4 "Five Years Among the Indians: Story of Olive Oatman," *Daily Evening Bulletin* (San Francisco), June 24, 1856; O. Oatman, "Narrative," 15; Stratton, *Captivity*, 138.

5 Stratton, *Captivity*, 135.

6 Stratton, *Captivity*, 136, 139.

7 Howe, *What God Hath Wrought*, 809.

8 Stratton, *Captivity*, 142–43.

9 Stratton, *Captivity*, 143–44.

10 Stratton, *Captivity*, 150, 153; O. Oatman, "Narrative," 15.

11 The Mohaves have never used the term *chief*. They prefer *captain*, *headman*, or *leader*. As psychoanalyst George Devereux explained, "The Mohave chief was, primarily, a servant of the tribe with little personal powers and many cares and duties." The leaders could exercise power temporarily, and their leadership was limited to a particular area such as war, celebration, or medicine. The tribe had no centralized government until the late nineteenth century. Devereux, "Mohave Chieftainship," 33.

12 Stratton, *Captivity*, 156–59.

LORENZO'S TALE

Epigraph. Oatman and Oatman, *Captivity of the Oatman Girls*, 97.

1 Stratton, *Captivity*, 91.

2 Stratton, *Captivity*, 103.

3 Stratton, *Captivity*, 106.

4 Stratton, *Captivity*, 109.

5 Wilder, "Oatman Massacre Recalled," 10.

6 Root, *Following the Pot of Gold*, 11.

7 Wilder, "Oatman Massacre Recalled," 11.

8 Stratton, *Captivity*, 11.

9 Woodward, *Journal*, 114.

10 Woodward, *Journal*, 55.

11 Heintzelman, *Transcription*, 26.

12 Heintzelman, *Transcription*, 12, 15, 21.

13 Heintzelman, "Post Return."

14 Heintzelman, *Transcription*, 17.

15 Heintzelman, "Post Return."

16 Quoted in Vogel, "James Colin Brewster," 129.

17 Heintzelman, *Transcription*, 79.

18 Love, *Hell's Outpost*, 19.

19 Woodward, *Journal*, 53–54; Browne, *Adventures in the Apache Country*, 57.

20 Heintzelman, *Transcription*, 21.

21 *Daily Alta California*, July 24, 1851.

22 Heintzelman, *Transcription*, 17.

23 Stratton, *Captivity*, 111; S. Hughes, "Murder at Oatman's Flat," 7.

BECOMING MOHAVE

Epigraph. Devereux, "Mohave Culture and Personality," 103.

1 Stratton, *Captivity*, 163.

2 Espaniole was technically a subchief under five more dominant leaders.

3 The names Olive used in *Captivity of the Oatman Girls* were probably Olive's—or Royal Stratton's—Spanish transliterations of Mohave names. Espaniole was also called "Espaniola" (Stratton, *Captivity*, 175) and "Aespaniola" (235).

4 A. Kroeber, "Olive Oatman's Return," 2.

5 Stratton, *Captivity*, 168.

6 Stewart, "Aboriginal Territory," 257. Though they are scarcely documented, some Mohaves had been associated with missions, possibly in the Yuma area. When explorer John Charles Fremont met six Mohaves in 1844, a Mohave who spoke fluent Spanish told him he had been a "mission Indian" before the mission system collapsed as a consequence of Mexico's independence from Spain. Gudde, "Mohave and Mojave," 171.

7 De Humbolt, *Political Essay*, 206–7; Hafen and Hafen, *Old Spanish Trail*, 74; Sherer, *Bitterness Road*, 6; Corle, *Desert Country*, 113; Shea, *History of the Catholic Church*, 342. Ironically, over half a century later, the military succeeded where the church had failed. Fort Yuma was built on the site of the old mission, specifically for the purpose of subduing local Indians.

8 Hine and Faragher, *American West*, 158; Sherer, *Bitterness Road*, 5.

9 Quoted in Sherer, *Bitterness Road*, 14.

10 Stewart, "Mohave Warfare," 57; Kroeber and Fontana, *Massacre on the Gila*, 132. On February 1, 1852, Sweeny noted in his diary, "We burned a number of villages, destroyed their planting grounds and did all the mischief that we could. We ran short of provisions before we got back, and had to kill some of our mules and live on the meat for two days. I liked it very well." Sweeny, "Military Occupation," 20.

11 A. Kroeber, *Handbook*, 745, 747, 752; Kroeber and Kroeber, *Reminiscence*, 7n6; Pamela Munro, interview with the author, February 15, 2005; A. Kroeber, "Olive Oatman's Return," 2.

12 Hine and Faragher, *American West*, 217; McWilliams, *Southern California*, 43.

13 United States Army Corps of Topographical Engineers, *Report of an Expedition*, 18–19.

14 Palmer, "Observations," 63.

15 Carlson, "Martial Experiences," 493; A. Kroeber, *Handbook*, 733; U.S. Congress, Message from the President, 589.

16 Mollhausen, *Diary of a Journey*, 244.

17 Stratton, *Captivity*, 172–73, 180.

18 Stratton, *Captivity*, 204.

19 Devereux, "Mohave Culture and Personality," 96–97; Devereux, "Psychology of Feminine Genital Bleeding," 238; Michael Tsosie, interview with the author, March 3 and 14, 2007; A. Kroeber, *Handbook*, 747–49.

20 A. Kroeber, "Olive Oatman's Return," 1; Pamela Munro, interview with the author, February 15, 2005.

21 Michael Tsosie says the name, also spelled "Owch," meant "water in the sky" and could designate anything associated with precipitation, including rain, clouds, thunder, and lightning. Michael Tsosie, interview with the author, March 3 and 14, 2007.

22 Gibbs, "Observations of the Indians"; Mowry, "Notes of the Indians," 10; Michael Tsosie, interview with the author, March 3 and 14, 2007.

23 Betty Barrackman, interview with the author, Needles CA, February 26, 2005. The name was subsequently mistranslated as "rot womb," probably because Oatman or others who recorded her story were embarrassed to say "vagina," says Pamela Munro, a linguist at the University of California, Los Angeles. Pamela Munro, interview with the author, February 15, 2005.

24 Pamela Munro, interview with the author, February 15, 2005; Tuttle, "River Colorado," 59. According to Devereux's Kinseyesque "The Psychology of Genital Feminine Bleeding: An Analysis of Mohave Indian Puberty and Menstrual Rites," the Mohaves loved fellatio (254) and loathed menstrual blood, particularly its smell (239). Men who had sex with menstruating women were considered lewd, though some men did it as a practical joke, after which they displayed their bloody penises before washing in the river (239, 246).

25 Sherer, *Clan System*.

26 Stratton, *Captivity*, 175–77.

27 Stratton, *Captivity*, 219.

28 Taylor and Wallace, "Mojave Tattooing," 5. This belief was shared by other Native American tribes, including the Sioux (Gilbert, *Tattoo History*). Many California and Arizona Indian tribes practiced tattooing. For most women in these regions, tattooing was restricted to the chin.

29 In *Captivity of the Oatman Girls*, they were called "ki-e-chook" (183), but the Mohaves have no such word; Stratton may have fabricated it.

30 By the early twentieth century, when the average Mohave weighed much more after adapting to the white diet, the standard changed, and a long face became the ideal. Michael Tsosie, interview with the author, March 3 and 14, 2007.

31 Whether or not Olive underwent a puberty ritual, and what it involved, is difficult to guess since she had probably reached puberty before she was adopted by the Mohaves, and puberty rites were individualized and partly determined by dreams (Michael Tsosie, interview with the author, March 3 and 14, 2007). Devereux described a four-day ceremony that included frequent visits by the girl's mother and grandmother, who told her how a woman should behave; buried her in hot sand to help her body develop properly for childbirth and give her shapely calves and arms and make her a good worker; massaged her; and advised against using body paint—believed to cause liver spots during menses, pregnancy, and childbirth. Devereux, "Psychology of Feminine Genital Bleeding," 241–42.

DEEPER

Epigraph. Whipple, *Pathfinder in the Southwest*, 257.

1 Stratton, *Captivity*, 181.

2 Quoted in Gordon, *Through Indian Country*, 10–11.

3 Gordon, *Through Indian Country*, 187.

4 Whipple, *Pathfinder in the Southwest*, 232, 245; A. Kroeber, *Handbook*, 749.

5 Whipple, *Pathfinder in the Southwest*, 245.

6 Whipple, *Pathfinder in the Southwest*, 235–36.

7 Whipple, *Pathfinder in the Southwest*, 236–37

8 Mollhausen, *Diary of a Journey*, 247–48.

9 Mollhausen, *Diary of a Journey*, 250–51, 257.

10 Mollhausen, *Diary of a Journey*, 245.

11 Sherer, *Bitterness Road*, 18.

12 Mollhausen, *Diary of a Journey*, 255.

13 Mollhausen, *Diary of a Journey*, 263.

14 Michael Tsosie, interview with the author, March 3 and 14, 2007.

15 Whipple, *Pathfinder in the Southwest*, 237.

16 Mollhausen, *Diary of a Journey*, 262–63.

17 Whipple, *Pathfinder in the Southwest*, 246–47.

18 Irataba's name was derived from the Mohave word for "bird," *yara*, modified by *teva* (wings), "spread out or loosened, as in flight" (Sherer, "Great Chieftains," 30n11). He was variously called Yara tav, Yara teva, Yarate:va, Arateva, Aratêve Yaratev, Eecheyara tav, and Irateba. The name "Aretev" is listed as the short form of Irataba's full name, Ichayer Aratev (Freed Bird), in Munro, Brown, and Crawford, *Mojave Dictionary*, 40.

19 Quoted in Whipple, *Pathfinder in the Southwest*, 252n4.

20 Mollhausen, *Diary of a Journey*, 249.

"THERE IS A HAPPY LAND, FAR, FAR AWAY"

Epigraph. Olive Oatman quoted in Stratton, *Captivity*, 188.

1 Stewart, "Mohave Warfare," 260–61. The sisters and daughters of *kwanamis* sometimes followed them to war, both to cheer them on and to help them finish a battle (267).

2 Kroeber and Kroeber, *Reminiscence*, 8–9.

3 Stratton, *Captivity*, 217–18.

4 A. Kroeber, *Handbook*, 746–47.

5 Wallace, "Dream in Mohave Life," 253.

6 Stratton, *Captivity*, 186–88.

7 Olive called it the Taneta tree (Stratton, *Captivity*, 188).

8 Stratton, *Captivity*, 188–93.

9 O. Oatman, "Narrative," 17.

10 Stratton, *Captivity*, 191–99.

11 Stratton, *Captivity*, 231.

JOURNEY TO YUMA

Epigraph. Olive Oatman quoted in Stratton, *Captivity*, 236.

1 Asa Abbott to John LeConte, September 12, 1851, Abbott Family private collection, Morrison IL.

2 John LeConte to Asa Abbott, October 15, 1851, Abbott Family private collection, Morrison IL.

3 "City Intelligence," *Daily Alta California*, March 3, 1851.

4 Lorenzo Oatman to Asa Abbott, May 19, 1854, Abbott Family private collection, Morrison IL.

5 Lorenzo Oatman to Asa and Sarah Abbott, May 19, 1854, Abbott Family private collection, Morrison IL.

6 Stratton, *Captivity*, 233–34.

7 Lorenzo Oatman to Asa and Sarah Abbott, May 15, 1855, Abbott Family private collection, Morrison IL.

8 Lorenzo Oatman to Asa and Sarah Abbott, January 5, 1856, Abbott Family private collection, Morrison IL.

9 Lorenzo Oatman to Governor J. Neely Johnson, January 2, 1856, photocopy in Patricia Carreon private collection, Foothills Ranch CA.

10 Stratton, *Captivity*, 270.

11 Olive Ann Oatman Papers, Center for Archival Collections, Jerome Library, Bowling Green State University, Bowling Green OH.

12 Stratton, *Captivity*, 236.

13 A. Kroeber, "Olive Oatman's Return," 2.

14 Stratton, *Captivity*, 259–62.

15 A. Kroeber, "Olive Oatman's Return," 3.

16 See Palmer, "Observations," 103. Michael Tsosie considers the episode apocryphal because, he says, no Mohave would have taken back a gift. Michael Tsosie, interview with the author, March 3 and 14, 2007.

17 Stratton, *Captivity*, 264.

18 O. Oatman, "Narrative," 22.

19 A. Kroeber, "Olive Oatman's Return," 3.

20 A. Kroeber, "Olive Oatman's Return," 4.

Epigraph. Sarah Bowman quoted in J. F. Elliott, "Great Western," 6.

1 Twain, *Roughing It*, 307.

2 According to Llewellyn Barrackman (interview with the author, February 26, 2005), the Mohaves dyed their hair using mesquite and clay to kill lice and control dandruff. Women also did it to make the color as black as possible.

3 Kroeber and Kroeber, "Olive Oatman's First Account," 311–12.

4 "Rescued from Captivity," *San Francisco Herald*, March 9, 1856.

5 "Rescued from Captivity," *San Francisco Herald*, March 9, 1956.

6 "Miss Oatman Rescued from the Mohave Indians," *Daily Alta California*, March 24, 1856.

7 Elliott, "Great Western," 4.

8 Sandwich, *Great Western*, 13, 25.

9 Sylvester Mowry to E. J. Bricknall, April 8, 1856, Collection of Western Americana, Beineke Rare Books and Manuscripts Library, Yale University.

10 Love, *Hell's Outpost*, 9.

11 Mowry, "Notes on the Indians of the Colorado."

12 Mowry was referring to what Sweeny called the "El-thu-dhik," which is probably a rendering of the "yak tadii" (also "yaly tadii" or "yaly tadiik"), the willow bark "apron" (according to Pamela Munro, interview with the author, February 15, 2005) that the Quechan women typically wore. Mowry, "Notes on the Indians of the Colorado."

13 Mowry, "Notes on the Indians of the Colorado."

14 U.S. Congress, Message from the President, 590.

15 Sylvester Mowry to E. J. Bricknall, April 8, 1856, Collection of Western Americana.

16 Woodward, *Journal*, 31, 61.

17 "Highly Important," *Los Angeles Star*, March 8, 1856.

18 Stratton, *Captivity*, 249.

19 "Rescue of Miss Oatman," *Los Angeles Star*, March 15, 1856.

20 O. Oatman, "Narrative," 23.

21 Beattie, "Diary of Ferryman," 101.

22 A. Kroeber, "Olive Oatman's Return," 5.

23 "Admissibility of Chinese and Negro Testimony," *San Francisco Evening Bulletin*, April 10, 1857.

24 "Rescue of Young American Woman from the Indians," *San Francisco Weekly Chronicle*, March 15, 1856.

25 "Rescued from Captivity," *San Francisco Herald*, March 9, 1856.

26. "Arrival of Miss Oatman," *Los Angeles Star*, April 12, 1856; "Olive Oatman: The Apache Captive," *Los Angeles Star*, April 19, 1856.

27 "Arrival of Miss Oatman," *Los Angeles Star*, April 12, 1856

28 Sansome, "The White Girl's Friend" (letter), *Daily Evening Bulletin*, April 26, 1856.

29 Root, *Following the Pot of Gold*, 29, 16, 18; S. Hughes, "Murder at Oatman's Flat," 4.

30 Barney, "Oatman Massacre," 18.

31 "Miss Oatman," *Los Angeles Star*, June 21, 1856

32 *Los Angeles Star*, June 28, 1856.

33 "Five Years Among the Indians: Story of Olive Oatman," *Daily Evening Bulletin* (San Francisco), June 24, 1856.

REWRITING HISTORY IN GASSBURG, OREGON

Epigraph. Stratton, *Church Government*; Stratton, *Captivity*, 284.

1 Hegne, "Captivity of Olive Oatman," 5.

2 Clark, Down, and Blue, *History of Oregon*, 236–37.

3 Moses Williams, Diary, entry of October 22, 1858.

4 Harrison Oatman to Jackson and Bina, March 20, 1858, Oregon Historical Society collections, Portland OR.

5 Reinhart, *Golden Frontier*, 166.

6 John Hughes to R. C. Williamson and Carie, July 22, 1856, Newberry Library Special Collections.

7 "The Captivity of Olive Oatman," *Table Rock Sentinel*, February 1982, 19.

8 Washburn in Vaughan, *Narratives*, xvii.

9 Derounian-Stodola, *Women's Indian Captivity Narratives*, 148.

10 Quoted in Derounian-Stodola and Levernier, *Indian Captivity Narrative*, 80.

11 Derounian-Stodola, *Women's Indian Captivity Narratives*, 148.

12 Hacker, *Cynthia Ann Parker*, 40.

13 Namias, *White Captives*, 50–51; Jemison in Derounian-Stodola, *Women's Indian Captivity Narratives*, 155–56; Brooks, *Captives and Cousins*, 186–87; Sides, *Blood and Thunder*, 243, 247. When Jemison's Seneca sister proposed taking her to see two white captives executed, her Indian mother scolded

her, "How can you think of conducting to that melancholy spot your poor sister . . . who has so lately been a prisoner, who has lost her parents and brothers by hands of the bloody warriors, and who has felt all the horrors of the loss of her freedom, in lonesome captivity? Oh! how can you think of making her bleed at the wounds which are now but partially healed?" The sisters stayed home and missed the spectacle, in which the prisoners were beheaded, cut up, and burned (quoted in Derounian-Stodola, *Women's Indian Captivity Narratives*, 155–56).

14 Hurtado, *Intimate Frontiers*, 58, 154n34.

15 Root, *Following the Pot of Gold*, 18.

16 Kroeber and Kroeber, "Olive Oatman's First Account," 313.

17 Harrison Oatman to Olive and Lorenzo Oatman, October 12, 1857, Richard Nolan private collection.

18 Moses Williams, Diary, entry of November 25, 1857.

19 C. Brooks, "Politics of Forgetting."

20 Stanton, "Report of the Secretary of War."

21 Anthony, *Fifty Years of Methodism*, 91, 130–31; Roberts, *Letters of William Roberts*, 222.

22 Stratton, *Captivity*, 283.

23 Stratton, *Captivity*, 34, 37.

24 Stratton, *Captivity*, 211, 200.

25 Stratton, *Church Government*.

26 Stratton, *Captivity*, 137, 163, 151.

27 Devereux, *Mohave Etiquette*, 5–6.

28 Stratton, *Captivity*, 185, 186.

29 Stratton, *Captivity*, 156.

30 Olive had lost track of both annual time and her own age by the time of her ransom, but she could calculate months, Mohave style, by lunar cycles. She told Burke that Mary Ann had died the previous year. Kroeber and Kroeber, "Olive Oatman's First Account," 312.

31 Woodward, *Journal*, June 12, 1853. Dendrochronological (tree ring) records show that the water level of the Colorado was above average in 1853, average in 1854, and 25 percent below average in 1855—enough to forestall the overflow the Colorado River Indians relied on for spring planting (McGinty, *Oatman Massacre*, 105), resulting in Mary Ann's death by late summer or fall.

32 Stratton, *Captivity*, 200–201.

33 Stratton, *Captivity*, 218.
34 A. Kroeber, *Report on Aboriginal Territory*, 12.
35 Stratton, *Captivity*, 224, 164–65, 163.
36 Stratton, *Captivity*, 229.
37 A. Kroeber, *Report on Aboriginal Territory*, 12.
38 Stratton, *Captivity*, 167.
39 Stratton, *Captivity*, 261.
40 Stratton, *Captivity*, 161, 282.

CAPTIVE AUDIENCES

Epigraph. Castiglia, *Bound and Determined*, 9.
1 The third edition inexplicably showed Olive back in her bark skirt, shaking Burke's hand, as Jennifer Putzi writes, "capturing the liminal moment in this transaction, the moment in which Olive is both white and Indian, 'civilized' and 'uncivilized'" (*Identifying Marks*, 35).
2 Stratton, *Captivity of the Oatman Girls*, 290.
3 Stratton, *Captivity of the Oatman Girls*, 10.
4 Vail, *Voice of the Old Frontier*, 22.
5 Derounian-Stodola, *Women's Indian Captivity Narratives*, xi.
6 Castiglia, *Bound and Determined*, 114.
7 Quoted in Derounian-Stodola, *Women's Indian Captivity Narratives*, 46.
8 Stratton, *Captivity of the Oatman Girls*, 231.
9 Carroll, *Rhetorical Drag*, 5.
10 Stratton, *Captivity of the Oatman Girls*, 3rd ed., "Notices," 2.
11 Stratton, *Captivity of the Oatman Girls*, 3rd ed., "Notices," 2.
12 Castiglia, *Bound and Determined*, 4.
13 Stratton, *Captivity of the Oatman Girls*, 113.
14 Stratton, *Captivity of the Oatman Girls*, 211.
15 As Robert Hughes explains in *American Visions* (185–88), the depiction of tribal Americans mutated throughout nineteenth-century America from the Noble Savage of empathetic artists such as Charles Bird King, George Catlin, and Karl Bodmer to the Demonic Indian of Charles Wimar's 1856 *The Attack on an Emigrant Train* to the Doomed Indian, crystallized in Tompkins Harrison Matteson's *The Last of the Race* (1847).
16 Quoted in Fryd, "Two Sculptures for the Capitol," 25.
17 *Rescue* remained on the Capitol steps until 1958. In 1939 the House moved (unsuccessfully) for its removal, proposing that it be "ground into dust,

and scattered to the four winds, that no more remembrance may be perpetuated of our barbaric past, and that it may not be a constant reminder to our American Indian citizens." In 1959 the sculpture was moved in preparation for the building's expansion then stored and forgotten until 1976, when it was dropped and broken as it was being transferred to a new facility. Fryd, "Two Sculptures for the Capitol," 17.

18 Hunt, *History of the College*, 11.

19 *Catalog of the University of the Pacific*, 6–19.

20 Collier, "Mohave Tattoo," 7.

21 Lorenzo Oatman to Asa Abbott, May 19, 1854, Abbott Family private collection, Morrison IL.

22 Moses Sperry to Asa Abbott, June 7, 1858, Abbott Family private collection, Morrison IL.

23 Stratton, *Captivity of the Oatman Girls*, 14.

24 Stratton, *Captivity of the Oatman Girls*, 279–81.

25 "Six Years' Captivity Among the Indians—Narrative of Miss Olive Oatman," *New York Times*, May 4, 1858.

26 "Indian Lectures: 'Lo! The Poor Captive!'" (advertisement), *New York Tribune*, May 10, 1858.

27 Olive Oatman to Abbott cousins, October 20, c. 1890s, Fields Family private collection, Morrison IL.

28 Royal B. Stratton to Asa Abbott, undated (probably 1861), Abbott Family private collection, Morrison IL.

29 *Minutes of the California Annual Conference*, 6.

30 Quoted in "Five Years Among Wild Savages."

31 "'Lo! The Indian' Captive!"

32 She was also the only documented white captive to go on the national lecture circuit, though, according to Derounian-Stodola, some captives taken during the Dakota war of 1862 lectured locally.

33 Grosz, "Intolerable Ambiguity," 56–57.

34 O. Oatman, "Narrative," 1.

35 O. Oatman, "Narrative," 2, 24.

36 O. Oatman, "Narrative," 39, 44.

37 O. Oatman, "Narrative," 183.

38 See "Female Figure" (artist unknown) in Furst, *Mojave Pottery*, plate 17, p. 120.

39 Palmer's sculpture, commissioned by former New York governor and sen-

ator Hamilton Fish, attracted three thousand viewers in two weeks when it was displayed in late 1859. Now in New York's Metropolitan Museum of Art, it was considered a turning point in the maturation of American art.

40 Quoted in Kasson, *Marble Queens*, 74.

41 Quoted in Kasson, *Marble Queens*, 80.

42 Quoted in Webster, *Erastus D. Palmer*, 30.

43 Kasson, *Marble Queens*, 82.

44 Quoted in Kasson, *Marble Queens*, 84.

45 *New York Times* article and review in the *Terre Haute News* both quoted in "Five Years Among Wild Savages."

46 "The Apachee Captive," *Rochester Daily Union and Advertiser*, April 28, 1865.

47 O. Oatman, "Narrative," 59.

48 Quoted in Matthews, *Rise of Public Woman*, 117.

49 Quoted in Piepmeier, *Out in Public*, 123.

50 Quoted in "Five Years Among Wild Savages."

51 Stratton, *Church Government*, 23.

"WE MET AS FRIENDS"

Epigraph. Washburn, *Indian in America*, 196.

1 Ives, *Report Upon the Colorado River*, 68–69.

2 Ives, *Report Upon the Colorado River*, 71–73.

3 Woodward, "Irataba," 56.

4 Edward Fitzgerald Beale was sent not only to blaze a path for emigrant travel and military operations in the West but also to test the feasibility of camels for military transport. His twenty-five camels, imported from Egypt and led by a Turkish camel driver named Hadji Ali, proved impractical because the pads of their feet were too soft for rocky ground and they spooked other pack animals (Martin, *Yuma Crossing*, 184). They were later sold to zoos and circuses or set free in the desert, where camel sightings were reported for decades. Beale's Wagon Road became Route 66 and was later absorbed into Interstate 40. At the time the Rose-Baley party used it (see Baley, *Disaster on the Colorado*), Beale considered his trail unfit for emigrant travel.

5 Sherer, *Bitterness Road*, 69n5.

6 Sherer, *Bitterness Road*, 101n3.

7 Woodward, "Irataba," 60.

8 Sherer, *Bitterness Road*, 102n6.

9 Carlson, "Martial Experiences," 492.

10 Quoted in Woodward, "Irataba," 62.

11 "Arrival of the Indian Warrior, Irataba," *New York Times*, February 7, 1864; "Indian Chieftains from the Far West," *Harper's Weekly*, February 13, 1864; quoted in Woodward, "Irataba," 62.

12 O. Oatman, "Narrative," 57–58.

13 Tuttle, "River Colorado," 61. Irataba's granddaughter later reported, "The White men taught him that that was the way to get land—to push people out by force. . . . My grandfather felt that even though this land (the Needles area) had been formerly his, the soldiers had taken it from him—just as he had taken the land around Parker from the 'Pima.' He therefore asked (the President) that the Mohave should be settled here [in Parker]." Devereux, "Mohave Chieftainship," 39.

14 Mollhausen, *Diary of a Journey*, 247–48.

OLIVE FAIRCHILD, TEXAN

Epigraph. "Her Veil Hid Scars of Indian Imprisonment," *Sherman Demo crat*, July 4, 1976.

1 "Apache Hank," *Reese River Reveille* (Austin NV), May 23, 1863.

2 Quoted in McGinty, *Oatman Massacre*, 182.

3 "Death of Rev. R. B. Stratton," *Worcester Evening Gazette*, January 25, 1875.

4 Worcester County Probates, case 57, 295: Royal B. Stratton.

5 Quoted in Clark and Clark, *Oatman Story*, 81; Collier, "Mohave Tattoo," 7; Hall, "Olive A. Oatman," 227.

6 Edna Oatman to Sarah Abbott, February 3, 1871, Abbott Family private collection, Morrison IL.

7 Lucena Oatman to Sarah Abbott, October 31, 1866, Abbott Family private collection, Morrison IL.

8 Wilson, *Taking the Waters*, 32–34. Mack had designed a speculum that he had produced by a local tinsmith, and in 1862 he claimed to have performed one hundred gynecological operations on women without complications. But he was best known for studying Florence Nightingale's nursing methods in London, opening in 1873 the first nursing school in

Canada to employ them. He died weeks after Olive left the Springbank; there is no record of whether he treated her directly.

9 John Fairchild to Asa Abbott, August 2, 1881, Abbott Family private collection, Morrison IL.

10 In her famous short story "The Yellow Wallpaper," Charlotte Perkins Gilman described a troubled woman going insane as a result of the rest cure. Gilman wrote the story in 1892, five years after emerging from the rest cure herself, as prescribed by her doctor, Weir Mitchell.

11 Will, "Nervous Origins of the American Western," 301.

12 Clark and Clark, *Oatman Story*, 83.

13 Hildebrandt's promotional broadside said the tattooing was ordered by the Lakota Sioux leader Sitting Bull, who wanted Hildebrandt as his "squaw." At the time, however, Sitting Bull had surrendered to U.S. troops and was being held at Fort Buford, Dakota Territory.

14 "Facts Relating to Irene Woodward," 2.

15 Bancroft's books include *History of the Pacific States of North America* (1882) and *History of Arizona and New Mexico, 1530–1883* (1889).

16 "Death of Rev. R. B. Stratton," *Worcester Evening Gazette*, January 25, 1875.

17 Olive Oatman to Sarah Abbott, January 9, 1889, Abbott Family private collection, Morrison IL.

18 "Items," *Arizona Republican*, March 27, 1893.

19 Derounian-Stodola, *Women's Indian Captivity Narratives*, 271, 309.

20 Derounian-Stodola, *Women's Indian Captivity Narratives*, 247.

21 "L. D. Oatman's Sudden Demise," *Red Cloud Nation*, October 10, 1901; "Lorenzo Dow Oatman," *Red Cloud Chief*, October 11, 1901.

22 Quoted in Pettid, "Oatman Story," 199.

23 "Mrs. Fairchild Dead: A Most Estimable Lady Called to Her Reward," *Sherman Daily Register*, March 21, 1903; "Mrs. Fairchild Dead: Wife of Major J. B. Fairchild Passed Away Monday Night," *Sherman Weekly Democrat*, March 26, 1903.

EPILOGUE

Epigraph. Deloria, *Playing Indian*, 191.

1 The third generation of the ten-member Oatman family consisted of just two people: Mamie and her cousin Royal (Lorenzo's son), who was the last blood Oatman relative. Because Mamie was adopted and Roy never

had biological children (he and his wife, Harriet Rants, adopted a son, named William Robert), the Oatman bloodline ended with Roy, though the family tree continued down the generations—a fitting denouement for a saga driven by strong adoptive relationships.

2 Robert Doman, "Tribal Atrocities Alleged in Divorce Suit Against Wealthy Mohave Indian Outdoes Fiction," *Arizona Republican*, April 30, 1922.

3 When the book was republished by Grabhorn Press in 1935, it featured a preface that perpetuated the myth that Olive had died in an insane asylum.

4 See Tinnemeyer, "Rescuing the Past"; and the introduction to Ruiz de Burton, *Who Would Have Thought It?*.

5 Ruiz de Burton, *Who Would Have Thought It?* xiii, xxxv.

6 Ruiz de Burton, *Who Would Have Thought It?* 17.

7 Ruiz de Burton, *Who Would Have Thought It?* 11.

8 Andrews, "The Lawless Have Laws," 1. The only significant factual biographical error in the script is the assertion, in the conclusion narrated by Reagan, that Oatman lived in San Francisco and Oregon for twenty years after her ransom. The scriptwriter, Robert Hardy Andrews, includes an author's note specifying that the details of the Oatman story vary and referencing two books as sources: Paul I. Wellman's *Death in the Desert* (which contains a one-paragraph footnote on the Oatman massacre) and Oscar Lewis's *The Autobiography of the West*. The latter, which contains six pages on Oatman's captivity, mostly excerpted from *The Captivity of the Oatman Girls*, is the source of Lorenzo's misspelled name. Andrews had also taken details about Mohave life from some unspecified edition of *The Captivity of the Oatman Girls*, which he calls "her diary" in the script (4).

9 Andrews, "The Lawless Have Laws," 11.

10 Andrews, "The Lawless Have Laws," 9.

11 Andrews, "The Lawless Have Laws," 22.

12 Andrews, "The Lawless Have Laws," 13, 31.

13 See Barbara Mortimer's essay "Resisting Rescue: The Problem of the Captive's Agency in *The Searchers*," in her book *Hollywood's Frontier Captives*.

14 Leonard, *Tonto Woman*, 2, 6. A striptease is a common prelude to Oatman's redemption. Stratton presents her bare-breasted on the riverbank at Yuma before her ransom, where she waits for an officer's wife to bring her a dress; newspaper accounts describe her prostrate in the sand for the

same reason; and in *Who Would Have Thought It?* Ruiz de Burton wraps Lola in a red shawl that slips off when she arrives in the Norval household, exposing "a little girl very black indeed" (16).

15 Leonard, *Tonto Woman*, 8, 13, 15.

16 Grayson, *So Wide the Sky*, 305.

17 Grayson, *So Wide the Sky*, 92.

18 Hawthorne, *Scarlet Letter*, 136–37, 111. For an insightful study of the body as text in the nineteenth century, including deeper analysis of *The Scarlet Letter*, see Putzi, *Identifying Marks*.

19 Lawton, *Ransom's Mark*, 126.

20 Vaughn and Clark, *Puritans Among the Indians*, 2. A self-described evangelist-historian named Little Bear Wheeler goes Lawton one better, casting the captivity not as the punishment for sin but as a metaphor for sin itself. In a six-minute segment on his CD compilation *Historical Devotionals*, Wheeler recounts the massacre and then takes a sudden turn into the story of Adam and Eve, explaining that the two sinners were "captured [by sin] and suffered great hardship, even worse than poor little Olive Oatman." In vertiginous associative leaps, Wheeler equates biblical sin with Indian captivity (the captives are imprisoned by their own worst impulses, as savage Indians are wont to do) and interprets the tattoo as its indelible result: "Many who have come back [to God] have been tattooed by the captivity of sin, and they still have scars in their hearts, but Jesus still loves us and he looks past those scars."

21 Deloria, *Playing Indian*, 22, 37.

22 National Park Service, U.S. Department of the Interior, "Ellis Island," http://www.nps.gov/elis (accessed May 11, 2007).

23 Whitman, "Song of Myself," 930.

24 Morely Winograd and Michael Hais, "The Boomers Had Their Day: Make Way for the Millennials," *Washington Post*, February 3, 2008.

Bibliography

ARCHIVAL SOURCES

Abbott, Arthur. "The Story of the Abbotts and the Sperrys: A Genealogical Sketch of the Ancestors of Asa McFarland Abbott 1820–1889 and his Wife Sarah Sperry Abbott 1822–1900." Unpublished manuscript. Collection of the New York Public Library.

Abbott Family. Private collection. Morrison IL.

Carreon, Patricia. Private collection. Foothills Ranch CA.

Collection of Western Americana. Beineke Rare Books and Manuscripts Library, Yale University.

Collier, Katherine. "Mohave Tattoo: The Captivity of Olive Oatman." Undated, unpublished manuscript. Arizona Historical Society.

"Facts Relating to Irene Woodward, The Tattooed Lady." 1882. Collection of George Arents Research Library, Syracuse University.

Fields Family. Private collection. Morrison IL.

"Five Years Among the Indians!" Malone NY: Heath and Seaver, 1859. Collection of the American Antiquarian Society.

"Five Years Among Wild Savages: The Renowned Apachee Captive, Miss Olive Oatman." Toledo OH. Collection of the Newberry Library.

Heintzelman, Samuel P. "Post Return, March 11, 1851." Archival Manuscript Collection. Library of Congress.

"'Lo! The Indian' Captive!" February 3, 1859. Sophia Smith Collection. Smith College.

"Miss Nora Hildebrandt, the Tattooed Lady." Undated broadside. Robert Bogdan private collection.

Mowry, Sylvester. "Notes on the Indians of the Colorado." March 23, 1856. Collection of Western Americana. Beineke Rare Books and Manuscripts Library, Yale University.

Oatman, Olive. "A Narrative." Photocopy of Olive Oatman's undated, handwritten lecture notes. Center for Archival Collections, Jerome Library, Bowling Green State University, Bowling Green OH.

Oatman, Olive Ann, Papers. Jerome Library, Bowling Green State University.

Oregon Historical Society collections. Portland OR.

Palmer, Edward. "Observations on the Mohave Indians Made in 1869, 1870, and 1876." National Anthropological Archives, Smithsonian Institution.

Pettid, Edward. "The Oatman Story." Unpublished manuscript. University of Arizona Library Special Collections.

Reminiscences of Jas. H. Miller (as told to Mrs. Geo. F. Kitt). MS 495. Miller Collection. Arizona Historical Society.

Sperry, Charles. "Pioneer Journal of Charles Sperry." In *That Great Sperry Family: The Genealogy of the Sperry Brothers by Families and Generations*, by Harrison Spenser Sperry. Collection of Church of Latter-day Saints.

Stearns, Avery Orson. *Reminiscences of Pioneer Days and Early Settlers of Phoenix and Vicinity (and) A Brief Sketch of the Life and Character of Samuel Colver: Including Six Letters of Transmittal to Mrs. Effie Taylor, Medford, Oregon, (1921–22)*. Photocopy of typescript. Collection of Jackson County (Oregon) Library.

Underhill, Ruth. "Material Concerning the Mohave." MS 7588. National Anthropological Archives, Smithsonian Institution.

Wilder, Willard. "The Oatman Massacre Recalled by Fellow Traveler." December 2, 1909. Collection of Richard Nolan (great-grandson of Harrison Oatman). Milwaukie OR.

Williams, Moses. Diary. Southern Oregon Historical Society collections. Portland OR.

PUBLISHED SOURCES

Andrews, Robert Hardy. "The Lawless Have Laws." Screenplay for *Death Valley Days* television series. July 2, 1965 (aired October 1, 1965).

Anthony, C. V. *Fifty Years of Methodism: A History of the Methodist Episcopal Church Within the Bounds of the California Annual Conference from 1847–1897*. San Francisco: Methodist Book Concern, 1901.

Baley, Charles W. *Disaster on the Colorado: Beale's Wagon Road and the First Emigrant Party*. Logan: Utah State University Press, 2002.

Bancroft, Hubert Howe. *History of the Pacific States of North America*. Vol. 12, *Arizona and New Mexico, 1530–1888*. San Francisco: History Company, 1888.

——. *The Native Races of the Pacific States*. Vol. 1. New York: Appleton and Company, 1874.

Barney, James M. "The Oatman Massacre." *The Sheriff Magazine* 7, nos. 11–12 (1948): 11–13, 24–25, 13, 14; 8, no. 1 (1949): 6–7, 18–19.

Beattie, George W., ed. "Diary of Ferryman and Trader at Fort Yuma 1855–1857." *Historical Society of Southern California Journal*. Los Angeles: McBride, 1928.

The Book of Mormon. Salt Lake City: The Church of Jesus Christ of Latter-day Saints, 1980.

Bourke, John G. "Notes on the Cosmogony and Theogony of the Mohave Indians of the Rio Colorado, Arizona." *Journal of American Folklore* 2, no. 6 (July–September 1889): 169–89.

Braatz, Timothy. *Surviving Conquest*. Lincoln: University of Nebraska Press, 2003.

Brandes, Ray. *Frontier Military Posts of Arizona*. Globe AZ: Dale Stuart King, 1960.

Brooks, Cheryl A. "Politics of Forgetting: How Oregon Forgot to Ratify the Fourteenth Amendment." *Oregon Humanities* (Fall/Winter 2006). http://www.oregonhum.org/politics-of-forgetting.php.

Brooks, James F. *Captives and Cousins: Slavery, Kinship, and Community in the Southwest Borderlands*. Chapel Hill: University of North Carolina Press, 2002.

Browne, J. Ross. *Adventures in the Apache Country: A Tour Through Arizona and Sonora, 1864*. Tucson: University of Arizona Press, 1974.

——. "A Tour Through Arizona." *Harper's New Monthly Magazine*, November 1864.

Burnham, Michelle. *Captivity and Sentiment: Cultural Exchange in American Literature, 1682–1861*. Hanover MA: Dartmouth College and University Press of New England, 1997.

Bynum, Lindley. Introduction to *Life Among the Indians: The Captivity of the Oatman Girls Among Apache and Mohave Indians*, by Lorenzo D. Oatman and Olive A. Oatman. San Francisco: Grabhorn Press, 1935. Reprinted in *The Captivity of the Oatman Girls*, by Lorenzo D. Oatman and Olive A. Oatman. New York: Dover, 1994.

Canniff, William. *The Medical Profession in Upper Canada 1783–1850. An Historical Narrative, With Original Documents Relating to the Profession. Including Some Brief Biographies*. Toronto: William Briggs, 1894. Available at Early Canadiana Online, http://www.canadiana.org/ECO/PageView?id=93cbd55e6f2464c1&display=00470+0511.

Carlson, Edward. "The Martial Experiences of the California Volunteers." *Overland Monthly and Out West Magazine*, May 1886.

Carroll, Lorrayne. *Rhetorical Drag: Gender, Impersonation, Captivity, and the Writing of History*. Kent OH: Kent State University Press, 2007.

Castiglia, Christopher. *Bound and Determined: Captivity, Culture-Crossing, and White Womanhood from Mary Rowlandson to Patti Hearst*. Chicago: University of Chicago Press, 1995.

Catalog of the University of the Pacific, for the Academical Year 1857–'58. San Francisco: Commercial Book and Job Steam Printing Establishment, 1858.

Caughey, John Walton, ed. *The Indians of Southern California in 1852: The B. D. Wilson Report and a Selection of Contemporary Comment*. San Marino CA: Huntington Library, 1952.

Clark, Hal, and Doris Clark. *The Oatman Story*. Las Vegas: H. and D. Clark's Quest, 2002.

Clark, Robert Carlton, Robert Horace Down, and George Verne Blue. *A History of Oregon*. Chicago: Row, Peterson, 1926.

Clinton, Catherine. *The Other Civil War: American Women in the Nineteenth Century*. New York: Hill and Wang, 1999.

Colley, Linda. *Captives: The Story of Britain's Pursuit of Empire and How Its Soldiers and Civilians Were Held Captive by the Dream of Global Supremacy, 1600–1850*. New York: Pantheon Books, 2002.

Conklin, E. J. *Picturesque Arizona: Being the Result of Travels and Observations in Arizona during the Fall and Winter of 1877*. New York: Mining Record, 1878.

Conn, Howard J. *The First Congregational Church of Great Barrington, 1743–1943: A History*. N.p.: The Anniversary Year Committee, 1943.

Corle, Edwin. *Desert Country*. New York: Dell, Sloan, and Pearce, 1941.

———. *The Gila: River of the Southwest*. Lincoln: University of Nebraska Press, 1951.

Dary, David. *The Oregon Trail: An American Saga*. New York: Knopf, 2004.

———. *The Santa Fe Trail: Its History, Legends, and Lore*. New York: Knopf, 2000.

Davidson, Cathy N. *Revolution and the Word: The Rise of the Novel in America*. New York: Oxford University Press, 1986.

Dawson, Muir. *History and Bibliography of Southern California Newspapers, 1851–1876*. Los Angeles: Dawson's Book Shop, 1950.

De Humboldt, Alexander. *Political Essay on the Kingdom of New Spain*. Translated by John Black. Vol. 2. New York: Riley, 1811.

Deloria, Philip. *Playing Indian*. New Haven: Yale University Press, 1998.

Demos, John. *The Unredeemed Captive: A Family Story from Early America*. New York: Knopf, 1994.

Denton, Sally. *Faith and Betrayal: A Pioneer Woman's Passage in the American West*. New York: Knopf, 2005.

Derounian-Stodola, Kathryn Zabelle. "The Captive and Her Editor: The Ciphering of Olive Oatman and Royal B. Stratton." *Prospects: An Annual of American Cultural Studies* 23 (1998): 171–92.

———. "The Captive as Celebrity." In *Lives Out of Letters: Essays on American Literary Biography and Documentation*, edited by Robert D. Habich, 65–92. Madison: Fairleigh Dickinson University Press, 2004.

———. "The Indian Captivity Narratives of Mary Rowlandson and Olive Oatman: Case Studies in the Continuity, Evolution, and Exploitation of Literary Discourse." *Studies in the Literary Imagination* 27, no. 1 (Spring 1994): 33–46.

———, ed. *Women's Indian Captivity Narratives*. New York: Penguin, 1998.

Derounian-Stodola, Kathryn Zabelle, and James Arthur Levernier. *The Indian Captivity Narrative, 1550–1900*. New York: Twayne, 1993.

Devereux, George. "Amusements and Sports of Mohave Children." *The Masterkey for Indian Lore and History* 24 (November 5, 1950): 143–52.

———. "Mohave Chieftainship in Action: A Narrative of the First Contacts of the Mohave Indians with the United States." *Plateau* 23, no. 3 (January 1951): 33–43.

———. "Mohave Culture and Personality." *Character and Personality: An International Psychological Quarterly* 8, no. 2 (1939): 91–109.

———. *Mohave Ethnopsychiatry: The Psychic Disturbances of an Indian Tribe*. Washington DC: Smithsonian Institution Press, 1969.

———. *Mohave Etiquette*. Southwest Museum Paper 22. Los Angeles, 1948.

———. "The Psychology of Feminine Genital Bleeding: An Analysis of Mohave Indian Puberty and Menstrual Rites." *International Journal of Psycho-analysis* 31 (1950): 237–57.

DeVoto, Bernard. *The Year of Decision: 1846*. New York: St. Martin's Griffin, 2000.

Didion, Joan. *Slouching Towards Bethlehem*. New York: Farrar, Straus and Giroux, 1968.

Dillon, Richard. "The Ordeal of Olive Oatman." *American History* 30, no. 4 (1995): 30–32, 70–72.

———. "Tragedy at Oatman Flat: Massacre, Captivity, Mystery." *American West* 18, no. 2 (1981): 46–59.

"Donation Land Claims in Oregon 1850–1855." *Rogue Digger* 38, no. 1 (Spring 2003): 3.

Drimmer, Frederick, ed. *Captured by Indians: Fifteen Firsthand Accounts, 1750–1870*. New York: Dover, 1985.

Dunn, J. P. *Massacres of the Mountains: A History of the Indian Wars of the Far West*. Mechanicsburg PA: Stackpole Books, 2002. First published 1886 by Harper.

Ebersole, Gary. *Captured by Texts: Puritan to Post-modern Images of Indian Captivity*. Charlottesville: University of Virginia Press, 1995.

Elliott, J. F. "The Great Western: Sarah Bowman, Mother and Mistress to the U.S. Army." *Journal of Arizona History* 30 (1989): 1–26.

"An Excursion to the Coco-Maricopa Indians Upon the River Gila." *The Ladies' Repository* (Cincinnati) 15 (1855): 15–16.

Faery, Rebecca Blevins. *Cartographies of Desire: Captivity, Race, and Sex in the Shaping of an American Nation*. Norman: University of Oklahoma Press, 1999.

Faragher, John Mack. *Women and Men on the Overland Trail*. New Haven: Yale University Press, 2000.

Farish, Thomas Edwin. *History of Arizona*. Vol. 3. Phoenix: Filmer Bros. Electrotype, 1915.

Fathauer, George H. "The Structure and Causation of Mohave Warfare." *Southwestern Journal of Anthropology* 10, no. 1 (Spring 1954): 97–118.

Faulk, Odie. *Destiny Road: The Gila Trail and the Opening of the Southwest*. New York: Oxford University Press, 1973.

Fiedler, Leslie. *Freaks: Myths and Images of the Secret Self*. New York: Simon and Schuster, 1978.

———. *The Return of the Vanishing American*. New York: Stein and Day, 1969.

Fryd, Vivien. "Two Sculptures for the Capitol: Horatio Greenough's *Rescue* and Luigi Persico's *Discovery of America*." *American Art Journal* 19, no. 2 (Spring 1987): 16–39.

Furst, Jill Leslie. *Mojave Pottery, Mojave People: The Dillingham Collection of Mojave Ceramics*. Santa Fe: School of American Research Press, 2001.

Galvin, Lynn. "Cloudwoman: The Life of Olive Oatman, an Old California Indian Captive." *The Californians* 13, no. 2 (1996): 10–19.

Gifford, E. W. "Northeastern and Western Yavapai." *University of California Publications in American Archaeology and Ethnology* 34, no. 4 (1936): 247–354.

Gilbert, Steve. *Tattoo History: A Sourcebook*. New York: Juno Books, 2000.

Godfrey, Charles M. "Mack, Theophilus." In *Dictionary of Canadian Biography Online*. N.p.: Library and Archives of Canada, 2000. http://www.biographi.ca/EN/ShowBio.asp?BioId=39800&query=mack (accessed June 7, 2004).

Gohres, Helen, ed. "San Diego History—In Documents: The Mexican Treaty, the Military, Railroads and Politics." *Journal of San Diego History* 18, no. 1 (Winter 1972). http://www.sandiegohistory.org/journal/72winter/historydocs.htm (accessed May 4, 2007).

Gordon, Mary McDougall, ed. *Through Indian Country to California: John P. Sherburne's Diary of the Whipple Expedition, 1853–1854*. Stanford: Stanford University Press, 1988.

Grayson, Elizabeth. *So Wide the Sky*. New York: Avon Books, 1997.

"The Great Western . . . An Amazon Who Made History." *Los Angeles Corral of the Westerners* 34 (June 1956): 4–8.

Greene, Max. *The Kansas Region: Forest, Prairie, Desert, Mountain, Vale, and River*. New York: Fowler and Wells, 1856.

Grey, Herman. *Tales from the Mohaves*. Norman: University of Oklahoma Press, 1970.

Grosz, Elizabeth. "Intolerable Ambiguity: Freaks as/at the Limit." In *Freakery: Cultural Spectacles of the Extraordinary Body*, edited by Rosemarie Garland Thompson. New York: New York University Press, 1996.

Gudde, Erwin G. "Mohave and Mojave." *Western Folklore* 7, no. 2 (April 1948): 169–71.

Hacker, Margaret Schmidt. *Cynthia Ann Parker: The Life and Legend*. Southwestern Studies 92. El Paso: Texas Western Press, 1990.

Hafen, Leroy R., and Ann W. Hafen. *Old Spanish Trail: Santa Fe to Los Angeles; With Extracts from Contemporary Records and Including Diaries of*

Antonio Armijo and Orville Pratt. Glendale CA: Arthur H. Clark Company, 1954.

Hall, Sharlot M. "Olive A. Oatman: Her Captivity with the Apache Indians and Her Later Life." *Out West* 29, no. 3 (1908): 216–17.

Hawthorne, Nathaniel. *The Scarlet Letter*. Mineola NY: Dover, 1994.

Heard, Norman J. *White into Red: A Study of the Assimilation of White Persons Captured by Indians*. Metuchen NJ: Scarecrow Press, 1973.

Hegne, Barbara. "The Captivity of Olive Oatman." *Eagle Point Historical Society* (November 1996): 3–6.

Heintzelman, Samuel P. *A Transcription of Major Samuel P. Heintzelman's Journal, 1 January 1851–31 December 1853*. Transcribed by Creola Blackwell. Yuma AZ: Yuma County Historical Society, 1989.

Hine, Robert V., and John Mack Faragher. *The American West: A New Interpretive History*. New Haven: Yale University Press, 2000.

Holmes, Kenneth. *Covered Wagon Women: Diaries and Letters from the Western Trails*. Lincoln: University of Nebraska Press, 1984.

Howe, Daniel Walker. *What God Hath Wrought: The Transformation of America, 1815–1848*. Oxford: Oxford University Press, 2007.

Hughes, Robert. *American Visions: The Epic History of Art in America*. New York: Knopf, 1997.

Hughes, Samuel. "Murder at Oatman's Flat." *The Arizona Graphic*, October 28, 1899.

Hunt, Rockwell D. *History of the College of the Pacific, 1851–1951*. Stockton CA: College of the Pacific, 1951.

Hurtado, Albert. L. *Indian Survival on the California Frontier*. New Haven: Yale University Press, 1990.

———. *Intimate Frontiers: Sex, Gender, and Culture in Old California*. Albuquerque: University of New Mexico Press, 1999.

Ives, Joseph C. *Report Upon the Colorado River of the West: Explored in 1857 and 1858*. Corps of Topographical Engineers, under the Direction of the Office of Explorations and Surveys. A. A. Humphreys, Captain Topographical Engineers, in charge. Washington DC: Government Printing Office, 1861.

Kasson, Joy. *Marble Queens and Captives: Women in Nineteenth-Century American Sculpture*. New Haven: Yale University Press, 1990.

Keckley, Elizabeth H., and James Olney. *Behind the Scenes, Or, Thirty Years a Slave and Four Years in the White House*. New York: Oxford University Press, 1988.

Krakauer, Jon. *Under the Banner of Heaven: A Story of Violent Faith*. New York: Doubleday, 2003.

Kroeber, A. L. *Handbook of the Indians of California*. New York: Dover, 1925. Reprinted 1976.

———. "Olive Oatman's Return." *Kroeber Anthropological Society Papers* 4 (1951): 1–18.

———. *Report on Aboriginal Territory and Occupancy of the Mohave Tribe*. New York: Garland, 1974.

Kroeber, A. L., and Clifton B. Kroeber. *A Mohave War Reminiscence, 1854–1880*. University of California Publications in Anthropology 10. Berkeley: University of California Press, 1973. Reprint, New York: Dover, 1994.

———. "Olive Oatman's First Account of Her Captivity Among the Mohave." *California Historical Society Quarterly* 41 (1962): 309–17.

Kroeber, Clifton B. "The Mohave as Nationalist, 1859–1874." *Proceedings of the American Philosophical Society* 109, no. 3 (June 1965): 173–80.

Kroeber, Clifton B., and Bernard L. Fontana. *Massacre on the Gila: An Account of the Last Major Battle between American Indians, with Reflections on the Origin of War*. Tucson: University of Arizona Press, 1986.

Launius, Roger D., and Linda Thatcher. *Differing Visions: Dissenters in Mormon History*. Urbana: University of Illinois Press, 1994.

Lawton, Wendy. *Ransom's Mark: A Story Based on the Life of Pioneer Olive Oatman*. Chicago: Moody Publishing, 2003.

Leonard, Elmore. *The Tonto Woman and Other Western Stories*. New York: Delta, 1998.

Lewis, Oscar. *The Autobiography of the West: Personal Narratives of the Discovery and Settlement of the American West*. New York: Holt, 1958.

Lossing, Benson John. "Extreme Western Tribes." In *A Pictorial History of the United States: For Schools and Families*. New York: F. J. Huntington, Mason Brothers, 1854.

Love, Frank. *Hell's Outpost: A History of Old Fort Yuma*. Yuma AZ: Yuma Crossing Publication Series, 1992.

Maloney, Alice Bay, ed. "Some Olive Oatman Documents." *California Historical Society Quarterly* 21 (1941): 107–12.

Martin, Douglas D. *Yuma Crossing*. Albuquerque: University of New Mexico Press, 1954.

Matthews, Glenna. *The Rise of Public Woman: Woman's Power and Woman's Place in the United States 1630–1970*. New York: Oxford University Press, 1994.

McGinty, Brian. *The Oatman Massacre: A Tale of Desert Captivity and Survival*. Norman: University of Oklahoma Press, 2005.

McWilliams, Carey. *Southern California: An Island on the Land*. Salt Lake City: Gibbs-Smith, 1973.

Meyers, Sandra L. *Westering Women and the Frontier Experience, 1850–1915*. Albuquerque: University of New Mexico Press, 1982.

Minutes of the California Annual Conference of the Methodist Episcopal Church. Held at Santa Clara CA, September 12–18, 1860. Committee of Publication: J. B. Hill, E. Thomas, W. B. May, and D. Deal. San Francisco: B. G. Sterett, 1860.

Mollhausen, Baldwin. *Diary of a Journey from the Mississippi to the Coasts of the Pacific With a United States Government Expedition*. Translated by Mrs. Percy Sinnett. Vol 2. London: Longman, Brown, Green, Longmans, and Roberts, 1858.

Mortimer, Barbara. *Hollywood's Frontier Captives: Cultural Anxiety and the Captivity Plot in American Film*. New York: Garland, 2000.

Munro, Pamela, Nellie Brown, and Judith G. Crawford. *A Mojave Dictionary*. Los Angeles: Department of Linguistics, University of California–Los Angeles, 1992.

Museum of the City of New York. "The Metropolitan Hotel." *Painting the Town*. http://www.mcny.org/collections/painting/pttcat23.htm (accessed June 7, 2004).

Namias, June. *White Captives: Gender and Ethnicity on the American Frontier*. Chapel Hill: University of North Carolina Press, 1994.

Oatman, Olive, and Lorenzo Oatman. *The Captivity of the Oatman Girls Among the Apache and Mohave Indians*. New York: Dover, 1994. Reprint of the 1935 Grabhorn Press edition.

Order of Services at the Installation of Rev. R. B. Stratton, as Pastor of the First Church, in Worcester, Wednesday, January 2, 1867. Worcester: E. R. Fiske, 1867.

Ortiz, Alfonzo, ed. *Handbook of North American Indians*. Vols. 9–10, *Southwest*. Washington DC: Smithsonian Institution, 1983.

Parry, Albert. *Tattoo: Secrets of a Strange Art*. New York: Dover, 2006. First published 1933 by Simon and Shuster.

Pettid, Edward. Introduction to "Olive Ann Oatman's Lecture Notes and Oatman Bibliography." *San Bernardino County Museum Association Quarterly* 16, no. 2 (1968).

———. "The Oatman Story." *Arizona Highways* 44, no. 11 (November 1968): 4–9.

Piepmeier, Alison. *Out in Public: Configurations of Women's Bodies in Nineteenth-Century America*. Chapel Hill: University of North Carolina Press, 2004.

Pilkington, James Penn. *The Methodist Publishing House: A History*. Vol. 1, *Beginnings to 1870*. Nashville: Abingdon Press, 1968.

Putzi, Jennifer. *Identifying Marks: Race, Gender, and the Marked Body of Nineteenth-Century America*. Athens: University of Georgia Press, 2006.

———. "'Tattooed Still': The Inscription of Female Agency in Elizabeth Stoddard's *The Morgesons*." *Legacy* 7, no. 2 (2000): 165–73.

Reinhart, Herman Francis. *The Golden Frontier: The Recollections of Herman Francis Reinhart 1851–1859*. Austin: University of Texas Press, 1962.

Remini, Robert V. *Joseph Smith*. New York: Viking Books, 2002.

Rice, William B. "The Captivity of Olive Oatman—A Newspaper Account." *California Historical Society Quarterly* 21 (1941): 97–106.

Richards, Leonard L. *The California Gold Rush and the Coming of the Civil War*. New York: Knopf, 2007.

Roberts, William. *The Letters of William Roberts*. Edited by John Hook and Charlotte Hook. N.p.: The Commission on Archives and History, Oregon-Idaho United Methodist Archives, 1998.

Root, Virginia V. *Following the Pot of Gold at the Rainbow's End in the Days of 1850*. Edited by Lenore Rowland. Downey CA: Elena Quinn, 1960.

Ruiz de Burton, Maria Ampara. *Who Would Have Thought It?* Edited by Rosaura Sánchez and Beatrice Pita. Houston: Art Publico Press, 1995.

Russell, Marian. *Land of Enchantment: Memoirs of Marian Russell Along the Santa Fe Trail*. Albuquerque: University of New Mexico Press, 1981.

Sandwich, Brian. *The Great Western: Legendary Lady of the Southwest*. El Paso: Texas Western Press, 1991.

Sayre, Gordon, and Paul Lauter, eds. *American Captivity Narratives: Olaudah Equiano, Mary Rowlandson, and Others*. Boston: Houghton Mifflin, 1999.

Schlissel, Lillan. *Women's Diaries of the Westward Journey*. New York: Schocken Books, 1982.

Schuster, David G. "Neurasthenia and a Modernizing America." *Journal of the American Medical Association* 290 (November 5, 2003): 2327–28.

Shea, John Gilmary. *A History of the Catholic Church within the Limits of the United States, from the First Attempted Colonization to the Present Time*. Vol. 4. New York: John G. Shea, 1892.

Sheldon, Francis E. "Pioneer Illustration in California." *Overland Monthly and Out West Magazine*, April 1888.

Sherer, Lorraine. *Bitterness Road: The Mojave, 1604 to 1860*. Ballena Press Anthropological Papers 41. Menlo Park CA: Ballena Press, 1994.

———. *The Clan System of the Fort Mojave Indians*. Los Angeles: Historical Society of Southern California, 1965.

———. "Great Chieftains of the Mojave Indians." *Southern California Quarterly* 48 (1966): 1–35.

Sides, Hampton. *Blood and Thunder: An Epic of the American West*. New York: Doubleday, 2006.

Smith, Gerald. *The Mohave Indians*. Bloomington CA: San Bernardino County Museum Association, 1966.

Smith, Joseph. *History of the Church of Jesus Christ of Latter-day Saints*. Vol. 3. Lamoni IA: Board of Publication of the Reorganized Church of Jesus Christ of Latter-day Saints, 1900.

Spier, Leslie. *Yuman Tribes of the Gila River*. New York: Dover, 1978.

Stanton, Edward M. "Report of the Secretary of War 1864." Notes: 40th Cong., 2d sess., House Executive, doc. 1, vol. 2. Series Set no. 1324. Abstract: p. 129. General Orders no. 33. Headquarters, Dept. of California, May 30, 1867.

Stevens, Charles Emery. *Worcester Churches 1719–1789*. Worcester MA: Lucius Paulinus Goddard, 1890.

Stewart, Kenneth. "The Aboriginal Territory of the Mohave Indians." *Ethnohistory* 16, no. 3 (1969): 257–76.

———. "A Brief History of the Mohave Indians Since 1850." *The Kiva* 34 (1969): 219–36.

———. "Mohave." In Ortiz, *Southwest*, 55–70.

———. "Mohave Warfare." *Southwestern Journal of Anthropology* 2, no. 3 (Autumn 1947): 257–78.

Stratton, R. B. *Captivity of the Oatman Girls: Being an Interesting Narrative of Life Among the Apache and Mohave Indians*. San Francisco: Whitton, Towne and Co., 1857; Chicago: Charles Scott and Co., 1857; New York: Carlton and Porter, 1858.

———. *Captivity of the Oatman Girls, a True Story of Early Emigration to the West*. Revised and abridged by Charles H. Jones. Salem: Oregon Teacher's Monthly, 1909; New York: Dover, 1994.

———. *Captivity of the Oatman Girls*. Lincoln: University of Nebraska Press, 1983.

———. *Church Government*. Albany NY: Weed, Parsons, 1862.

———. *Life Among the Indians: Being an Interesting Narrative of the Captivity of the Oatman Girls, Among the Apache and Mohave Indians, Containing Also an Interesting Account of the Massacre of the Oatman Family, by the Apache Indians, in 1851; The Narrow Escape of Lorenzo D. Oatman; The Capture of Olive A. and Mary A. Oatman; The Death by Starvation of the Latter; Five Years Suffering and Captivity of Olive A. Oatman; Also Her Singular Recapture in 1856; As Given by Lorenzo D. and Olive A. Oatman, the Only Surviving Members of the Family, to the Author, R. B. Stratton*. Introduction by Lyndley Bynum. Illustrations by Mallette Dean. San Francisco: Grabhorn Press, 1935.

———. *A Sermon, Delivered on Thanksgiving Day, November 24th, 1864, in the First Congregational Church*. Lee MA: J. A. Royce, Printer, 1865.

Sweeny, Thomas W. "Military Occupation of California, 1849–1853." *Journal of the Military Service Institution* (1909).

Taylor, Edith, and William J. Wallace. *Mojave Tattooing and Face-Painting*. Southwest Museum Leaflets 20. Los Angeles, 1947.

Tinnemeyer, Andrea. "Rescuing the Past: The Case of Olive Oatman and Lola Medina." In *Maria Amparo Ruiz de Burton: Critical and Pedagogical Perspectives*, edited by Amelia Maria de la Luz Montes and Anne Elizabeth Goldman. Lincoln: University of Nebraska Press, 2004.

Trafzer, Clifford E., and Joel R. Hyer. *Exterminate Them! Written Accounts of the Murder, Rape, and Enslavement of Native Americans During the California Gold Rush*. East Lansing: University of Michigan Press, 1999.

Tuttle, E. D. "The River Colorado." *Arizona Historical Review* (July 1928): 50–68.

Twain, Mark. *Roughing It*. New York: Signet Classics, 1871. Reprinted 1994.

United States Army Corps of Topographical Engineers. *Report of an Expe-*

dition Down the Zuni and Colorado Rivers, in 1851 [by] Lorenzo Sitgreaves. Chicago: Rio Grande Press, 1962.

U.S. Congress. House. Message from the President of the United States, to the Two Houses of Congress at the Commencement of the First Session of the Thirty-fifth Congress, on December 8, 1857. Vol. 942, sess. vol. 2. 35th Cong., 1st sess., H.Exec.Doc. 2, pt. 1. Containing a report by Sylvester Mowry, *Fort Yuma*, September 16, 1857.

US GenNet. "Royce Oatman." http://www.usgennet.org/usa/ga/topic/indian/oliveoatman.htm.

Vail, R. W. G. *The Voice of the Old Frontier*. New York: Octagon Books, 1970.

Vaughan, Alden T. *Narratives of North American Indian Captivity: A Selective Bibliography*. New York: Garland, 1983.

Vaughan, Alden T., and Edward W. Clark, eds. *Puritans Among the Indians: Accounts of Captivity and Redemption, 1676–1724*. Cambridge: Belknap Press of Harvard University, 1981.

Vitale, Gary C. "Whatever Happened to James Colin Brewster, the Boy Mormon Prophet?" *Desert Tracks* (newsletter of the Southwest Chapter of the Oregon-California Trails Association) (December 2007): 9–15.

Vogel, Dan. "James Colin Brewster: The Boy Prophet Who Challenged Mormon Authority." In *Differing Visions: Dissenters in Mormon History*, edited by Roger D. Lanius and Linda Thatcher. Urbana: University of Illinois Press, 1994.

Wagner, Randy. "The Road to California, 1849." Oregon Trails Association. http://www.octa-trails.org/JumpingOffToday/VirtualTour/CalTrailHistory.asp.

Wallace, William J. "The Dream in Mohave Life." *Journal of American Folklore* 60, no. 237 (July–September 1947): 252–58.

———. "Infancy and Childhood Among the Mohave Indians." *Primitive Man* 21, nos. 1–2 (January 1948): 19–38.

———. "Mohave Fishing Equipment and Methods." *Anthropological Quarterly*, n.s., 28, no. 2 (April 1955): 87–94.

Wallings, Albert G. *History of Southern Oregon*. Portland: A. G. Walling, 1884.

Washburn, Wilcomb. Foreword to *Captivity of the Oatman Girls*. Lincoln: University of Nebraska Press, 1983. Reprinted from the revised and enlarged third edition of 1858.

——. *The Indian in America*. New York: Harper and Row, 1975.

Webster, James Carson. *Erastus D. Palmer*. Newark: University of Delaware Press, 1983.

Wellman, Paul I. *Death in the Desert: The Fifty Years' War for the Great Southwest*. New York: Macmillan, 1935.

Wharfield, H. B. *Fort Yuma on the Colorado River*. El Cajon CA, 1968.

Wheeler, Little Bear. "Olive Oatman." *Historical Devotional*. Westward Expansion Series 8. CD 2, selection 6.

Whipple, Amiel Weeks. *A Pathfinder in the Southwest: The Itinerary of Lieutenant A. W. Whipple During His Explorations for a Railway Route From Fort Smith to Los Angeles in the Years 1853 and 1854*. Edited by Grant Foreman. Norman: University of Oklahoma Press, 1941.

Whipple, A. W., Thomas Ewbank, and Wm. W. Turner. "Report Upon the Indian Tribes." In *United States War Department Reports of Explorations and Surveys, to Ascertain the Most Practicable and Economical Route for a Railroad from the Mississippi River to the Pacific Ocean*. Vol. 3. Washington DC, 1855. http://memory.loc.gov/ammem/ndlpcoop/moahtml/afk4383.html.

Whitman, Walt. "Song of Myself." In *The American Tradition in Literature*. 7th ed. New York: McGraw-Hill, 1990.

Wilcox, Bernice F. *The Sperry Family*. Chili NY: Chili Mills National Historic Site.

Will, Barbara. "The Nervous Origins of the American Western." *American Literature* 70, no. 2 (June 1988): 293–316.

Wilson, Sheila M. *Taking the Waters: A History of the Spas of St. Catharines*. St. Catharines, Ontario: St. Catharines Historical Society, 1999.

Woodward, Arthur. "Irataba: 'Chief of the Mohave.'" *Plateau, Museum of Northern Arizona* 25, no. 3 (January 1953): 53–68.

——, ed. *Journal of Lieutenant Thomas W. Sweeny 1849–1853*. Los Angeles: Westernlore Press, 1956.

Wyllis, Rufus K. *Arizona: The History of a Frontier State*. Phoenix: Hobson and Herr, 1950.

Index

Page numbers in italics refer to illustrations.

IN THE WOMEN IN THE WEST SERIES

When Montana and I Were Young: A Frontier Childhood
By Margaret Bell
Edited by Mary Clearman Blew

Martha Maxwell, Rocky Mountain Naturalist
By Maxine Benson

The Enigma Woman: The Death Sentence of Nellie May Madison
By Kathleen A. Cairns

Front-Page Women Journalists, 1920–1950
By Kathleen A. Cairns

The Cowboy Girl: The Life of Caroline Lockhart
By John Clayton

The Art of the Woman: The Life and Work of Elisabet Ney
By Emily Fourmy Cutrer

Emily: The Diary of a Hard-Worked Woman
By Emily French
Edited by Janet Lecompte

The Important Things of Life: Women, Work, and Family in Sweetwater County, Wyoming, 1880–1929
By Dee Garceau

The Adventures of The Woman Homesteader: The Life and Letters of Elinore Pruitt Stewart
By Susanne K. George

Flowers in the Snow: The Life of Isobel Wylie Hutchison, 1889–1982
By Gwyneth Hoyle

Domesticating the West: The Re-creation of the Nineteenth-Century American Middle Class
By Brenda K. Jackson

Engendered Encounters: Feminism and Pueblo Cultures, 1879–1934
By Margaret D. Jacobs

Riding Pretty: Rodeo Royalty in the American West
By Renée Laegreid

The Colonel's Lady on the Western Frontier: The Correspondence of Alice Kirk Grierson
Edited by Shirley A. Leckie

Their Own Frontier: Women Intellectuals Re-Visioning the American West
Edited and with an introduction by Shirley A. Leckie and Nancy J. Parezo

A Stranger in Her Native Land: Alice Fletcher and the American Indians
By Joan Mark

The Blue Tattoo: The Life of Olive Oatman
By Margot Mifflin

So Much to Be Done: Women Settlers on the Mining and Ranching Frontier, second edition
Edited by Ruth B. Moynihan, Susan Armitage, and Christiane Fischer Dichamp

Women and Nature: Saving the "Wild" West
By Glenda Riley

The Life of Elaine Goodale Eastman
By Theodore D. Sargent

Give Me Eighty Men: Women and the Myth of the Fetterman Fight
By Shannon D. Smith

Bright Epoch: Women and Coeducation in the American West
By Andrea G. Radke-Moss

Moving Out: A Nebraska Woman's Life
By Polly Spence
Edited by Karl Spence Richardson

Eight Women, Two Model Ts, and the American West
By Joanne Wilke

CPSIA information can be obtained at www.ICGtesting.com
Printed in the USA
266812BV00002B/1/P

9 780803 235175